George Heller, AFTRA National Executive Secretary, 1946.

RITA MORLEY HARVEY

~~~~~~

Those Wonderful, Terrible Years

George Heller and the American Federation of Television and Radio Artists

Southern Illinois University Press

Carbondale and Edwardsville

Printed in the United States of America

Designed by Laury A. Egan

Production supervised by Kyle Lake

99 98 97 96   4 3 2 1

Frontispiece: AFRA Executive Secretary George Heller, 1946. Courtesy *Stand By!*

Library of Congress Cataloging-in-Publication Data
Harvey, Rita Morley, 1927–
Those wonderful, terrible years : George Heller and the American
Federation of Television and Radio Artists / Rita Morley Harvey.
p.   cm.
Includes bibliographical references and index.
1. American Federation of Television and Radio Artists—History.
2. Heller, George, 1906–   . I. Title.
PN1990.6.U5H37   1996
331.88′1179144′0973—dc20   95-34321
ISBN 0-8093-2022-3 (cl : alk. paper).—   CIP
ISBN 0-8093-2023-1 (pb : alk. paper)

The paper used in this publication meets the minimum requirements
of American National Standard for Information Sciences—Permanence
of Paper for Printed Library Materials, ANSI Z39.48-1984. ♾

In memory of my late husband, Ken Harvey,
a former president of the federation,
and all the others who made the union great

Contents

Illustrations following page 130

Preface

The American Federation of Television and Radio Artists, the national union of broadcasters, known as AFTRA, marked its fiftieth year in 1987. *Stand By!*, the official publication of the New York local (of which I had been a longtime contributor and cochairperson), was celebrating with a special, anniversary issue.

My assignment was to write an article on AFRA, the American Federation of Radio Artists, a predecessor of AFTRA, from its founding through its first landmark contracts with the giant networks. It would be based on interviews with one of AFRA's charter members (he holds pledge receipt no. 2) and still-active radio and television announcer Jackson Beck.

Like Jackson, I too loved radio. Since the age of six, in my home state of Connecticut, I had worked behind a microphone. I sang, tap-danced, acted, announced, hosted, even disc jockeyed my way though grammar and high school at stations around the area. Although I later trained in voice and piano at the Julius Hartt School of Music (University of Hartford), I decided to try my luck as an actress in New York City, the broadcasting center of the world.

It was a small miracle when, within days of my arrival, I landed my first job—a supporting role on *Studio One*, a CBS television drama produced by Worthington "Tony" Miner, directed by Paul Nickells, and starring the up-and-coming Charlton Heston. In that same moment, I won my badge of professionalism, of which I was immensely proud: membership in the New York local of the Television Authority (TvA), yet another predecessor to AFTRA. Soon, as a working actor on stage and in film, I would hold cards in Actors' Equity Association and the Screen Actors Guild as well; more on this redundancy later.

The early 1950s was the height of what we refer to, nostalgically, as the Golden Age of television. It was also the height of the so-called McCarthy Era. And more than anywhere else, perhaps, the excitement of one and the agony of the other was felt most keenly in the broadcast industry—particularly among members of the TvA.

I came to know of sponsor "clearances," of the CBS "loyalty questionnaire," of the existence of a secret, political blacklist. Soon I joined with others in speaking out against the insidious practice, which was apparently rife throughout the entire industry. And, in 1955, I ran on the Charles Colllingwood and John Henry Faulk middle-of-the-road slate against incumbents of the New York local board of (by then) AFTRA—a board that had become, for so many, the very personification of McCarthyism.

But, first, back to the Jackson Beck interview. One cannot speak of the early days of AFRA without speaking of Broadway actor George Heller, a founder and AFRA's longtime executive secretary (director), and of his close friends and cofounders Philip Loeb, Sam Jaffe, and Albert Van Dekker. Jackson Beck, already an established radio actor, was there at Heller's first organizational meeting one sweltering July night in 1937, and he recounted the old tales with gusto.

What a marvelous character George Heller must have been! And what a time! The middle of the Great Depression when working people everywhere came together to help one another, to protect one another. When a five-dollar-a-show radio performer rubbed elbows with the great stars of the day—Eddie Cantor, Jack Benny, Ed Wynn, Rudy Vallee, and so many others—to create a union in broadcasting. As Jackson talked on about Heller's charm, his dynamism, his ability to bring people together in a common cause, I became more and more fascinated. My memory of him was vague and clouded, at best.

What was the story behind this "glamour boy of the trade-union movement?" And what of Loeb, Jaffe, and Van Dekker? What events led to the creation of AFRA? And what roles did these men, the union boards, and General Counsel Henry Jaffe (no relation to Sam) play in those first, wonderful years—later, in those terrible years that would overtake and overwhelm them? This would be my next article, but I needed to dig deeper.

I turned to "AFRA-AFTRA, Twenty-Five Years of Labor Unionism," by William "Bill" Lipton, who played Chick on radio's *Chick Carter, Boy Detective*, among other roles. Written in 1963 as the Silver Anniversary Tribute, the manuscript sat for a second twenty-five years, unfinished and unread, high on a union shelf. "To expensive to publish," officials said at the time. Its pages were packed with fascinating details and loving commentary. As to McCarthyism and how it functioned within the union, however, Lipton dealt with it in a single paragraph:

> No purpose is served by recounting that period . . . in which activity of the extremes of political thought clashed in a convulsive struggle forcing those members who had little interest in either side to withdraw from the union arena lest they become involved themselves.

That much was surely true. But here was a time of stunning consequence in the lives of George Heller and his friends, in the lives of hundreds of others as well, all good, decent citizens, all once-busy, much-admired radio and television performers. Here was a time that bred such bitterness, such hatred—brother to brother, local to local—that it would take more than a generation to put it to rest.

I would attempt to deal with it. I *needed* to deal with it.

The New York Public Library at Lincoln Center houses vast collections on the performing arts—stage, opera, ballet, cinema, radio, and television. But here, as elsewhere, apart from a handful of old newspaper clippings, photographs, and other mementos, little else on AFRA and AFTRA existed.

The story must be built, then, from the bottom up, from interviews with George Heller's family, his friends, and his detractors; from the writings of the day; and from old AFTRA records. Surprisingly, it was in that least likely place, the minutes of meetings darkened now with age, that the real story—the compelling, sometimes amusing and, often, tragic story—came to life. Unless otherwise indicated, all quotes are drawn from those interviews, reports, and minutes of board and convention meetings; some are from private collections.

Years have passed. An article has grown into a record of an era. It has taken me many miles and many places. It has reintroduced me to old acquaintances and made me many new friends. It has walked me through the history of AFTRA, its members, and the industry in which they labored—through the glory days and the shame. My only regret is that I am unable to give the entire account as it happened in locals across the country.

This, then, is the story of the controversial, charismatic George Heller and his colleagues Philip Loeb, Sam Jaffe, and Albert Van Dekker.

This is the story of AFTRA—from the Golden Age of radio through the Golden Age of television—all told against the background of the House Committee on Un-American Activities and Senator Joseph R. McCarthy.

This is the story of what happened to the union, to the members, to the men.

Acknowledgments

My thanks go to dozens of wonderful people without whose help and keen interest this account could never have been written.

I send appreciation to Bruce A. York, executive director of AFTRA; to John C. Hall, Jr., former executive secretary of AFTRA; and to AFTRA staff members Terry Walker, Andy Schefman, Patricia Coleman, and Carol Keenan Kohl; to Stephen Burrow, executive director of the New York local; to Helayne Antler, former executive secretary; and to New York local staff Lorraine Tancona, Elba Aviles, Rose Ann Badamo, and Yvonne LoVerde Costagliola; to John T. McGuire, associate national executive director of the Screen Actors Guild, New York, and staff Maura Walker; to Harry Medved and Ellie Abrahamson, staff of SAG, Los Angeles; to Alan Eisenberg, executive secretary of Actors' Equity Association, and staff Willard Swire, Kenneth Greenwood, and Judith Anderson; to Meg McSweeney, director of the American Academy of Dramatic Arts; to John H. Slate of The Center for American History, the University of Texas at Austin; to Terri Lorenz and Joseph Garner of Westwood One; to Jeneane Murray and Martin Silverstein of CBS, Inc.; to the librarians of Darien, Norwalk, New Canaan, and Wilton, Connecticut; and to the New Canaan Writers Group.

My thanks go to Dick Moore and Associates; Helaine Feldman, editor of *Equity* magazine; and Dorothy Spears, editor of *Stand By!*, who helped get this work under way; to literary agent Gloria Stern, who encouraged me to keep going; to Jeff Stewart, who knew George Heller and believed this work should be published; and to editor Kathryn Koldehoff, for making it readable.

My deep appreciation goes to the AFTRA professionals who graciously shared their stories and photographs with me: Casey Allen, Leslie Barrett, Jackson Beck, Elise Bretton, Fran Carlon, Phoebe Brand Carnovsky, Cliff Carpenter, Lon Clark, Bert Cowlan, Esther Dekker, Robert Donley, Toni Garon, Madeline Lee Gilford, Sondra Gorney, Martha Greenhouse, Toni Heller Hall, Carl Harms, Cy Harrice, Helena Seroy Harrice, Bettye Ackerman Jaffe, Jim Jensen, Chris Karner, Ann Loring, Peg Lynch, Barbara Nelson Mach, Frank Maxwell, Tyler McVey, Arnold Moss, Jean Muir, Lillian Clark Oliver, Frances Reid, Kenneth Roberts,

Bill Ross, Abby Lewis Seymour, Bob Spiro, Margot Stevenson, and Ezra Stone.

Thanks to the "non-AFTRAns" as well: Joseph Balfior, Margaret Bauer, Mortimer Becker, Himan Brown, Tatiana Jolin Collingwood, Michael Collyer, John "Jack" L. Dales, Jr., Jan Dekker, Denise DuPont, David Elliot, Elizabeth Faulk, Walter Grinspan, Francesca Heller, Franklin Heller, Eilanna Hindle, David Jaffe, Henry Jaffe, Donald Janney, Harold Kocin, Audrey Mason, Chester L. Migden, A. Frank Reel, Alan Reitman, Anita Ross-Fein, Harriet Schwartz, Ethelle Shatz, Anthony Tollin, and Sanford "Bud" Wolff.

Special thanks go to Gene Francis, former officer of the TvA, and Mary Sagarin, Heller's private secretary, who offered me their own written memories to use as I would; and to Bill Lipton, former board member of AFTRA, for the same generosity of spirit. Finally, my particular thanks and deep appreciation go to Mrs. Clara Heller, who opened her home, her heart, and her life's precious memories to me.

For your inestimable help, I am indebted to you all.

THOSE WONDERFUL, TERRIBLE YEARS

The Actors' Forum

It was the fall of 1932, the low point of the Great Depression. The once-dizzying economy of the late 1920s had steadily, mercilessly slowed to a near halt. Sixteen million working Americans, one out of every three, were laid-off. Hundreds of thousands were evicted from their homes; farms were foreclosed; businesses were shuttered. Masses wandered with nowhere to go. Jay Gorney's and E. Y. Harburg's "Brother, Can You Spare a Dime?" was the ballad of the day. And Democrat Franklin Delano Roosevelt, governor of the State of New York, was campaigning for the presidency of the United States.

On Broadway too, with money scarce and in competition with inexpensive "movies" and the new, free radio, theater had begun a ten-year-long struggle simply to stay alive. New York productions numbering 239 in the 1929–30 season would drop to fewer than one hundred; permanent stock companies, from 165 to 30. Five thousand professional performers, some say more, were out of work.

Despite the mean and perilous times, what theater there was in 1932 was often brilliant and richly creative. Noel Coward's *Design for Living,* with Alfred Lunt and Lynn Fontanne; Eugene O'Neill's *Mourning Becomes Electra,* with Alice Brady and Judith Anderson; Cole Porter's *Gay Divorce,* with Fred Astaire and Claire Luce; and Jerome Kern's and young Oscar Hammerstein's newly returned *Show Boat,* with Dennis King, Norma Terris, Helen Morgan, and Paul Robeson had opened and were playing on the great white way.

Clara Mahr, daughter of Hungarian-born musical-comedy singer Julia Kelety and former member of the Repertory Theater of Pecs, was enjoying a budding New York career. Featured the previous season in Frances Hart's and Frank Carstarphen's *Bellamy Trial* on Broadway and in Fred Ballard's *Ladies of the Jury* opposite Alice Brady on the "subway circuit," she had just been set for a November opening of Don Marquis' *Dark Hours*, a "rewriting of the crucifixion," one reviewer would say.

Shortly into rehearsal, the producers decided that the play needed incidental music. They were bringing in a young composer named George Heller, better known on the street as an actor, singer, and dancer, whose musical arrangements for S. Ansky's *Dybbuk*, at the now-defunct Neighborhood Playhouse, had won him favorable notices. He would compose, conduct the chorus, and sing offstage the words of Jesus.

Clara Mahr remembered, "My first glimpse of George was in the dim, backstage light. He was off in a corner talking with some people when, suddenly, he broke away and started, rather briskly, in my direction.

"He was a little below average height, not much more than five-foot-six, lean and lithe with a wonderful head of wavy, chestnut hair, great dark eyes and a funny bump on his nose. A 'mistake,' I'd learn later, given him by a dance partner in some earlier show. 'Say-y-y,' he'd stopped directly in front of me, 'haven't I seen you somewhere before?' As an opening remark, it came as a bit of a disappointment, and I thought to myself, 'This is a pretty fresh young fellow—although, I must admit, he's awfully good-looking.' "

In that single moment, Clara Mahr could hardly have guessed that this "pretty fresh young fellow" would reshape not only her life but, within a very few years, the lives of thousands of others as well.

" 'Come on, now,' I answered, cutting the conversation short, 'that's such an old line.'

" 'No, really!' he insisted. 'You look so much like—ah—of course,' and now he was laughing, 'like my sister.'

"It sounded rather doubtful," Clara continued, "but in time I found it was true. George lost both his parents when he was still a teenager; from then on he was watched over by his two older sisters. And I looked so much like one of them that she could have been *my* sister as well!"

•

George Heller was born in Brooklyn, New York, on November 20, 1906, the last of four children and the first born in America. His parents, both deeply rooted in the Torah and the old ways of life, had immigrated from Pinsk, Russia, where his father had been a successful businessman. Without a hand trade, however, he floundered in the new country. To be a "common peddler" was degrading. He buried himself, instead, in one of the hundreds of sweatshops of the time and toiled there for years, so that his family could have a decent life. Suddenly and unexpectedly—on the morning of George's fifteenth birthday—he died of what was described later as "gastric complications."

Young George wanted nothing more now than to go on the stage. He could dance, and he sang beautifully. He wanted to follow in the footsteps of his older brother, Sam, who earlier had become an actor, albeit secretly, in New York's Yiddish Theater. But he knew it would break his mother's heart; he remembered the shame, the disgrace his parents had suffered when Sam's secret was finally discovered. George promised he would stay in school and continue with his piano studies.

It was not long before his brilliance at the keyboard brought him to the attention of concert artists Joseph Lhevinne and his wife, Rosina. The Lhevinnes took young Heller under their wing on a full scholarship. Their relationship and his studies continued on and off for many years.

Heller was eighteen when his mother died of cancer. It was then that he became involved with the popular Neighborhood Playhouse—the "miracle on Grand Street"—one of the avant-garde little theaters of the 1920s that, with its new plays and innovative production methods, so influenced the theater of the day.

He appeared there in *The Dybbuk*, in Richard Sheridan's *Critic*, and in Alfred Savoir's *Lion Tamer*, among others. Then, he was off to Broadway and the satirical revue *Grand St. Follies of 1927*, and *of 1928*, and *of 1929*. The up-and-coming James Cagney was his fellow song-and-dance man. Sandwiched between the several follies were four resounding flops, one of which he produced himself, losing every penny he had earned and more at his regular day job as a runner for a Wall Street investment firm.

Later, Heller toured for the Shuberts in a now-forgotten musical. It was there, on a Wednesday matinee in Detroit, that the famous "mistake" occurred. By the time he took himself to a doctor, the broken septum had knit, resulting in severe sinus trouble, which plagued him for months and eventually forced him to leave a new booking in the Chicago company of Ring Lardner's and George Kaufman's hit comedy, *June Moon*.

"I was pretty disgusted with the whole theater game by then," he wrote to his sister Kitty in Spring Valley, New York, in February 1930, "and could think of nothing but getting the hell out." The postmark, to Kitty's surprise, was not from the Windy City, where she had last heard from him, but from Cristobal, the Panama Canal Zone.

> You probably know about my interest in aviation, so when a friend told me about a job with vast potentialities starting on the ground floor of a very progressive aviation company, I was elated. The company, by the way, is called The Pan-American Airways, Inc.

One opportunity led quickly to another. With the help of some flyer friends, Heller became a candidate for the U.S. Army's Flying Cadet School: "I've studied all the angles of my situation," George wrote Kitty.

> Consider me: Talented a bit in an enterprise that is rapidly going on

the rocks—not very much interested in the dull complacent work of an office man and very much interested in a change so I may continually improve myself mentally and financially.

September 22, 1930, France Field, Canal Zone:

Dear Kitty and Sam, Have just received my appointment as Flying Cadet as of December. Your kind offer to help is appreciated but . . . I'm perfectly happy here on the $45 a month plus $2 extra for sharp-shooter pay. I also make $25 a month coaching some doctor in town who thinks he can sing, and I also make about $30 per for a little orchestra I've organized, so you see I pull in about $100 odd a month without even trying. . . . Honestly tho you never have to worry about me financially because I'll live on twenty cents a day if I have to and have a swell time doing it.

Sister Kitty was proved right, however, when she wrote George of her fear that he might be "too temperamental for this new venture." By the summer of 1931, he was back in New York City and living with sister Mildred, only one more of the growing thousands of "at liberty" performers seeking work in a field more and more constricted by the deepening depression. He wrote Kitty:

Haven't been able to close any of my leads—the musical comedy seems to have died an uneventful death from the most common of all theatrical diseases—i.e., lack of money. I did a broadcast at the Columbia Broadcasting abode . . . but the Jinx still seems to be following me around. I'm determined to stay with it through the month of August for that is the most promising of theatrical months. . . . I'm resolved to give this thing one good whole-hearted try . . . so that I won't have the necessity of calling myself a quitter.

And in December:

Dear Kitt, Can you send me a little money—I need a pair of shoes and a couple of other things. I've decided to go back to the Army. . . . I simply cannot see my way clear to accept any more help from you or Mildred. Please know that I shall always remember and appreciate what you have tried to do for me and I shall never forget.

Despite the shadowing jinx, despite a fire in Mildred's apartment that destroyed all his piano music, despite the numberless leads to nowhere, Heller managed to hang on. Finally, November 10, 1932, in what was surely a turn for the better:

Dear Kitt, Here's something you might like to see. I have a couple of tickets for dress rehearsal this Sat. night. If you cannot use them let me know. Everything is going nicely. With all my love, George.

The Dark Hours opened to a bare minimum of praise; even Heller's Voice of Jesus did not move the critics. The show ran only eight performances, long enough, however, for the relationship between Clara Mahr and George Heller to sweeten measurably. By closing, the two were a couple making the rounds of talent agents and producers together, looking for their next shows, picking up an occasional job in radio in the meantime.

"When we met," Clara remembered, "George was definitely on his uppers—broke, that is. Still, everything with him was fun. He was warm and charming, full of genuine good humor—the kind of fellow who had a hug for everyone. Women loved him." Clara most of all.

They found their new shows: she, Claire Kummer's comedy, *Amourette*; he, the first revival of Bertolt Brecht and Kurt Weill's *Three-penny Opera*. Edward Locke's oft-revived *The Climax*, starring Norma Terris (in which he played a concert pianist), was next. Then came the show that would be the pivotal moment in Heller's career—Kenyon Nicholson's and Charles Robinson's comedy *Sailor, Beware!* The couple found their future as well. They married late in the 1933–34 season.

•

"I remember one typical Heller moment," Clara told me. "We were newlyweds and had just moved into an apartment in Greenwich Village. What with our late-night schedules and the unpacking, it was long past midnight when we finally fell asleep. Around 7:30 A.M., from behind the common wall and directly overhead, someone started practicing scales on a piano—haltingly, at first, then louder, more confident and with more missed notes.

" 'Oh, no,' George moaned, and tossed fitfully. The practice continued, 'Oh, please,' he wailed, 'I can't sta-a-and it. Not another moment!' He leaped out of bed. 'I'm going over there and tell him he's got to stop!'

" 'You mustn't do that,' I protested, 'he has the right.' But George was already in his robe and out the door. I listened . . . all was silence. In a few minutes, he was back and under the covers.

" 'What did you say?' I demanded, 'How did you get him to stop?'

" 'Well, first of all,' he answered carefully, 'it's a *her*, not a him, and as cute as a bug in a rug. I was my most charming. I *begged* her to see it our way. I *pleaded* with her not to start *quite* so early in the morning. And,' now there was grin on his face and his eyes sparkled, 'I offered to give her piano lessons.' "

•

Sailor, Beware!, a "rowdy but funny farce," according to one review, opened at the Lyceum September 28, 1933, to uniformly good notices. There were accolades for the entire company and, with a top ticket of $3.85, big box-office receipts for the producers. But on Saturday night, pay night, a few weeks into the run, the three leading players were notified that beginning the following week their salaries would be reduced by 30 percent. The three refused the ultimatum to either accept the cut or leave the show. Monday morning, management gave them notice and proceeded to replace them with Junior Members of the Actors' Equity Association.

This money-saving maneuver, often used to prolong the life of a failing show, was becoming an all-too-common occurrence, even with the most successful Broadway productions. The players had been deceived; they were unhappy, but they were also helpless. An emergency plea to Equity was for naught. (Among the many agencies that the by-then President Roosevelt had created to rescue the failed economy was the joint industry and government National Recovery Administration [NRA], which set codes regulating profits and wages for hundreds of troubled industries throughout the country. Actors employed for two years or more were designated Senior Members of Actors' Equity; their salaries, forty dollars minimum per week. Those working less than two years, Junior Members, earned twenty-five dollars.)

"George was furious," Clara said. "What a reward for helping make *Sailor, Beware!* a hit. He called the cast together. I can hear him now—all passion, conviction, and direct to the point. 'Listen, if management is allowed to get away with this, it will be our jobs next. There's only one way to stop it. The threat of a full-company walkout!' "

Heller made sense, but was he right? And could his judgment be trusted? A decision was made. The next morning, en masse, with Heller at the head, the entire troupe handed in their notices. Confronted with having to close a hit, management did an aboutface. The original company—with their original salaries—returned to normal and a very respectable six-month run. The audacious George Heller, performing in a new but comfortable role of labor leader, had completed his first successful negotiation.

•

Actors' Equity Association, whose motto read "One for All and All for One," was the sole bargaining agent for all stage performers. Founded in 1913 by a group of prominent actors committed to ending the greed and heartlessness of producing managements, it struggled for six years and endued a bitter thirty-day strike before gaining recognition. It would be four more years and dozens more battles, however—one with a new company union, led by song-and-dance man George M. Cohan—before it secured a universal Equity shop and a standard minimum contract. By 1933, with a second office in Los Angeles and a membership of five thousand (cut by half in the first years of the depression), it stood in the field of legitimate theater as a respected, well-off, and highly influential organization.

"But it had grown lazy," Clara Heller told me, "and fallen out of touch with the average member—more like a social club than a labor organization."

Indeed, to emphasize its separateness from the traditional labor union, Equity named itself an *association*. The distinguished, well-loved Frank Gillmore—a founding member, leader of the 1919 strike, and Equity's first executive (1918–28)—had served as president for the previous six years. The council, Equity's governing body, was made up largely of matured, celebrated performers, several of whom were actor-managers. "And were, we felt," said Clara, "too closely aligned with the interests of the producing management."

Equity's Annual Spring Membership Meeting in the beautiful Grand Ballroom of the old Astor Hotel, at Broadway and Forty-fourth Streets, had an urbane elegance to it, a welcomed once-a-year gathering of thespians, many of whom had been out on tour and had not met for months. Scheduled for 1:00 P.M., rarely did it start before 2:00. "It was," as one teenaged member described it, "like a party—guys kissing girls, girls kissing guys, guys kissing guys—it was lovely!"

Incumbent officers were reliably reelected there. Matters of general importance were reported—the government's funding of Equity projects, the financial state of the fifty-year-old Actors' Fund and similar welfare projects (thousands of pairs of shoes and over one-half million dollars had been distributed to date to indigent actors and their families). Proper recognition was given and suitable tributes paid. Good-bye, we'll meet again next year.

No grievances were raised, nor criticisms made of the association's actions or inactions, as the case may be. That would have been undignified, unmannerly, or—in the troubled early 1930s—too foreign sounding, too radical, even communistic. Such incursions would be dealt with by President Gillmore's smart and silencing, "Out of Order."

True, Equity's first contract, achieved in 1919, had notably improved the then-prevailing conditions. Performers were at last protected from "spontaneous" firings and from being stranded on the road, unpaid and without means of returning home. An eight-performance week was established (no more unpaid extra performances or half-pay for particular weeks of the year); there was also the all-important arbitration clause. And what had been perpetual rehearsals—up to ten weeks for dramas, eighteen for musicals—were limited to four weeks for dramas and five for musicals—without pay, however. But in 1933, there were evermore problems crying out for solutions.

The *Sailor, Beware!* incident served to mobilize a number of dynamic young Broadway players. They too were troubled by management's abuses and Equity's seeming lack of response to dilemmas faced daily by working actors. Heller and his colleagues, just a handful to start, initiated what became regular, after-theater talk sessions at the Methodist Episcopal Church on Forty-eighth Street near Broadway. Long gone now but known fondly then as "the actors' church," it was where the hungry could get a real meal down in the basement for only thirty cents.

The apparent leaders of the group were George Heller; the brilliant, outrageously funny, veteran actor-director Philip Loeb of Howard Dietz's and Arthur Schwartz's *Band Wagon*, soon to open in John Murray's and Allen Boretz's *Room Service*; the gentle, wry-humored, scholarly Sam Jaffe, Kringelein in Vicki Baum's *Grand Hotel* and Czar Peter III opposite Marlene Dietrich in the film *The Scarlet Empress*; and the dynamic, ebullient, larger-than-life Albert Van Dekker, Baron Von Gaigern in *Grand Hotel* and, recently, of Victor Wolfson's *Bitter Stream*.

Interest grew steadily; the press took notice. Performers came from companies all around New York: Victor Kilian, Will Geer, Virginia Farmer, Will Lee, Burgess Meredith, and so many others. And from the Group Theatre they came: Moris Carnovsky, Phoebe Brand, Tony Kraber, J. Edward Bromberg, Elia Kazan, and Lee J. Cobb. Within five months, attendance had soared to nearly two hundred, some say as much to see Phil Loeb do his hilarious takeoffs on Equity incumbents as to discuss the issues.

Bound together by good fellowship, mutual respect, and a sense of adventure that comes from a shared purpose, the Actors' Forum (as George Heller named it) reached a consensus. They resolved to work for change from within the Actor's Equity Association, to be, in the best sense of the phrase, Equity's loyal opposition.

They would nominate and elect their own members to council to "stiffen the hands of the officers, fight for the needs of the average actor, and make the Council strong." Their platform called for rehearsal pay of twenty-five dollars a week, a "cuts board" to decide whether salary or cast reductions were justified, four membership meetings a year, election reforms, and of leading importance, a contract in the new field of radio broadcasting, where performers with little work in the theater were flocking for employment—performers accustomed to, and insistent on, protection by their union.

Esther Guerini Van Dekker, wife of Albert, herself an actress (she and Albert met and married during the 1922 Theater Guild production of Karel Capek's *R.U.R.*), told me, "George Heller was the driving spirit in the whole effort; a little dynamo. He was more formal, more specific than Albert, who was, by nature, a teller of stories. But George could electrify a crowd like no one I'd ever seen. He was a born leader—a tremendous presence.

"None of the Forum people cared one whit about power or personal status," said Esther. "They were moved only by their convictions. And that can be very upsetting to those on shaky ground."

Outside the caucuses, questions were being raised. What were the political ties of these "radical upstarts"? What was their financial backing? And what were their *real* motives? Was this, perhaps, a move to establish a new union? Were these young divisives even qualified to serve in high office?

In March 1934, at an Equity meeting called for the purpose of electing a nominating committee (one-fifth of the fifty-five-seat council was nominated and elected yearly), the Actors' Forum officially presented itself. With somewhat less than a warm welcome, it was greeted into the electoral process. "Why don't they tell us what they want?" asked President Gillmore. "Perhaps we can work with them."

With its fast-growing constituency, the Forum won several seats on Equity's nine-person Nominating Committee; and at the Annual Spring Membership Meeting several months later, now-candidates Heller, Loeb, Van Dekker, and Kilian were elected to the council for five-year terms. George Arliss, Eddie Cantor, Katharine Cornell, and Augustin Duncan, father of Angus Duncan (Equity's executive secretary from 1952 to 1972), were also elected or reelected the same year. Three others from the Forum won three-year terms. Sam Jaffe would run and be elected some years later.

Forum caucuses continued, however, with the knowledge and agreement of President Gillmore, so that "actors could be provided with an opportunity to discuss and formulate additional plans for the strengthening of the Association." And from that moment on, Equity was never the same.

The year 1934 must have been a nightmare for the staid Mr. Gillmore and friends. For the previous decade, he and Executive Secretary Paul Dullzell, with the ever-reliable support of the council, had accomplished the routine business of a national organization in a congenial, unpressured atmosphere rarely interrupted by member dissent—and then only on issues not having to do with operating procedure. All had been in near-perfect order.

Then, the administration was besieged by seven articulate, highly motivated, well-informed "troublemakers from the outside." Supported by an activist caucus as well as by several like-minded councilors, they scrutinized, analyzed, and otherwise demanded change in old policies to meet current needs.

They called for the abolishment of the junior minimum wage and the setting of a single minimum of forty dollars per week, rehearsal expenses of twenty-five dollars per week for principals, fifteen dollars for extras, and only Equity members to be employed as extras. They pressed for the cuts board, prohibition of agents in default, regulation of summer stock, closer cooperation with other unions, and enactment of unemployment insurance. (Although Forum councilors were not Communists, the American Communist Party was the first to make unemployment insurance a major cause and can be credited with raising the cry that resulted in its ultimate passage.)

Strangely, the majority of the council, the regulars (represented as having sharply divergent views from the Forum), offered no program of their own. Rather, they labeled the movement dangerous, accusing it of attempting to subvert the association. Fourth Vice President Peggy Wood, leading lady of John Van Druten's *Old Acquaintance* and Otto Harbach's and Jerome Kern's *Cat and the Fiddle*, spoke in defense at the tumultuous First Quarterly Membership Meeting:

> I assure you the Council has not sat with folded arms . . . but could not lay down rules without knowing how they would work out, or make rules and then wait and see what would happen. As for the Forum claims that they were responsible for the institution of the 'cuts board,' the idea had been presented earlier, and, on occasion, managers had been required to bring in their books to verify cutting salaries.

The firing point between the two sides, Miss Wood would have one believe, was not of substance but rather of timing, of manners, of style.

Heywood Broun, many years a columnist for the *New York World-Telegram* and sometimes actor, wrote in the May 1935 issue of *The Nation* magazine:

> The rulers of Equity have been less than scrupulously fair in meeting the drive of the Forum. They have raised the red herring and whirled it over their heads with fury. At a meeting March 1, a policeman was called in to remove a member who demanded the privileges of the floor. It is true . . . that some of the newer theatrical groups are heavily represented . . . but many have allied themselves upon the simple belief that Frank Gillmore has been president too long and

has grown just a wee bit inefficient. One could hardly think that this constituted communism.

•

"I was the 'gofer' for the Actors' Forum," said Ezra Stone, who played the young Henry Aldrich in Clifford Goldsmith's *What a Life!* on Broadway and again on the radio series *The Aldrich Family*. (He would direct then show when it moved, later, to television.) "I was seventeen, a young rebel, and a recent graduate of the American Academy of Dramatic Arts where Phil Loeb was my stern, unrelenting teacher and my beloved second father.

"For years, my contribution to the Forum was rounding up the necessary one hundred signatures of members in good standing on petitions Phil needed to present to council the following Tuesday. I'd report in at the Playhouse for 'half hour' [the thirty-minute period prior to curtain when all actors must be *in* the theater] on a given Saturday matinee—all thanks to Phil, my earliest job was as understudy to the great Teddy Hart in Holm's and Abbott's *Three Men on a Horse*. Then I'd set off on a carefully plotted route covering all backstages in the district. By evening half hour, I'd returned—victorious and full of pride—my mission was a success!" And this is how Ezra Stone earned his nickname: it was then the time of the Spanish Civil War. A woman, a spellbinding orator and militant leader of the Spanish left, had risen to worldwide attention for the dangerous missions she undertook on behalf of her suffering people. Considered an authentic Spanish Joan of Arc, she was known as La Pasionaria, the passion flower. In honor of Ezra's "grand service to the cause," Loeb, with his usual tongue-in-cheek, dubbed him "La Petition-aria."

•

Opposition to the Forum leaders continued to mount. It welled up and spilled over; invectives, such as "those bastards," "those Reds," were regularly and recklessly hurled. But nowhere did passions run higher than in the offices of the Equity administrators.

November 1, 1935, the gauntlet was flung. President Gillmore announced that he and Paul Dullzell would step down from their posts if the policies and procedures of the "Forumites," as he markedly called them, were upheld by membership vote. A highly publicized, much-discussed special meeting, "never before heard of in Equity's history," was called. It would be the public contest between the left and the right, the young and the old, the regulars versus the Actors' Forum. Two thousand members jammed the Astor Hotel ballroom to witness the fray.

Gillmore made his case. In a lengthy, impassioned speech, he accused the Forum of a laundry list of misbehaviors: obstructionism, disrupting the normal manner of doing business, creating a schism, and trying to tie the association with Communist groups.

"Under the persistent prodding of the Forum," spoke the harassed Gillmore,

> we have been stampeded into a orgy of new rules which make it more difficult for the managers to produce, which has increased the cost of production. When a person (like an industry) is sick you try to give him a rest, you don't add to his burdens, that is unless you wish to kill him off entirely.

Philip Loeb refuted each of Gillmore's accusations. On the point of "tying up with Communist groups," he explained that the Forum supported the Lundeen Unemployment Insurance Bill because it was the only bill to come out of Congress that specifically included actors. Loeb read a list of fifty-five non-Communist organizations, state and city governments, as well as labor unions—the Screen Actors Guild, the Musicians Local No. 802, and the Dramatists Guild included—who were also in support. "So if the Forum is Red because it backed the worker's bill," said Loeb, "then everybody is Red." The hall was thrown into chaos.

Heywood Broun attempted to calm the waters: "Well, you can't say it's a bad thing . . . to have a meeting as big as this. When you promise a fight, everybody turns out.

"Now, as a labor leader, like Mr. Gillmore"—Broun was the founder and then president of the American Newspaper Guild—"I know there is an organized group in opposition." He went on,

> Sometimes I am with the opposition, sometimes I am against it. . . . I have gotten into violent controversy and called people God-damned liars in open meeting. After, I apologized and we shook hands, and I realized it was an excellent thing to have a lively opposition in a vital labor group. . . . Actors' Equity ought to decide that it is . . . a part of the labor movement and not just a semi-professional kaffee klatch of geniuses and people of high talents.

Executive Secretary Dullzell spoke:

> The Forum is a comparatively small group but it has gained force and power far beyond its size. . . . It is obvious that [it] is trying to . . . alienate the actors' understanding of Equity [and] to undermine [its] prestige, goodwill and good name with the public, the government and all the crafts in the theater.

The association long prided itself on its relationship with government officials and members of Congress and relied on their high regard for generous funding of projects for unemployed members.

Fierce protests and weighted statements favoring one side, then the other continued for nearly three hours. Some urged that it not come down to an either-or vote: "There are those of us who wish [Gillmore and Dullzell] to stay and who also approve the actions of the Forum." A motion from the council endorsing the executives and deploring as dangerous "all gatherings of members except under the auspices of Equity" was presented and voted upon. Ballots were taken out to be counted; the highly charged atmosphere calmed.

Next on the agenda–and of far greater concern to most—was what actors currently on relief could expect from the newly established Works Progress Administration (WPA) and its Federal Theater Project. Despite 150 petitioners' making this discussion, properly, a *first* order of business, the item was dropped. President Gillmore announced that the time allotted for the use of the hall was up.

"Mr. Chairman" and "Point of Order" rang from all corners, to no avail. There were appeals for an informal discussion to follow, for a motion for a special meeting, but neither would be entertained by the chair. Nor would Gillmore assure the outraged members that their requests would be considered in a timely fashion.

Sam Jaffe demanded from the floor, "Are we to be guided by constitutional procedure or not? A motion had been made and seconded. The floor should be opened for discussion. This is not a one-man operation!" The Forum's use of *Robert's Rules of Order*—overuse it was said—was the bane of the administration's existence.

Gillmore called for a motion to adjourn. "No-o-o," echoed throughout the hall. Nonetheless, he spun out in an instant, "All in favor, say 'aye'; opposed, say 'no'; the 'ayes' have it; you stand adjourned!"

At that moment, a teller rushed in carrying the results of the previous ballot. Gillmore signaled for quiet and announced that the motion upholding the administration had passed by a vote of nearly three to one. Supporters roared their approval. Several Forum leaders were observed rushing onto the platform. "Then," as editor Alfred Harding of *Equity* magazine observed, "something extraordinary happened."

Through the din, the Forum reported that the Astor Hotel had agreed to an additional fifteen minutes, and that time would be used to open discussion on the Federal Theater Project. Gillmore angrily denied them the right to do so, declaring, "This is not an Equity meeting." His supporters crowded the dais shouting threats and curses, refusing to allow the discussion to begin. Then, from the floor, "In the wildest and most unexpected ending an Equity meeting ever had," Harding wrote, a Forum leader leaped upon a chair and shouted instructions into the crowd.

Whereupon, some five hundred persons rose as one and departed the premises.

"If the Forum wished it," commented a member left behind, "they could not have staged a better demonstration of their particular brand of harassment than the one just performed."

Nevertheless, from *Equity* magazine we learn that, as uncompromising a situation as it appeared, two significant actions came out of that day: "Council has agreed to a series of membership discussion meetings the first Friday of each month . . . beginning immediately; the agenda and presiding officer to be designated by Council." And George Heller advised President Gillmore by mail that "all future Actors' Forum meetings are hereby cancelled."

"The clash had cleared the air," the administration wrote, "and, because of it, Equity will enjoy better mutual understanding and fewer strained relations. And if that has come to pass, the meeting at the Astor and everything for which it stood has been worth the effort."

But not quite yet. Two months later, Equity received a letter:

> I *demand* you take *definitive punitive action* . . . over the behavior of *George Heller* and *Albert Van Dekker*. The disgraceful incident on Friday . . . is *sickening*, but definite proof of what these men and their "group" *represent* and stand for. . . . I again demand that they be *expelled* from the Council at once . . . a Council whose activities have never been in question until the birth of this undeniably communistic movement. . . . Stop them *now*, in their tracks. Fight them as they *deserve* to be fought.

In yet another first, the January 1936 *Equity* magazine tells us that Heller and Van Dekker were brought to trial and charged with conduct unbecoming members of the council.

The "disgraceful incident on Friday" occurred at the Fourth Quarterly Membership Meeting, during the final stages of a debate concerning the Federal Theater Project's proposed wage scales. George Heller was speaking from the dais, pointing up the inadequacies of the government's offer. From the front row, directly beneath the speaker, one Laurence O'Sullivan, "a member frequently in opposition to the administration and now in opposition to the opposition," began to heckle.

"Heller could have appealed to the chair," the report continued,

> but, instead, elected to reply himself . . . and, although witnesses disagree as to the particular epithet which provoked the action, there is no doubt as to what happened. Suddenly, Mr. Heller jumped from the platform, ran directly to O'Sullivan, now risen to his feet, and swarmed all over him.

Clara Heller remembered the incident: "I was there and heard it. O'Sullivan called him 'a dirty Jew.' It was right that George do it—it was also very funny."

"O'Sullivan, several inches taller and many pounds heavier," the magazine wrote,

> made no attempt to strike his smaller opponent, but contented himself with defending himself. All over the hall, people were on their feet; there was a surge forward. . . . Because of the manner in which he extended his sympathy and support, members present believe Councilor Van Dekker . . . aided and abetted Heller in the attack.

The hearing was scheduled for the next bimonthly council meeting. Van Dekker, who would be screen-testing at Warner Brothers Pictures for his first film, *The Great Garrick* starring Olivia DeHavilland, was unable to attend. He wrote to President Gillmore:

> The letters of my Christian friends . . . that furnish the material for this trial are to my mind characteristic of letters written to governors . . . by sick people in state institutions. Usually they are signed by Napoleon or the King of the Sahara and . . . treated accordingly.

Van Dekker had been a psychology student at Bowdoin College and visited just such institutions.

> The indictments are so vague and the language so confused that I don't know what the plaintiffs are talking about. There are to be sure . . . several slanderous statements for which 100 years ago I would have challenged more capable representatives to a duel.

Heller appeared on his own behalf. Apologizing to the council, he declared that "only the disputed epithet would have driven him to such an extreme." Prepared neither to expel him nor to accept his apology as "sufficient reparation for his breach of the peace and disregard for the dignity of his office," the council suspended Heller for a period of ten weeks. There being no real evidence to connect Van Dekker, charges against him were dropped.

" 'Van' hated council meetings," Esther Van Dekker told me, "the hostility and personal vituperation he and the others met there was beyond his patience to endure. He'd walk around the West Forty-seventh Street block, one or more times, before he could face going inside. 'What has this got to do with being an actor?' he'd fume at me. George and Phil were better able to work their way through."

But the uncompromising Philip Loeb, the constant critic of the administration, who remained on the council long after both Van Dekker and

Heller left, would feel the sting of public reprimand as well. He too was vilified as a "rabble-rouser," as a "dirty Jew," as a "Communist."

Though there was eventually praise for Heller—Gillmore would one day describe him as "an indefatigable, faithful worker and most able Councilor"—he and his colleagues had radically shaken the decorum of the association and in so doing had bruised many powerful old-liners. These political wounds would fester; and some sooner, some later, Equity's loyal opposition, each in his own way, would be made to pay the price.

•

"Still, those were wonderful years for George and me," Clara Heller said. "Council was revitalized and opened up to the problems of the workaday actor. The reforms the Forum put in place then are still in effect today. And George, unlike so many others in the business, was working regularly."

In 1935, Heller appeared with Elia Kazan, Lee J. Cobb, Russ Collins, Roman Bohnen, and Dorothy Patten in the Group Theatre production of Clifford Odets' revolutionary one-acters *Waiting for Lefty* and *Till the Day I Die*. Later the same year, he played in the Soviet farce *Squaring the Circle*, by Yevgeny Petrov Katayev, adapted by Nikolay Ostrovsky.

Fran Carlon, who played Lorelei on *Big Town*, among many other roles on stage and radio, saw him in that production. "George was a brilliant actor," Fran said, "with a dynamic presence on stage. And as a Communist Party chief embroiled with two newly married couples in the same room, he was marvelous—and very, very funny."

But Heller's biggest break was still to come. While attending the theater one night, George and Clara were approached by Bill Liebling, a well-known talent agent of the day.

"George," Liebling began, "you don't happen to play the xylophone, do you?"

"Yes, of course I do," I said, without blinking an eye. Bill did a 50-foot broad jump.

"Well, grab your xylophone and follow me," said Liebling. "You're just the man Kaufman and Hart have been scouring the city for!"

At that point I admitted that I didn't *exactly* play the xylophone. Actually, it was a "patala," a Burmese instrument I'd mastered while at the Neighborhood Playhouse—very much like the xylophone, though. Liebling was convinced and took me to Kaufman and Hart.

I pleaded with them, "Look, fellows, just give me a week." And they agreed.

For seven days in a second-rate hotel near Broadway, I boned up—even learned a couple numbers by Beethoven. By the time they heard me, I wasn't perfect, but I was good enough to get the part." (From an interview in the *New York World-Telegram*.)

George Heller opened at the Booth Theater, December 15, 1936, as the young husband in the Pulitzer prize-winning comedy *You Can't Take It with You*. Brooks Atkinson's review in *The New York Times* was a rave for the show, the stars—Henry Travers and Josephine Hull—and the entire company: "The best comedy Mr. Hart and Mr. Kaufman have written."

Clara Heller's review: "George was absolutely charming in it—simply delightful."

•

One Actors' Forum promise was, as yet, unkept: a contract in radio broadcasting.

Equity surveys of the field confirmed that radio was in total disorder. Actors, announcers, and singers had no idea, from one show to the next, how long they would work and how much or, in some cases, *if* they would be paid. As the field grew more and more crowded, certain performers began bidding against one another's services, driving the small, erratic fees even lower.

The association deplored the conditions but chose to wait for the NRA to assign an administrator to review the field and establish a code—"a fair and strong code," President Gillmore said, "to which Equity should be consulted in the final revision and given a place on the authority designated to administer [it]."

By January 1936, the NRA had collapsed under the weight of a U.S. Supreme Court decision invalidating its compulsory-code system. Now, one year later, the situation for performers had worsened, not only in New York, the broadcast capital of the country, but in all radio centers, large and small, coast to coast. It was time to take the initiative; Heller pressured the council. We must organize the field ourselves!

•

2

~~~~~

First, Radio Equity

From a few experimental wireless stations dotting the country—notably Lee De Forest's Radio Telephone Company in New York in 1907, and two years later, Charles Herrold's fifteen watt-station (soon to be KCBS) in San Jose, California—evolved the great, sophisticated radio networks of today, under the marketing genius of men like David Sarnoff and William Paley.

By the early 1930s, some thirty million Americans, who knew little of electromagnetic waves, audion tubes, or regenerative receivers, were grateful only that in this grinding, never-ending depression they were blessed with one modern-day miracle. For, with but a twist of the dial, any citizen could tune in the world: from the ominous rumblings out of Europe to President Roosevelt's fireside chats, to sporting events, concerts, religious services, informational programs, and—for the pure, unmindful joy of it—the wonderful world of entertainment.

Fred Allen, Jack Benny, Amos and Andy, and their gangs; Fibber McGee and his Molly; Will Rogers; the voices of Jessica Dragonette, Arthur Tracy, and Vivienne Della Chiesa; the dramas of Norman Corwin; and the horror stories of Arch Oboler were but a few of an evening's delights.

In daytime, too, there were the heart-wrenching "serial dramas" to help lighten household chores—*Our Gal Sunday, Backstage Wife, Ma Perkins*, and dozens of other stalwarts soon to come. Radio was richly diversified, easy to understand, and best of all, it was free for the listening.

All programs were originally "aired" unsponsored. Soon, promoters of small, affordable items—cigarettes, patent medicines, beauty products—recognized the potential of this incredible new marketplace. Advertising agencies vied to buy up radio time from which to hawk their sponsor's goods, prompting President Herbert Hoover to warn that the airwaves—the people's airwaves—could be "taken over by a lot of advertising chatter." Nonetheless, a faithful public gobbled up any product that, whether sung or talked about, brought them their favorite shows.

By mid 1937, while President Roosevelt in his second inaugural address despaired that "one-third of this nation is ill-housed, ill-clothed, and ill-nourished," radio networks, sponsors, and their advertising agencies were sitting in the catbird seat of an immensely popular and profitable industry. The Golden Age of radio was in full flower.

"For performers it was chaos," said Jackson Beck, *The Cisco Kid* and narrator on *Superman* ("Faster than a speeding bullet . . ."), among many others. "Unless you were the star of the show, and they earned in the thousands, you never knew what your income would be." And every producer at every station in New York—the Federal Communications Commission (FCC) acknowledged seven; *Billboard* magazine said twelve; but Beck counted twenty-one at the time, "some you couldn't even hear"—had his own set of rates.

"When you worked for Frank and Anne Hummert, of Blackett, Sample and Hummert, on one of their fifteen-minute daytime serials, for example, you took home exactly $11.88. On a thirty-minute nighttime show you'd get five bucks for a small part, maybe $35, occasionally $50 for a lead. Sometimes, you'd get an additional five for a rebroadcast." Before the transcontinental hookup linked the networks' owned-and-operated stations (the o & o's), performers returned to the studio three hours after the initial broadcast to repeat it "live" for the West Coast. "Those figures sound ridiculous today," said Beck, "but if you hustled, you could make two hundred a week. With rent about $140 a month for a three-room apartment, that was pretty good money. If you got really busy, you'd hire a stand-in to cover the rehearsals you couldn't make. I did it myself for Carl Eastman, lead on *Life Can Be Beautiful*—it was a great entree into a director's 'stable.' If your shows were spread out around town, a tip to the elevator operator and a waiting cab (some guys used an ambulance) got you through the day."

As the marketplace continued to expand, established producers balked at paying higher fees than their new competition, and rates headed down. Although the one-hour rehearsal for a fifteen-minute show allowed an actor to work several shows a day, rehearsals for nighttime were "endless." Seven hours was not unusual for a thirty-minute show—at no additional pay. "They don't give you time to eat," and, "There's nowhere to sit," and, "I was let go with no pay, just before air," were regular complaints.

"All that was before George Heller," Jackson Beck remembered, "when members of Equity council, in the great tradition of the 'thea-tah,' looked down their noses at the new medium—performers were 'readers not actors.' Adding radio to their jurisdiction was deemed 'unnecessary.' " Producers concurred for their own reasons: "To organize 'our' performers would be an impossibility!" one told the press.

"But once George got on council," Beck continued, "and started pushing and pulling for a radio contract—and maybe because he became such a 'pain in the ass'—they finally gave in." In June 1937, Actors' Equity established a radio division, naming Heller to head it. He quipped to Clara, "They kicked me upstairs."

July 12 marked Heller's first organizational meeting. "Boy, I'll never forget that night," Beck said. "It was stifling in New York. But despite the heat, 123 of the 125 radio stars George invited showed up.

"I came, too," said Beck. "By then, I was a regular on a couple of shows. Since 1934, I'd built a pretty darned good career with no help from anyone; I didn't need a union to represent me. Then I met George Heller. He was special—his dynamo drive, his brilliant mind—what an inspiration! In that one night, he turned me around to make me what I am today—a union man."

Heller touched and fired everyone that night. Without exception, they pledged for Radio Equity to become the agent for collective-bargaining purposes in the field of broadcasting. The Membership Committee and the Working Conditions Committee were set into motion; a steering committee was established then replaced eight days later by a temporary board of directors, slated to serve for only two months, or until a general election could be held.

•

Los Angeles entertainers had been "walking down the same street." Drawing on another great pool of talent, motion picture performers, major LA stations had developed their own network programming; the town had become the second-largest production center in the country.

But there, fees for supporting players were lower than in New York. A modest earlier effort to organize was met with company threats: "If there is any talk of union, none of you will work again." By 1937, however, a group of 150 actors, headed by Frank Nelson (the neighbor on *Blondie*), Norman Field (Charlie's principal on the *Edgar Bergen and Charlie McCarthy Show*), and John Gibson (Ethelbert on *Casey, Crime Photographer*), had banded together once again under the name Radio Artists Guild (RAG).

And in another part of town, James Wallington (announcer for *The Burns and Allen Show*, among others) told this story: "I was stopped at a light on Santa Monica Boulevard when Dick Powell pulled up beside me. Said he wanted to talk. Seems an agency in town was tying up actors at twenty-five dollars a week. They'd use them a couple of times but, in between, the guys weren't allowed to take any other work. Dick and I met again," said Wallington. "This time with Eddie Cantor, George Burns, Gracie Allen, Bob Hope, Bing Crosby, announcer Ken Carpenter, Edgar Bergen, Gene Hersholt, and some others. We discussed how bad things had gotten for the average performer. That's when we decided to say 'yes' to George Heller and a national union of broadcasters." Only days after New York, Hollywood held their first organizational meeting. Every performer who "is now or hopes to be working in radio" signed a pledge for Radio Equity (Lipton 1963).

It was, indeed, the stars of radio, many of whom were up-and-coming players during the long, painful birth of Actors' Equity, who came through for the workaday performer. They knew what to say, whom to say it to, and how best to say it. To their everlasting credit and alongside Heller, Loeb, and all the others, they rolled up their sleeves and became union organizers.

Equity's President Gillmore, now generous in his praise for "Heller's tireless and efficient organizing efforts," volunteered his guidance and his offices to the "reformed vagabonds of radio." And in Hollywood, Kenneth Thomson, executive of the four-year-old Screen Actors Guild (SAG), opened wide his doors as well.

•

If conditions were bad in the major centers, they were even worse at the smaller stations across America. Word of Radio Equity spread like wildfire, by phone, by letter, by chance, by visiting celebrity. Within weeks, Equity's Dullzell was obliged to report,

> Applications were signed by the hundreds and frantic calls came to us for help from all over the country. It was at this point, we realized that the problems facing radio people were peculiar unto themselves and would require the concentrated attention of a separate organization.

On August 16, 1937, Actors' Equity Association relinquished jurisdiction and, with a charter issued by its parent organization (the Associated Actors and Artistes of America), a new entity was born: the American Federation of Radio Artists. With it went the wholehearted moral support and financial sponsorship of Equity and SAG.

Jackson Beck remembered, "They said to George, 'You want a union for radio? Well, go out and organize one—and here's ninety thousand from each of us to float it. We expect you to pay it back in ten years—if you last that long.' " AFRA paid it back in seven.

•

Chicago, the serial drama capital of America, was the country's third-largest radio-production center; some sixty-eight network shows originated there each week. And there reigned Irna Phillips, the prolific creator-writer of the fifteen-minute form and employer of scores of underpaid, local talent. The sponsor of many of her shows was the Procter Gamble Company, maker of assorted cleansing products. From her longtime commitment with P & G, a fan magazine would one day name Phillips the Queen of the Radio Soap Opera, and upon her crowning a new term in broadcast culture was coined.

Actor Raymond Jones recalled: "I was one of three to get a letter from George Heller in late July asking what the conditions were in our area and if we'd be interested in organizing radio artists. I answered that I'd be *most* interested—wages and conditions here were a mess. But we feared management reprisals—there was a lot of antiunion feeling here. Heller advised that we keep our activity undercover.

"Sixteen of us met, clandestinely," Jones went on. "We promised one another that we wouldn't tell who was there. We mapped out our campaign. At precisely eight o'clock on the morning of August 30, each of us would walk into a studio where a show was rehearsing. We'd hand out AFRA applications and ask if the performers were interested in joining. We got over two hundred members in that one morning and a hundred more in our nighttime visitation. Management couldn't stop us then because there were so many of us, and we were their key people."

Anne Seymour, Mary on *The Story of Mary Marlin* and one of the sixteen, wired Heller on August 31: "Response excitingly favorable. Already have first one hundred dollars in the bank." Orientation meetings began September 1; on the seventeenth, one month and one day after New York and Los Angeles, Chicago received its AFRA charter (Lipton 1963).

Cincinnati, Ohio, the site of the Midwest's largest single radio station, the 500,000-watt WLW, joined one month later, followed by San Francisco (home of the long-running dramatic series *One Man's Family*), then Montreal, and Detroit. Everywhere, pledges were signed for AFRA to bargain for radio performers. Heller, Loeb, Van Dekker, and Jaffe had spawned a national movement whose time had come, and none too soon.

•

Who were these broadcasters at the more than six hundred stations around the country, soon to become "militant freshman" in the field of labor? Many were professional singers and actors; others had been teachers, salesmen, lawyers, engineers, and architects. A number were journalists and editors. Still others came from business and management. AFRA was blessed with a membership that had a broad range of skills and a diversity of intellect unique in the trade-union movement (Lipton 1963).

AFRA's cofounders agreed that a single labor contract, obtaining throughout the country and governed from one major city—like that of Equity in New York and SAG in Hollywood—would not work in the multicentered field of radio broadcasting. They conceived, instead, of a federation of autonomous locals, one in each center, whose executive secretary (chief administrator and negotiator) would bargain for contracts tailored to the area's staff and freelance artists. In addition, a principal or national office would be established in New York to negotiate and protect the contracts of artists working at the networks.

The federation would be governed wholly by its members; the previous tumultuous years at Equity had firmed that conviction. Policy making and management would be vested in a national board of directors, one director for approximately every one hundred members in good standing. The board would be elected by the membership and in proportion to that membership: 50 percent for New York and the East, 30 percent for Los Angeles and the West, 20 percent for Chicago and the Midwest.

Directors would be working members, representatives of the professions employed in broadcasting: singers, actors, and announcers (including sportscasters). There would be no nominating committee in the national AFRA.

Three membership classifications were established: Active, persons who had appeared in at least thirty broadcasts in any capacity or ten as a principal player; Associate, persons who had not appeared a sufficient number of times to qualify as Active; and Nonresident, persons who are citizens neither of the United States nor of Canada. Dues were based on the prior year's earnings: twelve dollars a year for those members earning less than two thousand dollars, plus a ten-dollar initiation fee, sliding upward to one hundred dollars for those earning over fifty thousand, plus a twenty-five-dollar initiation fee. Initiations were waived for Equity members.

AFRA policy would be formulated through a system of participatory democracy, stemming from a yearly convention attended by elected delegates from each local. The convention would rank as the supreme governing body—higher than the AFRA National Board—and could direct or overrule the board on any matter. There, contract proposals would be gathered from the major locals, debated, and approved. Finally, even above the authority of the convention would be a national referendum—the will of the entire membership.

•

"Originally, we wanted Phil Loeb to head AFRA," Bill Ross, stage manager, director, and former Equity councilor told me, "but Phil insisted that George Heller had the superior skills."

Most agreed that the position of national executive secretary was the "natural spot" for Heller, but opposition by Equity and SAG officials soon reduced that likelihood. Some complained of his youth—he was thirty at the time—others of his prominence in the militant Actors' Forum. The split, which brought formation briefly to a halt while aspirants maneuvered for position, ended amicably on August 31, with the appointment of a compromise candidate, Mrs. Emily Holt.

A graduate of the Cornell University School of Law and an organizer of the first NRA Federal Theater, Mrs. Holt was then associate counsel at Equity, in charge of arbitrations. The first woman leader of an AFL union, she would be paid a salary of seventy-five hundred dollars a year. Heller, elected earlier to the office of treasurer, was named part-time associate executive secretary at thirty-five hundred a year.

Equity's Paul N. Turner was appointed general counsel. One of his associates-to-be was Laurence Beilenson of SAG in Hollywood; he would tend AFRA's interests west of the Mississippi River. Turner's associate in the East was the tough, blunt, brilliant Henry Jaffe, then of the new Guild of Musical Artists. For Henry Jaffe—again, no relation to Sam—the appointment would be more than a job. He would become George Heller's closest friend, his lifelong associate, his brother.

In what seemed like only a moment in time—barely eight weeks—the federation had written its constitution, opened seven locals, and scheduled its first national convention. Membership topped three thousand. Thirty-five of a projected fifty-five-member board (including officers) were selected from candidates in the major locals; the remaining seats were held open for locals yet to be established.

The roster of officers, volunteers all, was a glittering array of celebrities: Edward Arnold, Jack Benny, Edgar Bergen, John Boles, Bing Crosby, Martin Gable, Helen Hayes (though she soon resigned to tour in Laurence Housman's *Victoria Regina*), Warren Hull, John McGovern, James Melton, Ray Middleton, Grace Moore, Osgood Perkins (holder of Equity card no. 1 and father of young Anthony), Dick Powell, Lanny Ross, Margaret Speaks, Paul Stewart, and Rudy Vallee, to name a few.

Eddie Cantor, radio's most popular star, an early activist for supporting players on stage and later in film (he served as president of SAG, 1933–35), was elected AFRA's first president. Vice presidents were Norman Field (also named executive of the Los Angeles local), violinist Jascha Heifetz, operatic baritone Lawrence Tibbett (he would serve as president of the New York local, 1940–45, and as president of the national AFRA in 1945), announcer James Wallington, and recording secretary, Lucille Wall (Portia on *Portia Faces Life*).

•

It was the winter of 1937. President Roosevelt had begun his second term in office. Everywhere, conditions for working people and the labor movement as a whole—an integral part of the New Deal's plan—were visibly improved. The economy was showing signs of recovery. And in this more favorable economic climate and generally free of the harassment and Red-baiting that had so shaken unions before it, the American Federation of Radio Artists was launched and well under way.

"We were full of optimism," said Clara Heller. "We were helping put working America back together again."

•

3

~~~~~~~~

"Building a Floor in the Jungle"

AFRA was four months old when it finally entered into its first negotiations with the radio networks for a contract covering sustaining (unsponsored) broadcasts, and then only after President Eddie Cantor sent out a "brace of telegrams" to Presidents Lenox Lohr of the National Broadcasting Company (NBC) and William Paley of the Columbia Broadcasting System (CBS) as well as to Bamberger Broadcasting (soon to be WOR, New York), WGN (Chicago), the Agricultural Broadcasting Company, and Don Lee Broadcasting System (West Coast). Cantor advised, "It would be in the best interests of the industry to meet with AFRA negotiators." A joint committee was established, and in early January 1938, the sessions got under way.

Jackson Beck remembered, "We had Holt, Heller, Henry Jaffe, Beilenson from Los Angeles, and Ray Jones, now head of the Chicago local, on our side. Of prime importance was the recognition of AFRA as sole bargaining agent. Then, we wanted to be paid on a per-program basis, not per day or per week, as the companies were demanding. We wanted better fees—the average was five dollars for a fifteen-minute sustaining show—and standardized fees, pay for rehearsals, and a rebroadcast fee.

"The networks were adamant about keeping different scales for their stations in New York, Chicago, LA, and San Francisco," Beck continued, "but 80 percent of all shows originated from those stations. If they prevailed, it would have been death for the federation. That's where the fight centered." AFRA found, however, that it had a "friend at court," and he too wanted to make order out of the existing chaos.

AFRA' general counsel, Henry Jaffe, told me, "Isidor Schultz "Zack" Becker, director of business affairs at CBS, was *the* most important person in AFRA's history—and that's including George and me! Zack Becker was a brilliant man, a shrewd man. He wasn't an attorney but he knew more than all of them. He believed a performers' union was inevitable and that it might as well be done the right way.

"He gave us all sorts of hints as to who to talk to and what to do next," said Jaffe. "If we made a bad move, he'd call George up at home (he thought the world of George). 'You know,' he'd say, 'that was not a good idea.' But he never showed bias at the table—never sold his employers out. Zack Becker worked diligently and successfully for the good of CBS—for the good of the others as well."

•

You Can't Take It with You was running into its second year. Actor-xylophonist-treasurer and associate executive secretary George Heller juggled AFRA's negotiations and his Broadway schedule with an ex-dancer's dexterity and split-second timing.

Abby Lewis, a member of the company, recalled, "It was at a critical moment in the talks, one early afternoon, when George remembered to his horror, 'It's Wednesday matinee!' He excused himself, saying he had to use the men's room, then raced to the Booth Theater.

" 'Put my understudy on for me, will you?' he asked of our very worried assistant stage manager, Franklin Heller [no relation]. 'I'm in the middle of negotiations.'

" 'OK,' said Franklin, 'go ahead,' And off George ran.

"Then, like a shot from across the street—where producer Sam H. Harris had his office—appeared our general manager.

" 'Fire George Heller!' he ordered.

" 'You better check with Mr. Harris first,' said Franklin. 'Remember the big split up in 1919 with his partner, George M. Cohan? Well, that was all about the new Actors' Equity. Cohan hated it and was out to destroy it; Harris was basically sympathetic to it. He believes actors need a union. I think you'll find him on Heller's side.'

"With all the friends George made," Abby continued, "he also had some powerful detractors. And they spread the word that he and his Forum friends were all communistic. I knew it wasn't fair or correct, but that's the way progressive people are often described by those who don't know any better. Nevertheless, our company felt uncomfortable about it and steered away from discussions with him about unions or any other labor-management affairs.

"But when the run of *You Can't Take It with You* began to wind down and Sam Harris came to us for salary cuts, it was George our leading lady, Josephine Hull, turned to for advice.

"With the absolute fairness that made him so beloved by the broadcasting companies, George answered, 'Mrs. Hull, on this, I'm on the side of management. Business is off; it's clear they're losing money. I recommend we take the cuts.'

"That's the way George Heller spoke," said Abby, "simply, directly to the point, and without any artifice."

•

It took six long months of hard, sometimes bitter bargaining. "We just didn't agree on anything," one network official remembered. But Emily Holt and George Heller finally succeeded in convincing the companies that indiscriminate "price cutting" was damaging the industry, that to create a worthwhile broadcast culture, competition should be based on quality, not cost. And on July 19, the Minimum Sustaining Agreement for Network Radio, AFRA's first major contract, was won.

By then, there were thirteen locals across the country. AFRA's paid-up membership, representing nearly 90 percent of all persons heard on the air, had grown to fifty-five hundred. St. Louis, Missouri; Denver, Colorado; Racine, Wisconsin; Shreveport, Louisiana; Birmingham, Alabama, and Toronto had joined. Smaller and, as yet, unchartered groups were organized in Washington, D.C., and Schenectady, New York; and in Boston, Pittsburgh, and Miami Beach.

With the Minimum Sustaining Agreement, an essential principle was secured. Performers on shows broadcast nationally, from any point of origin, would be paid standard network rates. Performers on network shows originating from Chicago, Los Angeles, or San Francisco and broadcast only within those regions would be paid lower rates but still standard.

The standard network rates were, in part, actors and solo singers, seventeen dollars for a fifteen-minute show, twenty-one dollars for a thirty-minute show, and twenty-five dollars for a one-hour show (each with specified rehearsal hours included in the rate); an additional four dollars an hour overtime; and a 20 percent discount for a guarantee of five shows a week. Singing duos, trios, and quartets (per person) would earn twelve dollars for a fifteen-minute show, fifteen dollars for a thirty-minute show, and eighteen dollars for a one-hour show. Singing groups of five or more (per person) were eleven, thirteen, and fifteen dollars, respectively. Rates for group singers on staff were forty-five dollars per person, per week. Broadcast repeats would earn 50 percent of the regular rate.

There were further gains: paid auditions, full pay when a performer was dismissed without cause, and children on adult shows to be paid the same as adults. Like Actors' Equity before it, AFRA minimums would be inviolable; no deductions (read: commissions) would be allowed—this in reaction to the network-owned artist bureaus that, while booking and promoting talent for the company, charged that talent additional, and often excessive, service or production fees. (In 1941, in an opinion supported by the FCC, the union established a clear conflict of interest. The bureaus were sold off, and AFRA began the franchising of talent agents and regulation of allowable commission. "Scale plus 10 [percent]" would be the minimum, were an artist represented by an agent.)

Spoke one network official at the time, The AFRA agreement

> was as beneficial to the employer as it was to the employee. By the nature of the competition that exists in all fields, employers tend to hire help as cheaply as they can. For the New York performer, the old $5 fee for a 15-minute show went to $17 (we frequently paid more than $17 on top shows), but Los Angeles rates were raised by more than 300%. (Lipton 1963)

From *Variety*, the entertainment weekly, July 20, 1938: "ACTORS UNION RATIFIES CONTRACT WITH WEBS, BUT SOME GRUMBLE—New York Members Accept First Two-year National Pact—Chicago, Los Angeles, San Francisco Meetings Follow.

> Acceptance by overwhelming majority was not without dissent from a small but vociferous minority objecting to what they termed "steam-roller" tactics. . . . Mark Smith [president of the New York local] stated that every drop of juice had been squeezed out of the networks. George Heller, assistant executive secretary, admitted there were "bad clauses as well as good," but urged acceptance. Among those expressing disappointment . . . were actors Ray Collins, Helene Dumas, Joe Julian and Jackson Beck.

•

AFRA struggled to win its Minimum Sustaining Agreement, but a harder fight lay ahead as talks opened several days later with the advertising agencies and independent radio producers—for a contract covering commercial broadcasts using the facilities of the networks and their o & o's.

Holt and Heller had earlier extracted a significant understanding from the networks: only signatories to AFRA codes could buy network time. This put the agencies and independents under tremendous pressure to make a deal. But there were nearly two hundred fifty of them, and each had its own set of rates. Not only did they differ widely from one another, but they differed in each production center as well. New York's Blackett, Sample and Hummert (BS & H) agency, the biggest employer of daytime radio talent—and the lowest paying—would be AFRA's main target.

A union shop and uniform, minimum rates were once again the central demands. Negotiations were on and off for five long months. Giants like the Young and Rubicam agency and the Batten, Barton, Durstine and Osborne agency, while they had been "very receptive" at the outset, now openly labeled AFRA's proposals "ridiculous" and "preposterous." Dissension grew white-hot at the bargaining table, inside the radio studios, and in the halls of the union as well. Most AFRA board members were, after all, regulars on the agencies' shows.

By year's end, despite the network's not-so-subtle pressure that advertisers settle, all attempts at reaching common ground had failed. The twenty-four delegates to the First AFRA National Convention in St. Louis that December authorized the board (with some misgivings, it was said) to call a strike, if there was no solution.

On January 21, 1939, with still no apparent movement, the major locals voted unanimously for strike approval. AFRA walked out; sister unions pledged full support. U.S. Secretary of Labor Frances Perkins announced she was prepared to enter the talks as mediator. The broadcast industry faced its first national shutdown.

Then, on the morning of January 23, William Wrigley—"Anyone can make chewing gum, but *I'm* the only one who can sell it"—contacted Holt indicating his interest in making a deal. She and Heller flew directly to Wrigley's Chicago office. When they returned that evening, they carried with them a signed commercial contract.

Bright and early the next morning, Glenn Sample, of the targeted BS & H, called. He had heard of the Wrigley meeting and was seeking a private session of his own. Following a lively several hours of bargaining, AFRA won its second major signatory. With the defection of two of their top people, the other agencies capitulated. Talks resumed two days later. National strike action was deferred.

In what became a four-day, three-night bargaining marathon, rotating shifts of management were pitted against the single team of Emily Holt, George Heller, and Henry Jaffe. With barely enough time to print up the newly agreed-on terms, rewrite the old ones, and get back to the table for the next round, there was little sleep those nights: "Not more than an hour at a time from Monday to Thursday," Holt reported. Agreement was reached on the National Code of Fair Practice for Commercial Broadcasting with sixty-five agencies and independent producers; within weeks, the number grew to 170.

Jaffe told me, "Our little trio versus the shifts of management was a plus for us. We knew everything that was going on; we had all the facts—the agencies didn't. And chief negotiator Emily Holt was a remarkably accomplished lady, who juggled it all with amazing skill."

AFRA won its union shop:

[The union] agrees that it will continue to keep its membership roles open and will admit eligible radio artists whom [the company] engages on commercial broadcasts. [The companies] will use the services only of performers, actors, singers and announcers who are in good standing—or become such members prior to their appearance.

And AFRA won its uniform scales: actors and announcers would earn fifteen dollars for a fifteen-minute show plus a ten-dollar repeat fee; twenty-five dollars for a thirty-minute show, a $12.50 repeat fee; thirty-five dollars for a sixty-minute show and $17.50 for a repeat; one-hour rehearsal required, six dollars per hour rehearsal thereafter. If a producer of a fifteen-minute serial drama guarantees a thirteen-week, noncancelable engagement, then a discount of up to 15 percent of salary would be allowed. Program extras with no individual lines would earn $7.50 and five dollars for a repeat. Actors in dramatized commercials would earn fifteen dollars for a fifteen-minute show, twenty for a thirty-minute show, thirty for a sixty-minute show, with 50 percent repeat fees. Announcers on the Giants and Dodger baseball games were guaranteed fifty-five dollars per broadcast. Solo singers would earn forty dollars for a fifteen-minute show, fifteen dollars for a repeat; fifty dollars for a thirty-minute show, twelve for a repeat; seventy dollars for a sixty-minute show, $22.50 for a repeat; six dollars an hour rehearsal after the first hour. Rates for singing groups of two to four voices were thirty, thirty-five, and forty-five dollars each, respectively; groups of five to eight voices, twenty-four, twenty-eight, and thirty-six dollars each, respectively; groups of nine or more, fourteen, sixteen, and twenty dollars each; four dollars per hour rehearsal after the first hour.

Mrs. Holt would comment later:

> The Code of Fair Practice gave the highest rate of pay for union members in any union contract in any country in the world. . . . When [it] and the AFRA Shop agreements were signed, I knew the union was on its way. We had been through all the growing pains and we came through with little strain on both the members and the industry. That was very important. Because if there's strain on the industry, the members suffer. (Lipton 1963)

On the eve of final settlement, however, the union was confronted with an incredible situation. The agencies refused to sign. They maintained that they were not employers of talent (even though, in fact, they were payers of talent); they were simply acting as agents for the sponsors in commercial radio. A year earlier, the networks maintained that, as they themselves produced no commercial shows (at the time), the would negotiate wages and conditions only for those they considered their employees—those on sustaining programs. Who, then, was there to sign this deal?

"I don't know who thought the thing up," said one network official, "but . . . whoever did was pretty darn smart; it must have been the AFRA people; they were much smarter than we were" (Lipton 1963). The solution, which remains in practice today, was that the networks—NBC, CBS, and the new Mutual Broadcasting System and their major stations—would sign the commercial code as acknowledged employers of talent. The agencies would then deliver a Letter of Adherence to the networks and to AFRA, agreeing to "accept and conform" to the terms and conditions of the code, as if they themselves had signed it.

The February 8, 1939, issue of *Variety* heralded the news. The simple two-word headline said it all to AFRA members across the country: SWEEPING VICTORY!

Years later, speaking to the delegates of the Thirty-sixth AFTRA National Convention in Atlanta, Georgia, then President Ken Harvey would comment: "The union built a floor in the jungle. And we don't have to love it to understand that we would all be a little more predatory, and even the poorest of us would be poorer, if AFRA had not existed."

•

By the time the industry adopted the first commercial radio code, AFRA had organized, either by way of chartered locals or by national membership, nearly every important center in the country (defined as having four stations or more). Kansas City, Missouri; Dallas–Fort Worth; Milwaukee, Wisconsin; Des Moines, Iowa; and Cleveland, Ohio, were now part of the federation of radio artists, bringing the number of locals to eighteen and membership to seventy-five hundred. Next to join would be AGRAP, the American Guild of Radio Announcers and Producers, the first on-the-air union in broadcasting.

"AGRAP was organized in July 1935," said founder Kenneth Roberts, father of actor Tony and writer Nancy, "two years before AFRA and one day after the passage of the Wagner Act. Originally, we were a union of CBS staff announcers in New York—the likes of Del Sharbutt, Ted Husing, Frank Knight, Andre Barauch—along with several assistant producers. Later, we expanded to other cities and other stations. By 1939, our membership was up in the hundreds."

From the advent of the first commercial radio station in 1920—KDKA out of Pittsburgh—it was the golden-voiced staff announcer who literally held the broadcasting schedule together. Scriptless and often by the seat of his pants, he worked ten or eleven hours a day, sometimes seven days a week, putting a show on the air, then taking it off again, successfully and on time.

Savvy, stylish, a master of the dictions of the world, the announcer ad-libbed his way through morning "wake-ups," luncheon "remotes," and evening concert halls, capped off by Guy Lombardo or the Vincent Lopez orchestra "coming direct" from one hotel or another around town. Something had to give.

Kenneth Roberts told me how AGRAP achieved its first contract: "CBS informed us that they were fully prepared to negotiate with us. They gave us the hours and the salary we wanted—that part was fairly easy. But they would *not* budge on our demand for a union shop. Bargaining went on for weeks, and for weeks we refused to sign. One morning, CBS founder William Paley strode into the session. 'What the *hell* is going on here?' he demanded. 'Why is this taking so long?'

"I explained, 'We're simply asking that when a new employee comes on staff, he should have to agree to join our union.'

"Paley thought a moment; then he said, 'In the circles I travel, I'm considered a liberal. You make me feel like a conservative—and I don't like the feeling. You can have your union shop.'"

The quality of life for staff was vastly improved. The men now had a base salary of fifty-five dollars with a forty-hour week, time and a half for overtime, vacation with pay, plus five dollars additional for every program they announced (commercial fees deducted, however).

"In those days," Roberts said, "there were no freelance announcers; only staff competed for all commercials heard on the air." Still, the station jealously controlled their men. If an announcer crossed over to another network for a show, he was told to resign. If his income rose beyond a certain point—as would happen to Roberts in the 1940s—he would have to take a leave of absence.

"Despite that," said Roberts, "the man felt a strong allegiance to the company—it was like the old school ties. We loved CBS and had huge respect for top management.

"From the moment AFRA was born they began courting us," Roberts, a future officer of the federation, continued. "They wanted our announcers—desperately! But we were wary of joining and, perhaps, getting lost in a union of predominantly freelance actors. After all, the actors' situation was far different from ours: we had *regular* hours and a *regular* salary."

It was years before AGRAP agreed, and then only if AFRA would give them autonomy within the union. This established the so-called category system and, although AFRA rules and regulations would undergo a number of changes over the years, that system remains in place. Staff announcers—now newsmen and -women as well—on both local and network stations approve their own terms before the full contract is submitted for board approval.

•

Even before young AFRA could fully savor its considerable victories, it was confronted with a test on whose outcome hinged its ultimate success or immediate failure. It happened, coincidentally, on the eve of an election at KMOX, a CBS o & o station in St. Louis, an election in which staff announcers could either choose or reject the radio federation as their bargaining agent.

A question had been brought to the National Labor Relations Board (NLRB): Is AFRA an appropriate bargaining unit for both freelancers and staff performers? Management was confident that this was the perfect issue with which to slow down and divide up the fast-expanding union. Surely, no CBS staffer in his right mind would want to entrust his career and company pension to a bunch of indiscriminate actors and singers.

A hearing was called for mid-July 1939. "It was a blistering day," Henry Jaffe said. "Fifteen lawyers representing the networks and various ad agencies were there." A number of witnesses had been heard. The pattern of questioning was clear. Next on the stand was KMOX staffer Marvin Miller, who would become known in the mid 1950s as the dour bestower-of-gifts on the television series *The Millionaire*. A CBS attorney proceeded with the examination:

Mr. Miller, have you joined AFRA?
Yes.
Have you read the constitution?
Yes
Do you know everyone in the union has an equal vote?
Yes, I do.
There are 10 staff announcers at KMOX but there are 150 freelancers in St. Louis, who could force you, at any time, to go out on strike. Do you want to be dominated by these freelancers? (Lipton 1963)

In one quick sentence, epitomizing the issue and bringing the hearings to an end, Miller answered: "I'd much rather be dominated by my fellow performers than by the network."

The subsequent NLRB decision favored AFRA. The federation's basic strength—the mutual support of a diverse membership—was tested and affirmed. The common interests of all members and all locals, great or small, were made exquisitely clear.

•

The curtain came down on *You Can't Take It with You* in the winter of 1938. It marked the end of Heller's performing career, which had begun with an appearance in the Children's Chorus of the Metropolitan Opera at age eight, encompassed twenty-one New York theatrical productions, and then ended on a high note in a great American classic.

In January, Heller was elected executive secretary of the New York local, a position held in addition to his spot on national AFRA. He commented later,

> During the first two years of AFRA, I'd get calls from casting offices offering me one part or another. But don't ask me if I want to go back on the stage; AFRA's my stage. And there are compensations; I get a big kick out of doing things for other actors.

Heller was free now to focus on building the union and, with Clara, building a family. In April 1939, the Heller's first daughter, Toni, was born—the Chicago local wired AFRA requesting that Miss Toni Heller be granted honorary membership. And in February 1944, Francesca arrived, completing the picture.

●

Francesca Julia Heller, now with her own child, Jordan Heller-Skolnik, told me, "What I remember most about my father was the feeling he gave me, from the time I was a very little girl—that I was safe with him, that I was protected. If something went wrong—he would make it better, he would fix it. He could fix anything.

"And I remember the music—there was always music. I still see him as he danced around the room, pirouetting across the coffee table—while my mother tore her hair out. Later, I remember the duets—him at the Steinway, me on the flute. And the walks and talks—playing ball, raking leaves, making bonfires—all the wonderful, ordinary, fun things one does when living in the country."

●

And there was now time to build friendships.

"Our circle of intimates was always small," said Clara Heller. "In the early days, there were the Sam Jaffes, Phil Loeb, and, of course, the wonderful Van Dekkers and their three children, who, at every visit, no matter when or where, came bearing baskets of glorious, home-cooked foods. There were Andy and Rose Stewart—we were pregnant together in Washington Park—and actress Paula Bauersmith and her husband, Warren. And, of course, our closest friends, Henry Jaffe and his wife, Jean Muir, and their three children. And Clayton Collyer—everyone called him 'Bud'—and Marion, with their three.

"Bud was one of New York's busiest radio actors," said Clara. "Among the many parts he played was the double role of Clark Kent and Superman—roles he kept secret for years, afraid it would hurt his serious acting career. He was on the AFRA board from its inception—he was key in writing the AFRA Constitution. He was a lovely, charming person; we adored him. Our children, too, became good friends."

Jan Dekker, the oldest of the Van Dekker children, told me, "When our families got together, as they often did before we moved to Hollywood [leaving the "Van" from the family name behind], George loved nothing better than to be with us children. I was only a kid then, but I felt like a full human being when George was there. He never patronized; never talked down. He spoke to us in a kind-of ecstatic way. My mother described him as 'a radiant spirit.' "

"I don't want to sound metaphysical about it," Michael Collyer, one of Bud's three children, said, "but George Heller had a wonderful aura about him. He was small and delicate and extremely handsome. It was always a special occasion when we visited with the Hellers. My father, of course, was devoted to George. I mean, deeply loved him."

These, then, were the Hellers' friends. These were the happy times, the growing times. No hint, yet, of the dark and dreadful years to come.

•

4

~~~~~~~

Heller's Good Right Hands

Mary Sagarin, author and editor of scholarly books for the young, arrived in New York in 1932, by way of the Albany Night Boat down the Hudson River from Schenectady. Orphaned and with three younger brothers to care for, she came to the City to make her fortune.

"My first job was as a legal secretary. I earned twenty dollars a week and felt like a millionaire. As a sideline, I wrote 'romances' for confession magazines." And in 1937, Mary Sagarin took her "big chance" and opened a public stenography office on West Forty-fifth Street. Her first paying client and her favorite still was the new federation of radio performers, which had just opened an office across the street. Mary was hired on a freelance basis to take minutes of conventions and other meetings. "By hand, mind you, with pen and ink, not machine. George Heller took rather a liking to me and often asked that I come work for him full time. I always refused; I couldn't see myself tied to a regular office job—not then, anyway."

Mary's youngest brother was killed in World War II. Shattered by his death, she closed her business. Years passed before she felt ready to return to work. Then, one day, she made her way back to AFRA to have a little talk with by-then National Executive Secretary George Heller.

"As I entered his office, I felt a distinct change in the man I knew only a few years before. There, sitting behind his desk, was *my boss*. From that day to this, out of my respect for that exceptional man and the way he conducted the union, I never called him by his first name—I wouldn't have dared!

"Mr. Heller was a delightful man to work for. He was enormously good-looking with an indescribable magnetism; everyone felt it. When he walked into a room, it was like a shot in the arm. Harold Hoffman, AFRA's office manager before he went on to head the Screen Actors Guild in New York, said, 'If he was taller, he'd be a movie star.'"

Mary Sagarin remained Heller's protective right hand throughout his tenure. She spoke proudly of the admiration "the little, cigar-smoking ex-dancer" earned at the bargaining table—his peers describing him as "colorful but tough negotiator" and "a man who can be trusted." Heller's board of directors apparently shared this fine opinion, even those with mixed feelings.

"One day," said Mary, "I found a letter that had been inadvertently dropped by an AFRA officer. 'I don't like Jews running the union,' it read, 'but George can get us better contracts than anybody else—and we can trust him.' Mr. Heller tore the letter up, saying, 'Forget you ever saw it.' Whatever he felt inside, his friendly relationship with the writer continued as before.

"Yet he was capable of and, in fact, famous for a most spectacular temper," Mary continued. "He claimed he was allergic to stupidity, and his command of four-letter words while suffering an allergic reaction was astounding. When he'd take off at someone (management, usually), everything in the office stopped, and we'd listen in awe and wonder. But I learned that that temper, that toughness, was under full control and, like a good actor, he used it carefully and for maximum effect."

When it came to AFRA members, however, Heller had an unwritten law. The office staff—he liked to call them "his AFRAdities"—was to treat everyone, whether on welfare or earning one hundred thousand dollars a year, with equal courtesy and respect. No matter what problem they brought to the union.

And problems would come, by the carload.

•

Gene Francis was a kid actor with the Eva LeGallienne Civic Repertory Theater production of James Barrie's *Peter Pan*. By late 1935, when he attended a special meeting of Actors' Equity, he was a teenager and a Senior Member of the association.

"Everyone in town had read the blistering editorials against the Actors' Forum group," Francis told me, "and we were all alerted to attend; two thousand of us showed up. It was at the tail end of the meeting. A battle had broken out about extending the time. Members were shoving and calling names; it was bedlam. Then, in the middle of it all, this little guy leaps up on a chair and shouts out, 'If they won't let us talk here, we'll talk at our own meeting. Follow me!'

"That was my first real introduction to George Heller and his fine fury. And, suddenly, there I was—one of a mob of five hundred others—marching out of the Astor Hotel, Heller in the lead, up Broadway and into the old actors' church." That was the beginning of Francis' long, rich association with the man he described as an "extraordinary human being."

"George could whip up the emotions of an audience better than anyone I've ever seen," said Francis. "And he never really changed much over the years—a firebrand; a revolutionary with a genius for reasoned leadership; a man of compassion, with a keen, innovative mind; an innate business sense, and an understanding of the doctrines of law—all this and a good-looking, serious, electrifying actor!"

Francis' own theatrical career took him away from New York to Hollywood and the role of Algernon in the East Side Kids film series. "Although I didn't participate with George in the founding of AFRA, I had the pleasure of becoming a member of the LA local when I worked on the *Lux Radio Theater*, then hosted by Cecil B. DeMille."

•

It was late 1940, and AFRA was now three years old and enjoying a robust growth. It counted twenty locals and a national membership of 10,500. AFRA contracts grew as well. In the first renegotiation of the sustaining radio code, Holt and Heller won improvements averaging 15 percent overall, plus a first cost-of-living provision, whose importance at that time could scarcely be imagined. News commentators, reporters, home economists, and editorial analysts were added to the people covered. Mrs. Holt reported to the 1940 convention: "AFRA contracts, apart from the network agreements, now cover 225 stations in 65 cities across the country."

The Code of Fair Practice for Transcriptions and Recordings for Radio Broadcast Purposes was added in May 1941. It covered the making and the use of programs and advertisements at a later time in the broadcast schedule. Along with the new code, AFRA established a system—the mandatory Producers Reports—to track the fees owed to recording artists upon the use of these and any other "electrical reproductions now or hereafter devised."

The transcription agreement presaged a whole new phase in the method of sponsorship and the repeated use of programs, in particular the repeated use of commercials. New definitions came into being: a *custom-built* transcription was for use by a single sponsor, one time only, from any major station; and an *open-end* transcription was for use by any number of participating sponsors in any number of smaller stations where various local messages could be inserted.

Performers' fee schedules, while still based on the length of a program, grew more complex. Actors and announcers in custom-built, for example, earned a minimum of from two dollars for a one-minute transcription up to twenty-eight dollars for a sixty-minute program; solo singers, $3.33 for a one-minute transcription (these were the jingle singers), up to $43.75 for a sixty-minute program. Group singers, depending on their number, earned from $3.66 to $6.66 for one minute and up to fourteen to twenty-eight dollars for a sixty-minute program. Artists employed on dramatized commercials earned twelve dollars on a fifteen-minute program and up to twenty dollars on a sixty-minute program. And for all, there was a six-dollar-an-hour rehearsal fee.

Radio's unsung auxiliary players, the sound-effects men, asked to be included with performers in the transcription code, but it first needed to be established whether soundmen were radio *technicians* or radio *artists*. "OK, you want a knocking at the door," they said. "Who's doing the knocking—a French maid or the iceman?" For bargaining purposes, the soundmen proved their point and were welcomed into the federation. Salary for staff soundmen would be three hundred dollars a month for a thirteen-week, noncancelable contract. For freelancers, it would be $7.50 per hour, plus equipment (Lipton 1963).

The practice of "live" repeats continued for several years, however, until 1946, when Bing Crosby, unable to get NBC's permission to record *Kraft Music Hall*, left the network for the new, more accommodating American Broadcasting Company (ABC) and a show of his own.

With by then three major national contracts to administer and police, it was no longer efficient for AFRA to handle all matters from the principal office alone. It divided itself into regions; the top negotiator in each region would be its director. Holt and Heller remained with the established locals making up the eastern section (including New York City); Raymond Jones led Chicago and the locals of the new Central Section; Claude McCue, then executive of the San Francisco local, moved down to head Los Angeles and the new Western Section. All that was missing was somebody to put out the fires in the emerging locals in towns and cities in between.

A national, or field, representative was added: Hy Faine, who would go on to head the Guild of Musical Artists from 1946 to 1970, and Nellie Booth of St. Louis were the first. Wherever there was a group of broadcasters too small to afford a negotiator or unable to handle a special situation, or if the region's executive was somehow unavailable, the national rep was there to help. This rare bird—organizer, negotiator, troubleshooter, family therapist, and speaker in the local tongue—was, and still is, an essential part of the operation of the union (Lipton 1963).

•

On December 7, 1941, the Japanese attacked Pearl Harbor. In one moment, the isolationist stance of the United States was ended, and we were catapulted into World War II. Every American institution refocused its goals and rallied to help in the war effort. Radio people too played an essential part in that effort, as did the entire theatrical community. More than three thousand union members, nearly one-third of AFRA, went into active duty. Hundreds of others, under the banner of the United Service Organizations (USO) and often within rifle sight of the enemy, entertained the troops. Radio "doublers"—mimics of any voice in any language—were called on to issue bogus orders from enemy "commanders" so as to confound operations.

AFRAns at home broadcast some sixty half-hour shows a week by shortwave from New York to the European theater; thousands of records, or "platters," featuring AFRA singers and actors were flown to fifty-five stations overseas to bring a little cheer to our fighting men. In the first six months of the war alone, those in and on radio were credited with selling $707 million in U.S. War Bonds.

George Heller was too old for the military but his contribution as an organizer in the war effort was as great as that of any person in the entertainment field. As vice president of the United Theatrical War Activities Committee in the East, he helped mobilize the entire industry not only to entertain but to establish and maintain Stage Door Canteens, assist in Treasury Bond drives, blood-donor campaigns, USO camp shows, hospital shows, and all other entertainment for our armed forces.

James E. Sauter, head of War Entertainment Services for New York State and then president of Air Features, Inc., production arm of the BS&H agency, said: "All the wonderful things George did for other people . . were because he was young at heart and good at heart. We knew each other well as part of an industry—many times we were adversaries—but he was always the first person I thought to turn to for support, help, comfort, and understanding" (Lipton 1963).

•

Cecil B. DeMille may have parted the Red Sea in a desert outside of Hollywood, but he could not move the Los Angeles local of AFRA from its firmly grounded principles. In 1942, antiunion advocates, intent on dismantling the protections granted labor unions under federal law, placed a so-called right-to-work initiative on the California ballot. Essentially, the bill would do away with the provisions of a union shop. The LA Central Trades and Labor Council responded, mounting a huge campaign to oppose it and calling upon all state unions to participate.

"Prior to that time," said actor Tyler McVey, a future president of the LA local, "our board was against getting involved in anything outside of the union—we wouldn't support any cause, back any candidate, or take sides on any political issue.

"But this was different—this was something that affected the very existence of all unions. We decided to help fight it. We'd get our stars to cut radio spots that broadcast the union message. To pay for air time, we'd levy a one-dollar assessment on each member."

Notice of a meeting to discuss and vote on the board's recommendation was sent to the entire membership, including Mr. DeMille. There, it was approved with a resounding and unanimous "yes." The recommendation was further approved by the national board. It was then publicized with a provision allowing thirty days for receipt of the assessment and a warning of disciplinary action for those who did not comply.

Film producer DeMille, smarting since 1938 because he was obliged to join AFRA so he might continue hosting the *Lux Radio Theater*, was understood to be one of those behind the initiative. He chose not to attend the meeting where he might have argued his point of view; indeed, Mr. DeMille attended no meeting in the years he was a member of AFRA. However, he adamantly refused to pay the one dollar or allow anyone else to pay it *for* him on the grounds that it was a "political assessment" and would nullify his opposition.

The stress on the local was evident. DeMille was a very important man; he was in a position to hire hordes of actors. But he was also an AFRA member; he would be given every opportunity to reconsider. A second meeting, to which he was expressly invited, was called. Again, DeMille was absent; again, LA members supported the board's action. Finally, after weeks of tussling with the decision, DeMille was put on suspension.

He promptly filed suit against AFRA, Holt, Heller, and the LA board (the twenty "John Does"). The case, with attorney William Berger representing the federation, wound its way slowly and painfully through the process, through restraining orders and appeals; DeMille lost at every step. Finally, it reached the California Supreme Court where, again, DeMille lost—as had the right-to-work initiative, as had the *Lux Radio Theater*, when its $5,000-a-week host was expelled from AFRA.

California Supreme Court Justice Emmett Wilson declared in January 1945:

> I have been unable to find a sustaining ground upon which it could be held that a union may not expend its funds for the purposes . . . [of] the betterment of the conditions of its members, as long as it is not used in political activities, and I do not regard such activities as including the support of legislative measures that advance their lawful aims or the opposition to those that frustrate them.

The threat to California unions—to all unions—was blocked by the Los Angeles local of AFRA, and the landmark precedent set by the court tolled the death knell for right-to-work movements across the country for years to come.

The situation, however, had become a cause célèbre, with DeMille leading on all fronts. Even after Judge Wilson's decision, the producer's arguments were still heard on national radio. AFRA officers, announcer Ken Carpenter or actor Edward Arnold, would then appear to refute them. In a time of growing discontent with labor, public opinion favored DeMille. They missed his austere, slightly cranky presence and resented those who, for whatever reasons, had taken it away.

"The result to the LA board was," Tyler McVey said, "we wound up being labeled a bunch of rabble-rouses and Communists. Nobody in the industry wanted to have anything to do with us. The funny part was that most of the board—Frank Nelson, Stanley Farrar, Lurene Tuttle, Bob Bruce (who led the effort against the initiative), I, and others—were all conservative Republicans. But we were union people first, and we didn't feel that this right-to-work thing was good for labor. It's possible, you know, to be a conservative and still be a good union man."

•

Executive Secretary Emily Holt delivered her final report to the AFRA National Convention preceding her retirement later in 1946.

> We have emerged, within the War Labor Board restrictions [of 15 percent on wage increases over 1941 levels], as a debt-free, powerful and respected union—an example of the best traditions of labor union activity and administration. We boast a national membership of 24,000 and are 28 locals strong.

Miami, Boston, and Cincinnati were now chartered locals, as were Rochester, New York; Pittsburgh; and Louisville, Kentucky. Nucleus memberships were growing in Portland, Oregon; Fort Wayne, Indiana; and Atlanta.

•

In early 1945, two of the Hellers' good friends, playwrights James Gow and Arnaud d'Usseau (*Tomorrow the World*), presented George with a copy of their new play, *Deep Are the Roots*. The first drama since those of Eugene O'Neill to deal seriously with problems of race, it told of the tragic events surrounding the return of a black World War II army officer to his home in the Deep South.

"George found the play terribly exciting," Clara remembered. "He felt it must be seen on Broadway—and that Elia Kazan must direct!" Heller would have loved to present it himself but, now, with his posts at both the national AFRA and the New York local, it was impossible; he would have to have a coproducer. With an enthusiastic go-ahead from both boards, he asked his friend Kermit Bloomgarden to join him. (Bloomgarden later produced *The Crucible, Death of a Salesman,* and *Music Man,* among others.)

The critics raved. Edwin Schloss of *The Philadelphia Record* wrote: "Let the trumpets speak! . . . The theater has stopped cutting out paper dolls . . . the first play of significance and distinction has arrived. . . . Consummately cast and superbly staged." And at its New York opening, Burton Rascoe of *The New York World-Telegram* headlined: "THE FABULOUS INVALID PERKS UP. . . . This play has strength, power, beauty, dignity and intelligent earnestness . . . it is an occasion for the emergence of a theatrical star of the very first magnitude—Barbara BelGeddes."

Deep Are the Roots ran for more than a year in New York; a second production played in London. Playwright d'Usseau's inscription in the working manuscript read: "For George, who proves a leprechaun can produce a play."

Clara remembered, "George's entire earnings that year at AFRA went to pay taxes on profits from the show." Later, NBC offered him sixty thousand dollars a year if he would come over to them as vice president in charge of labor relations. "I must confess," said Clara, "there was a glint in my eye—it was three times what his union salary was then. But he said, 'Honey, I can't sit across the table from my own people.' That closed the subject. Of course I agreed."

"It saddens me greatly," Clara went on, "that, although George led the federation for eighteen years, he brought so little home with him about the day-to-day goings-on. I knew there was always turmoil there, but if it weren't for those angry—often violent—telephone calls that later interrupted our life at home, I never would have known what a terrible personal predicament he was in. And I'd quickly close the bedroom door against his 'colorful language' so the children wouldn't hear. But, of course, they heard—George Heller could be heard down to New York City.

"When I'd ask him to share the burden with me, he'd answer, 'Please, I have it all day! If I can forget about it for a little while at home, I'll be happy.' He never did," said Clara. "It was with him to the end. Only when he played the piano did he forget.

"Not till I went back to work (Clara produced the weekly five-hour-long children's show *Wonderama* at Dumont TV in 1956) and found myself in the center of a nasty political fight did I understand what George meant—and understood, too, how his silence was his way of protecting me and the children from the anguish he suffered alone for so many years."

•

Television—a whole new world of broadcasting (the first-known transmission was from WGY, the General Electric experimental station in Schenectady in 1928)—became operational at President Roosevelt's official opening of the 1939 New York World's Fair. NBC's flagship station (CBS would follow some months later) promptly initiated what might be called regular television service. For several hours daily, the company served up a variety of simple entertainment for their several thousand New York City subscribers, featuring, for the most part, little-known radio or local nightclub performers.

Some called it "radio with pictures." It was, at best, primitive. From the *Radio and Television Talent Directory* magazine of September 1939 came these comments:

> Trouble with television . . . is the low fees and long rehearsals. Compared to AFRA [radio] scale, television is peanuts to talent that'd otherwise jump at the opportunity. Apparently the opportunity has arrived; as many know, few admit, [it] is alive with commercial plugs. . . .
>
> FCC regulations say no commercial television. The gimmick lies in giving the "sponsors" free use of the facilities. . . . Actually, these telecasts are regarded as experimental shows which isn't far from wrong.
>
> Since they want their commercials done as smoothly as possible "sponsors" have started using professional talent and paying for it. Between NBC and commercial fees an actor will find television closer toward being worth the while.

Television time was, indeed, "given away" to advertising agencies. Sponsors could not be expected to buy time until a far-larger marketplace had developed; and consumers could not be expected to purchase expensive television receivers until there were worthwhile things to see.

World War II abruptly decided the matter; commercial television was put on hold for the duration. But its promise for professionals remained ever exciting. If, or when, this thing actually got going, it could mean tremendous work opportunities for hundreds, even thousands, of technical, engineering, and production people.

After the war, technological freezes were slowly lifted and, by early 1946, four television networks stood prepared to develop and transmit programming. In addition to the formidable NBC and the fast-rising CBS, ABC and the smaller Dumont TV were established. The experiment had become reality.

The 1947–48 television season, in which baseball's World Series was carried for the first time by NBC, was essentially the daylong, diversified schedule we enjoy today—with one major exception. It was all live—totally, spontaneously, dangerously live.

A number of stars had skillfully, albeit tremulously, made the transition from behind the microphone to on-camera performance. Comedian Milton Berle, the first to move over, appeared on the *Texaco Star Theater*, as did Henry Morgan on his short-lived variety show *On the Corner*. Arthur Godfrey moved over on his *Talent Scouts*; Ed Sullivan too on *Toast of the Town*; and there were newcomers Sid Caesar and Imogene Coca on *Your Show of Shows*—all welcomed regulars.

There were dramatic programs, some known by the names of their sponsors: the Kraft (the first on television), Philco, and Chevrolet television theaters, in addition to *Hollywood Screen Test* and *Studio One*, where hundreds of new, often brilliant writing, producing, directing, and performing talents were seen by the American public for the first time.

There were news and public-affairs offering: commentator Pauline Frederick, *We the People*, and *America's Town Meeting of the Air*. There were quiz shows and, after 10:00 P.M., the perennial wrestling and boxing matches.

With dozens more variety, mystery, and adventure series in the offing, plus situation comedies, soap operas, and musical transplants from mother radio soon to follow, for actors, announcers, singers, dancers, and other artists, television would be a bonanza.

•

5

~~~~~~

The Authority in Television

Big trouble was brewing in the chambers of the Four A's (the Associated Actors and Artistes of America), a chartered member since 1919 of the American Federation of Labor (AFL) and the parent organization of all performers' unions. The International Board of Directors, the governing body of the Four A's, was made up of executives and elected officers of each of its nine member unions, known as branches. Its primary duties, in addition to issuing charters to new branches and "securing united action for the common good," were "to determine . . . the relations of the branches to each other in matters of jurisdiction, infringement of territory and all other matters of like nature." On these counts, in mid 1948, the international board was having particular difficulties.

Except for the Hebrew and Italian actors' unions, each of the remaining seven branches—Actors' Equity Association, Chorus Equity Association, AFRA, American Guild of Musical Artists (AGMA), American Guild of Variety Artists (AGVA), and LA-based SAG and Screen Extras Guild (SEG)—shared a vested interest in the rights of jurisdiction in the emerging field of television. Each had claimed these rights for itself and none was ready to back down. It had become, as one member described it, "a hopeless snarl."

How the branches should deal with television had been a constant, unanswered question since its first practical demonstration in 1938. The earliest Four A's discussions centered around the possibility of merging all the branches into one great, national television union, representing "all performers in the entertainment world." Equity President Frank Gillmore wrote George Heller in 1939 that "a serious attempt will be made by Equity, Screen Actors Guild and AFRA and any other organization desiring [it] to arrive at a definite consolidation whereby its members will no longer be faced with dual membership and duplicity of dues."

In late 1939 and again in early 1940, meetings were held with merger as the major topic of discussion. An unnamed SAG representative, agreeing that union offices should be consolidated as "the first step toward unity," predicted continuous jurisdictional battles "if we continue along our way as separate autonomous and, may I say, selfish organizations. If the members knew of the waste, the extravagance and the stupidity of our present method of operation, it would not be long before they would take action." No action was proposed, but a merger study, the first of its kind, was called for. In it, CPA Bernard Reis strongly recommended an all-branch merger (Cole 1960).

Again in mid-November 1941, following the FCC's granting of commercial licenses to the NBC and CBS networks, branch meetings were held to set "consolidated" wage scales and working conditions. Within three weeks, however, Pearl Harbor had been attacked and commercial television postponed. But from that time on, no AFRA National Convention failed to discuss the future of television coincident with a merger of the branches. And by the middle of 1948—with television production in full swing and still no consolidation of either rates or real estate—the situation on the international board had become explosive.

AFRA Executive Secretary George Heller (who succeeded Emily Holt upon her resignation several months earlier) stepped in with a ingenious compromise. Although he had been a spokesman for radio artists for more than ten years with the very companies now programming for television, he announced his willingness to relinquish AFRA's claim and proposed, instead, the establishment of a new bargaining agent to speak on behalf of all branches.

"Gentlemen," Heller admonished the Four A's, "let's stop this fighting! Let's get an agreement first, and, later, performers themselves can decide which union they want to represent them—if any of us." The eastern branches came to agree: "Television cuts across all the old established craft lines and should be represented by a separate, overall organization."

To that end, a television committee was established, with Heller as its chair; he was directed to open negotiations with the networks. When the first sessions showed "very good promise," he moved quickly to replace the committee with a proper organization, one that could negotiate, administer, and police a contract, an organization independent of the international board, an "authority" in the field of television.

Hoping to persuade SAG and SEG to concur with the single-bargaining-agent strategy, Heller and a small delegation went West. After days of "exploratory meetings," however, the guilds' executives notified the Four A's that they would not participate with the "live" entertainment unions in the East, that it was not in their best interests to bargain jointly in what had been their fifteen-year-long, never-questioned, exclusive jurisdiction in film. They maintained that, whether shown on a movie screen or on a television screen, film was theirs and theirs alone.

Heller pressed on, mindful of the guilds' fear of being overtaken.

The five Branches have agreed to relinquish claim and assign it to the authority. It is only fair and proper that the Guilds do likewise. It is not a new union but a collective effort to merge interests and join together for the purpose of benefiting the members. . . . It would be impractical and possibly fatal to divide the new medium into two.

AFRA counsel Henry Jaffe concurred:

We can't go to the networks with half a package. The industry requires indivisible television bargaining. And you know the employer loves a union dispute. . . . It means a delay of months or years and by the time it's over there may be a new economic cycle, or maybe TV is superseded by a new art.

As that controversy ripened, a second one was in the making: a movement—this time in response to suggestions by AFL executives—to merge into one national union. In late 1948, a conference of branches was held; certain basic principles on the need for merger were agreed upon; and a report was issued. Each branch was asked to present alternate proposals for approval so that "at last the desired objective can be accomplished" (Cole 1960).

How do seven disparate organizations, each with its own unique structure, personality, and constitution, unite? For months, all possibilities and combinations of possibilities—full merger, partial merger, merger of the eastern branches only, joint partnership, joint venture—were hashed, rehashed, voted, and ultimately rejected by SAG (and SEG).

Adding to the general muddle, in early September 1949, Hollywood film producers declared their unwillingness to recognize the Four A's as the bargaining agent for film on television. They would, however, recognize SAG and SEG, and the guilds so announced to the Hollywood trade press. The Four A's responded sharply:

No Branch has the right at present to negotiate or claim jurisdiction in TV without the approval of the International Board. . . . The SAG is directed not to sign any agreement with producers which . . . is a derogation of the Four A's Television Committee's authority over 'live' or film television.

It was a flaw in the Four A's' constitution that no provision existed for an impartial hearing process; disputes were expected to be resolved by the disputing leaders themselves. So while the branches hassled, back at the newly equipped television studios, performers in the field and the scores of out-of-towners arriving monthly to break in were being consistently overworked and underpaid.

Ezra Stone, director of Irving Berlin's *This Is the Army*, still young Henry on *The Aldrich Family*, and by then director of NBC TV's zany *Olsen and Johnson Show*, reported to Heller that people were working for twenty-five dollars a week and were "being fired for asking for a half-hour lunch. . . . They rehearse three days and are fired with no pay. . . . It takes five weeks before some get their first paycheck. We're in a desperate situation here!"

In late September 1949, a four-day conference of the Four A's International Board of Directors was called for the purpose of taking action on the proposed authority. The initial turndown by the guilds had served to unify the eastern branches "as they never had been before." As Heller put it, "It crystallized our efforts to create a practical, workable instrument for the benefit of television performers."

All ranking branch officers convened in New York City, including from Hollywood Executive Director John "Jack" L. Dales, Jr., of SAG, its general counsel William Berger; President Ronald Reagan; officers Dana Andrews, Lee Bowman, and Richard Carlson; and from the guild's office in New York, administrator Florence Marston and counsel Herman Gray. Executive H. O'Neil Shanks of SEG and its counsel, Robert Gilbert, also attended.

Hopes ran high that in this arena hard-core differences would finally be resolved. Hopes faded early. Not only were jurisdiction and the securing of "united action for the common good" thrashed out, but power, parochialism, and basic differences on trade unionism were at issue as well.

"We had made our position clear," Jack Dales told me. "We were adamant with respect to film on television. To us, it presented no new or different problems to warrant a new organization. And, as Equity's Frank Gillmore said to me, 'You are a union of actors; we are a union of actors; AFRA is not.' But the international was weak—unlike other internationals I've known. It was the individual branches that mattered there, and clearly they were being directed by Jaffe and Heller."

Dales continued, "On one occasion, when the board made a decision in favor of the Guild, George later said to me and Bill Berger—not as a threat, but as a fact of life—'Forget about that; you're not going to live to enjoy it.' I called him on that remark and got an apology."

On day three, the guilds presented what would be their final offer: a relationship of "cooperation." Heller responded that this plan, in which joint membership meetings are precluded and wages and working conditions proposals are subject to a guild veto, "is essentially *non*-cooperative, impractical, and will not be in the best interests of the television performer." After lengthy debate, the offer was rejected by the East. Equity officer Philip Loeb suggested the Four A's seek outside mediation. That offer was rejected by the guilds.

On the fourth day, the resolution authorizing formation of the Television Authority (TvA)—with jurisdiction over all performers—was put on the table. A fiery debate erupted that lasted for hours; then the situation took an unexpected turn.

"We were asked to excuse ourselves," said Dales, "while the rest of the board caucused on a particular matter. We stood outside the room for over an hour, and we were getting pretty damned restless. No one going in or coming out would give us any information or say what the heck was going on in there. So, I said to my group, 'Fellows, we're going home.' "

Hollywood reentered the hall; Reagan took the floor. Reading from a long, *pre*-prepared account of the Four A's' continuing failure to recognize the guilds' position, he concluded:

> If this resolution is passed . . . it means the beginning of a fight and we have no fear of the outcome—TV cannot live without motion pictures. . . . You have no right to give to a proposed new union any part of our jurisdiction. The Guild will resist . . . by every means within its power and pledges its entire resources to this end. . . . Nor will we obey any orders from the . . . International Board to do so.

SAG and SEG exited the conference; they exited the Four A's as well. A motion to recess left authorization of the TvA on the table. The rancorous meetings were over.

"You know Reagan," was Henry Jaffe's comment to me, "he's a stubborn pain in the ass! The idea of sharing anything with anybody was anathema to him. Based on a bunch of internal meetings, they figured, 'Why should we give up anything? We have all the strength and all the stars.' "

Personal dislike and distrust were also operating. "Reagan felt George was a Communist," Jaffe said, "and I, the principal advisor of a Communist. And here's this nervy, little guy from New York City coming in and saying, 'Your jurisdiction is ours!' The fact that my closest friend, Laurence Beilenson—partner with Bill Berger and, at one time, Reagan's personal lawyer—knew better and told him so made absolutely no different to him."

From Loeb's report to the Equity Council:

> In the face of SAG's set, provocative, blustering and at times insulting attitude, the delegates of the five Branches refused to allow themselves to retort in kind. The offer of mediation is sufficient proof of

a willingness to deal fairly and bring about a just and amicable settlement. It will, I believe, point the way to avoid the jurisdictional war with 'no holds barred' threatened by President Ronald Reagan.

On October 6, 1949, *The New York Times*, on page one, reported: "Motion picture stars of Hollywood declared an 'open fight' on . . . performers in the East." Jack Gould, radio and television editor, wrote:

> In a move that threatened to precipitate the most serious upheaval in the entertainment world in a decade, Screen Actors Guild raised the possibility of [making] another alliance in organized labor and pointedly emphasized its amicable relations with James C. Petrillo, president of the American Federation of Musicians.

On November 16, following two mass membership meetings in Hollywood, one pro and one con (which succeeded only in widening the breach), the international board voted to establish the TvA, a two-year trusteeship, granting it *overall* jurisdiction in the field of television. Loans of one hundred thousand dollars from Equity and from AFRA, twenty-five thousand dollars from Chorus Equity, five thousand from the Guild of Musical Artists, and "to the best of its ability" from the Guild of Variety Artists, set the new organization on its feet.

Paul Dullzell, then president of the Four A's, emphasized when issuing the announcement, "It is with the express understanding that TvA agrees to mediate all matters that may be in dispute with the Guilds," and further, "any organizational work or signing of contracts would be held up until such agreement was reached."

For months, the guilds carried out their promise "by whatever means within our power," publicly disputing and denouncing the existence of the authority. The issue remained deadlocked; memberships on both coasts were split. Within the TvA, SAG was seen as meanly and foolheadedly delaying the organization of television; within the guilds, the TvA was seen as recklessly and arrogantly attempting to raid SAG's and SEG's jurisdiction. The guilds announced their intention to organize the field of made-for-television films by and for themselves.

At the TvA's First National Convention, one year later, Heller would comment, "With the Guilds flooding the industry and membership with statements in opposition . . . it's an everlasting wonder that we were able to accomplish anything at all."

•

In December 1949, the national board of the TvA convened its first meeting. Ten ranking members from each of the five branches were selected as delegates. George Heller was elected executive secretary by unanimous vote; he took a two-year leave of absence from AFRA. Henry Jaffe was appointed general counsel; he, however, stayed on with the radio union.

Officers were chosen and given the title "chairman" until proper elections could be held. They were Chairman Lawrence Tibbett, who was then president of AGMA and past president of AFRA; First Vice Chairwoman Virginia Payne, a vice president of AFRA, and Ma on the long-running *Ma Perkins*; Second Vice Chairman Ralph Bellamy, starring on Broadway in *Detective Story* and a vice president of Actors' Equity; Third Vice Chairman Bob Spiro of Chorus Equity, formerly a cantor and then chorus singer in *High Button Shoes* on Broadway; Fourth Vice Chairman Ken Carpenter, past president of AFRA and announcer on the *Edgar Bergen and Charlie McCarthy Show* and the *Kraft Music Hall*; Treasurer Phil Foster, AGVA officer and popular television and nightclub comedy headliner.

Heller's first executive hurdle was in deciding when and where to meet. Broadcasters (AFRA) worked day and night; opera and ballet (AGMA) and theater people, represented by Actors' Equity and Chorus Equity, worked nights plus Wednesday and Saturday afternoons; nightclub entertainers (AGVA) worked all night until 2:00 the next morning. Each delegation jealously guarded its own prerogatives and each, having lived through months of dissension and maneuvering at the Four A's, was somewhat distrustful of the other.

Heller suggested two meetings a month at 5:00 P.M.—after all, everyone had to eat! And there being no room at the office (the TvA took space at 15 West Forty-fourth Street, down the hall from the recently moved AFRA offices), he booked a private dining room at the popular Cherios restaurant. To assuage the fear that, with the expected absenteeism of busy performers, all branches would not be heard equally, a system of alternate delegates was devised: enter, Equity council member Gene Francis, alternate to actor-director Margaret Webster.

Among others on the board (or their alternates), there were entertainers Gypsy Rose Lee, Georgie Price, Joe Smith (from the comedy team of Smith and Dale), Jackie Bright, and Dewey Barto; actors Mady Christians, Sidney Blackmer, Kathleen Meskill, Frances Reid, Hume Cronyn, Paul McGrath, Frank Silvera, Mildred Dunnock, and Hiram Sherman; singers Leon Bibb, Lanny Ross, Jerry Wayne, Eleanor Steber, Muriel Rahn, and Margaret Speaks; dancers John Bubbles (from the team of Buck and Bubbles) and Chris Karner; radio actors Clayton Collyer, Vinton Hayworth, Jack Arthur, William P. Adams; and announcers Nelson Case and Ben Grauer, to name a few. All these folk, together with the union executives, AFRA's A. Frank Reel (formerly Heller's associate, then executive secretary), Equity's Paul Dullzell and Louis Simon,

AGMA's Hy Faine, AGVA's Henry Dunn, and Chorus Equity's Ruth Richmond (who was soon replaced by attorney Rebecca Brownstein) made up—for better or for worse—the TvA.

Gene Francis, then the romantic lead opposite Eva Marie Saint on television's *One Man's Family*, recalled, "Meetings were sometimes hilarious but, most often, they were hot and heavy and late into the night. Many had not even heard of *Robert's Rules of Order*. In AGVA politics, you just yelled out whatever was on your mind—sometimes to tell a good story, sometimes to have a good fight."

Francis continued, "It was a perfect choice that George represent this amalgamation. Not only for his negotiating skills and his brilliance at bringing opposites together in common cause but for his understanding and love of performers—all performers. He was the only executive I know of whose office was situated where, with the door open, he could see members as they walked in—and, more important, members could see him."

Heller credited his board with the ability and the intelligence to govern themselves. And he established procedures in the TvA, as he had earlier in AFRA, that would ensure that they continue to do so with the least possible interference from the executive. While not a unique concept, it was unique in practice.

"At meetings," Francis said, "he'd introduce an item, give full background on it, then sit back and let the discussion roll. He valued every member's opinion—no matter what their point of view. He would, of course, urge us always forward with one project after another, but it was the board—the representatives of their respective memberships—not the executive, who set TvA policy.

"As diverse a group as we were," Francis added, "we came to work well with one another." And in the beginning, at least, everybody loved and respected George Heller.

•

On April 16, 1950, with all possibilities for mediation between the TvA and the two screen guilds exhausted, the Four A's lifted their restrictions and gave the go-ahead for the TvA to resume bargaining for a network contract—for live television only. "It had been a long time coming," said Francis. "The complications of a five-branch package of proposals were enormous, but we'd done our homework; George was raring to go." And he was bringing with him some mighty tough and innovative demands.

Negotiations bogged down early and dragged on fruitlessly for months. A major sticking point was Heller's demand for *full* payment for *all* performers, including extras, each time a program was rebroadcast, by "whatever technical means available at this time or to be developed in the future." Heller explained: "We are not seeking to increase . . . wages but to discourage the re-use of programs within the same locality [where produced], thus guaranteeing steady work for our performers." The argument was not working.

On Saturday afternoon, November 18, Dumont TV quit the talks and walked out; they were struck within the hour. The other companies split apart and they too left the table. The talks were over. Heller had failed in his first round with the television industry. Strike orders were issued for NBC, CBS, ABC, and the New York independent WOR TV to begin Sunday, 8:00 A.M. Despite the air of combat between the TvA and SAG—and to the dismay of network officials—the guild directed its members not to appear on any live network show against which a strike had been called.

A. Frank Reel of AFRA told me, "At that point, a strike in television was no big threat. It would, in fact, have been a boon to the networks. For years they'd been pouring money into a medium whose time hadn't come yet, and there was no income to show for it. But a strike in the still-profitable field of radio, that was something else again. And it was implicit that we at AFRA, who had just begun our own negotiations with the companies, were ready, willing, and able to back Heller up—100 percent."

"Somehow," said Gene Francis, one of the negotiating team, "George was able to get the NBC guy back into a secret session sometime after midnight. We waited outside the conference room on the sixth floor of NBC at 30 Rockefeller Plaza and drank black coffee. One hour, two hours, three hours—all the while the remarkable comic Phil Foster regaled us with his 'borscht circuit' stories."

At 3:45 A.M., a deal was struck. Heller notified the NBC broadcasters to continue working. The other networks had no choice, now, but to settle. By 4:30, CBS was back in; ABC and WOR soon followed. The TvA Code of Fair Practice was signed by the parties at 7:25 A.M.—thirty-five minutes before the strike deadline. Picket lines in front of Dumont, the first to quit and the last to make a deal, came down just before noon the following day. Founder Dr. Allen B. Dumont signed for his company.

Overnight, the TvA had become a force to be reckoned with in the trade-union movement.

•

"George was pure genius at the negotiating table," Gene Francis told me. "And he knew it! And he enjoyed it! So did his adversaries! He could spend an entire morning pounding the table with such fervor that even *we* were exhausted. And teamed with attorney Henry Jaffe, the two were magnificent! Nobody negotiated a contract the way those two did, and there's been nothing like it since—in any of the performers' unions."

Heller empathized so strongly with the struggling performer that whatever was being wrangled over at the moment—even a cleaning fee for the use of personal wardrobe—he would get carried away. "He'd stand up," said Francis, "and go into a great performance about what it means to a guy who's got only one good suit, and how he's forced to wear it on a TV show and how, if it gets soiled, he has to take it to a dry cleaners. 'The actor shouldn't have to pay for that out of his own pocket! If this was Hollywood or even Broadway, you'd be *giving* him a suit to wear! But, no, you make the guy wear his *only clothes*! No where else but in television does anyone do that!' and on, and on, and on.

" 'George, please,' Henry, the wise, friendly counselor, would interrupt, 'George, enough! Gentlemen, you'll have to forgive my colleague—he cares so much. Look, all we're talking about here is $1.69. Can't we find a way out of this?' "

Henry Jaffe told me, "It was George who devised the strategy. He was the thunder and fire and I'd be the ameliorating influence—as if I was trying to convince him to go easy. We did that together for eighteen years and it always worked. We'd get them down, finally, to giving us more than what we asked for."

Davis Snell, in *The New York World-Telegram and Sun* of December 9, 1950, wrote:

> Odds are you'd never figure a male ballet dancer for top billing among the two-fisted gentry who boss the labor unions. Not unless you sat across the bargaining table from George Heller who has just executed a grand jete into the number one spot in the new TvA, emerging thereby as a labor czar whose powers over his domain are not matched by those of John L. Lewis.
>
> Heller can win arguments either up, down or crosswise and the view is close to unanimous that this enormous bargaining power couldn't have been handed to a nicer guy—an opinion grudgingly shared by captains of the television industry. . . . We found him fair. . . . He's a very gracious winner. . . . He can be vitriolic and tough as hell. . . . When he throws a tantrum it's only partially an act.

Heller won a two-year agreement, including full recognition of the TvA as bargaining agent for live performers, a union shop, and substantially all minimum rates and working conditions originally demanded, which were, in part, actors, solo singers, and solo dancers on camera would earn seventy dollars for a fifteen-minute show, $125 for a thirty-minute show, $170 for a sixty-minute show; announcers (voice-over), fifty dollars for a fifteen-minute show, ninety dollars for a thirty-minute show, and $125 for a sixty-minute show. Performers and announcers doing multiple shows in a given week would have slightly discounted rates as the number of shows increased. Performers who spoke five lines or under would earn fifty dollars, $62.50, and seventy-five dollars; walk-ons and extras, twenty, thirty-five, and forty-five dollars. Announcers and performers in a dramatized commercial within a show would earn sixty, seventy-five, and ninety dollars. Specialty acts (nightclub and circus performers, etc.) would earn two hundred dollars for a single performer and up to $475 for an act with four performers. Sportscasters, Class A (baseball, football, and boxing), would earn two hundred dollars per event or $550 per week; Class B (all other sports), $150 per event or $350 per week; assistants and colormen, Class A, $125 per event or $350 per week; Class B, one hundred per event or $225 per week. Chorus singers would each earn forty-five dollars for a fifteen-minute show, sixty dollars for a thirty-minute show, and seventy-five for a sixty-minute show; chorus dancers would each earn from seventy dollars to eighty-two dollars, depending on the size of the group, for a fifteen-minute show, $100 to $112 for a thirty-minute show; and $125 to $137 for a sixty-minute show. A specific number of unpaid rehearsal hours were included in each category. And a specific number of rehearsal days were allowed for each show, within a proscribed span.

But chorus dancers' "included hours" were forty within a six-day period for a one-hour variety show. That meant almost seven hours of dancing a day, nearly twice that of a solo dancer. And while all other performers earned five dollars an hour overtime, chorus dancers (chorus singers too) earned only $3.50. Often unappreciated and generally overlooked, chorus dancers—the Broadway "gypsies"—were understandably less than happy with Heller's deal.

Group dancer Christine Karner of the TvA board (she danced on the *Colgate Comedy Hour* and on Sid Caesar's show) said, "In radio, there were actors, singers, and announcers, basically. George and Henry were familiar with their work and their required rehearsal hours. But in TV, suddenly there was a whole bunch of dancers. What are they going to do with them? They could cost the networks a lot of money!

"Jaffe, in particular, could not realize what a physical hardship forty hours was. We didn't have 'idiot cards' or TelePrompTers; every dancer had to know their routines cold. We talked and talked to them about it; all through negotiations we talked, but we got nowhere.

"They'd come out of the conference room each time, saying, 'We tried, kids; we tried.' But we weren't kids anymore—we'd trained for ten, twelve years to be good enough to get into a [Bob] Fosse or DeMille musical. We became very cynical. We felt we were given away to the networks so the announcers could get what they wanted."

"George started too low," said chorus singer Bob Spiro. "He used the Equity minimum as his bargaining figure. I told him that Chris, I, and hundreds of others would vote 'no' at the ratification meeting.

" 'Bob, I had to start somewhere,' he said. 'We'll catch up next time.' " In labor negotiations there's always a next time. But for these group performers, who lent such style and distinction to variety entertainment, in dollar terms there never was a real catch-up.

Minimums in other performers' unions in 1950 were, for Actors' Equity, on Broadway, seventy-five dollars a week for all players, one hundred dollars a week for all players on the road, and in summer stock, fifty dollars a week for all; SAG basic minimums were fifty-five dollars a day and $175 a week.

•

Sometimes during that private, early Sunday morning session, the NBC negotiator asked George Heller, "Do I have to go through this all again with the Screen Actors? Can't you get your brothers in the guild to accept this deal too?" What an opportunity Heller had been handed—to mend fences and to make the crucial step towards "a single bargaining agent for TV." He went to one phone to call Jack Dales; announcer Nelson Case went to another to call Ronald Reagan.

In the wee hours of that triumphant morning, Heller pleaded with Dales, "Jack, let's forget our differences; let's get together. We've just made a great deal—it covers all performers on television, from all branches, forever. We're handing it to you—it's yours!" Dales and Reagan rejected the offer and stood firm on their original position: film shown on television belonged to the guild and the guild alone.

•

In this historic, nearly perfect first television contract, Heller was ultimately able to rescue what was thought to be lost at the table. In Provision XIII of the TvA Code, it read: "Kinescope recordings," which was the only existing method for immediate rebroadcasting, "can be played within sixty days of the original telecast, but only in areas where the program was not previously broadcast." And the next paragraph read:

TvA intends to establish restrictions on the showing of a kinescope in any area where the program was previously carried. Pending the working out of such restrictions, no kinescope will be shown in any area where the program was previously carried, without the written consent of TvA.

When the first request came before the TvA board some months later, it ruled that "payment shall be the full original fee" of every performer, including extras. The quality of kinescope, however, was generally poor and its use fairly limited. (Kinescope would be replaced, beginning in 1955, by the far-superior videotape.)

SAG, more concerned with getting money up front, would cut a poorer deal for filmed program reruns in their first (1952) contract with the Alliance of TV Film Producers—or so it would seem at the time: no fee for the first and second reruns, 50 percent of minimum for the third and fourth combined, 25 percent for the fifth, and a 25 percent buyout for the sixth and all others. Of far greater importance to screen actors than program reruns was that they would receive *no payment at all* when their movies ran on television.

Jackson Beck remembered, "Heller and a select committee went out to the Coast to try to bring them to their senses. Bud Collyer, a very bright, very logical guy, known for being able to talk his way around anything, was one of the group. They said to the guild, 'We're getting full fees for program repeats, and you're going for reduced rates. It's crazy; what are you guys doing? You should be coming up to us!'

"Ronnie Reagan answered something like, 'Who's going to watch a show on television twice, anyway?' Well, one thing led to another. Bud lost his cool and went for him. It took the rest of the committee to pull 'em apart."

The great disparity between the two replay schedules would one day be the undoing of Heller's achievement. "But," said Gene Francis, "he went to his grave secure in the knowledge that he left this legacy to his beloved members." That legacy included a schedule of fees for repeated commercial announcements, known as "residual payments," which were "never tampered with, only improved."

•

As part of that 1950 first round with the television industry—and fourteen years before it became the official position of the U.S. government—Heller proposed, and won, the adoption of the Industry Statement of Policy, which concerned the employment of black performers, then rarely seen on the new medium. The statement read:

Negroes take part in every phase of life in our country today, as citizens, as workers, and as the consumers whose buying dollars help pay the costs of television entertainment.

It is our purpose to secure representation of Negroes on television matching their role in everyday life and providing opportunities for the employment of the many qualified Negro artists among the membership of TvA.

We believe that this is both honest and fair, as well as good business practice, and we are sure that the vast majority of people in this country will welcome and applaud this policy.

To this end, we call the attention of our writers, producers, and directors, to the above statement, and request them to help carry out this purpose, by the employment of Negro specialty acts, by the integration of Negro singers and dancers in chorus groups, by the employment of Negro actors in the many dramatic roles reflecting their participation in everyday life, and by the creation of new program ideas to realize the purpose set forth above.

But even before the hurrahs died down, a force was set loose on the American scene that would strike the TvA membership—and the broadcast industry as a whole—with a blow so severe that more than a decade would pass before they and labor-management relations would return to normal.

•

6

The Stage Is Set

The Great Depression inflicted such hardship, such deprivation as had never been seen in this country before. And no one suffered it more than those who labored on the farms, in the mines, and in the factories large and small. They had survived union busting, beatings, and sometimes killings by company goons; now they were without work, without a livelihood, without their self-respect. How would they ever rise from this misery?

For many foreign-born workers, creative artists and intellectuals as well, the Communist Party of the United States—more than ten thousand strong in the early 1930s and growing—offered the most militant and compassionate leadership. Although party rhetoric was often punctuated with calls for revolution, artists (better dreamers than warriors, it was said) marched to its call for labor reform, social justice, and civil rights for blacks. Whatever their politics, most Americans were demanding change from the bankrupt policies of the Hoover administration—and change they would have. In 1932, Franklin Delano Roosevelt and a Democratic Congress were swept into office on the promise of recovery, reform, and relief. In that same election, William Z. Foster, the perennial Communist candidate, received a mere 0.26 percent of the vote, proof that the vast majority of the nation remained committed to more traditional solutions to its problems.

The first hundred days were highlighted by voluminous legislation, fifteen bills in all, and Roosevelt, "the great experimenter," enjoyed almost universal support. It was not long, however, before radicals, from the right and the left, began an assault on him and his reform programs, the former for not doing enough, the latter for doing too much—initiating costly relief programs, such as Social Security and unemployment insurance, stepping up the income tax, and favoring trade unions—in all, severely endangering the American free-enterprise system.

Despite the opposition, Roosevelt's New Deal created a climate where, unfettered by stop orders from federal courts (the Norris–La Guardia Anti-Injunction Act), unions were allowed not only to exist but to function freely (the Wagner, or National Labor Relations Act). It was now legal for workers to organize, to bargain collectively, to arbitrate grievances, and—all else failing—to strike.

"A traitor to his class," proclaimed the right. He was leading the country into socialism—worse, into communism. And only fifteen years before, in the most stunning political upheaval in modern history, Russian workers had risen up, toppled their leaders, expropriated the land and the factories, and under the red banner of communism, overtaken the machinery of the state. It could happen here! It could happen now!

But the American Communist Party, established in 1920 and legal since 1923, was having trouble simply holding on to its members. The attraction at the outset of the depression had cooled. Once willing to undergo the rigors of membership, many found they could no longer put up with the dogma, the personal sacrifice, the demands for unconditional loyalty to a rigid, made-in-Russia policy—a policy that held too little regard for American needs, American interests. And so, in the mid 1930s, they exited the party.

In the fall of 1937, however, Roosevelt called for collective security measure to block fascist Germany abroad. Communists, who had found little to admire in the New Deal, now embraced the president in a common cause against Russia's most despised enemy. The party flourished here; it even found a measure of respectability. By the summer of 1939, membership, including sympathizers, had zoomed to an estimated ninety thousand.

Harvey Klehr wrote, in *The Heyday of American Communism: The Depression Decade* (1984),

> American Communists had come a long way. . . . Few liberal organizations were without a significant Communist presence. . . . Politicians . . . vied for Communist support, albeit quietly. Hundreds of prominent intellectuals, artists and performers applauded the Soviet Union's every action. Well-known Communists held leading posts in the trade union movement.

That trade-union movement prospered under the leadership of the flamboyant John L. Lewis, head of the Committee of Industrial Organizations (CIO), a breakaway from Samuel Gompers' more conservative AFL. Aided by militant Communist labor leaders, the CIO launched spectacular organization drives in the country's basic industries: automobiles, steel, rubber, and shipbuilding. Union membership soared from two million at the beginning of the New Deal, to nine million six years later. Power between workers and owners became more evenly distributed.

•

Threatened by the dynamic upsurge of the militant left and strengthened by gains in the 1938 congressional elections, House Republicans allied with southern Democrats to establish the Special House Committee on Un-American Activities (HUAC). Its purpose was to investigate charges of "un-American propaganda activities." While not the first official body in the twentieth century to investigate possible subversion, it would become the most controversial, the most raucous, and the longest lasting. Democrat Martin Dies of Texas, said to be the head of the hunting party out to destroy the New Deal, was named chairman.

As one of its first targets, HUAC chose the successful Federal Theater Project, one of the several WPA white collar welfare programs that, in its first three years, had rescued so many out-of-work actors, playwrights, directors, set designers, musicians, and even journalists from outright destitution. It employed more than eight thousand persons—seasoned and novice, black and white, young and old—in twenty-two states across the country. It brought theater, circus, and children's shows to some thirty million Americans, many of whom had never seen a live performance. It had Yiddish units and black units; its radio division brought listeners the first-heard works of Henrik Ibsen and Shakespeare. It was the training ground for many notable talents: John Huston, Burt Lancaster, John Houseman, John Randolph, Will Lee, Will Geer, Canada Lee, E. G. Marshall, Orson Welles (Welles' Mercury Theater developed there), and playwright Arthur Miller, to name just a few. A vocal minority in the Federal Theater, however, had "created the image of a Communist-controlled project racked by controversy and committed to something more than just relief" (O'Connor and Brown 1978).

The HUAC investigation earmarked twenty-six of the theater's vast repertoire for political scrutiny. Some of the twenty-six were contemporary pieces, some were theater classics, but most were the popular living newspaper productions, docudramas of real-life problems, such as slum housing, inadequate health care, and racial prejudice, each of which ended with a call for immediate government action.

The closed-door hearings convened in August 1938. They were preceded (and accompanied) by a barrage of sensational charges in the press. Said committeeman J. Parnell Thomas: "[The] Project not only is serving as a branch of the Communist organization but is also one more link in the vast . . . New Deal propaganda machine." Unable to observe, reporters printed only the chairman's version of the proceedings. All but a few of the witnesses were said to be disgruntled WPA employees. Despite her constant entreaties, National Director Hallie Flanagan, former head of experimental theater at Vassar College, was not called until months later. Even then, her refutation of the charges was not entered into the official transcript. Regional officials, wishing to support her testimony, were not allowed a hearing (O'Connor and Brown 1978).

> That there were Communists and Communist sympathizers associated with the project is unquestionable in view of the social context of the times, the numbers of the personnel. . . . But the contention . . . that 26 Federal Theater plays were un-American, anticapitalist, and therefore pro-Communist was never proved. (Vaughn 1972)

What was proved, however, by HUAC's first foray into show business was that investigations of the entertainment industry drew maximum attention, that accusations of un-American activity need not be validated, that accusations in themselves could get the desired results: the silencing of opposing political opinion.

Despite the efforts of many theater luminaries to save the project, it was too late. Southern Congressmen were uncomfortable with its racial mix; others with its "protest" aspect; still others felt it was no longer a relief agency, rather, a national theater in competition with private enterprise.

In June 1939, Congress cut out all appropriations for the Federal Theater Project in a pending relief bill. As recounted by O'Connor and Brown (1978), President Roosevelt had little choice: "His veto would have ended the entire work relief program the very next day. As he signed the bill, he remarked, 'This singles out a special group of . . . people for denial of work in their profession. It is discrimination of the worst type.' "

Chairman Martin Dies and HUAC had won in the end. The voice of the dynamic, provocative Federal Theater was stilled forever, and the official campaign to link progressives in the arts with the Communist Party was launched and well under way.

•

Dies' search for a second site from which to launch an investigation of "Communist subversion in entertainment" turned to Hollywood, the home of the motion picture industry and the publicity capital of the world.

There, since 1936, despite the national policy of isolationism, a vigorous international movement had sprung to life. Likened to the European Popular Front, it was the community's response to harrowing accounts of

Nazism by filmmakers recently abroad and those who had fled Germany to find safe haven in Los Angeles.

While many cities had their early, often unpopular fighters against fascism, based on the size and population of the hometown of motion pictures, the Hollywood Popular Front was notable. The Anti-Nazi League, the Committee to Aid Republican Spain, and the Joint (with New York) Anti-Fascist Refugee Committee were only three of its vehicles of protest. The founders were predominantly screen writers (many had helped establish the Screen Writers Guild). Their supporters numbered in the thousands, from technicians to studio executives, and the community calendar was crowded with glamorous consciousness-raising and fund-raising events (Ceplair and Englund 1980).

Politically, the movement was a coalition of liberals, moderates, and a small number of Communists. They fought fascism not only abroad but at home as well—be it the American Nazi Party, the Ku Klux Klan, the new Dies Committee (as some called it), or its counterpart in California, the Tenney Committee (chaired by State Senator Jack Tenney). Actor Melvyn Douglas, an organizer of the Anti-Nazi League, would comment later that it was the Communists who were the "fellow travelers" of the liberals and not vise versa (Ceplair and Englund 1980).

Chairman Dies hit back. On a coast-to-coast broadcast, he charged that, although most in the Anti-Nazi League were probably not themselves Communists, they were dupes and their organization a creature of a small clique of loyal apparatchiks. HUAC, he stated, would hold hearings in Hollywood in September 1938 "at which members of the film colony would be afforded an opportunity to reply to charges that they were participating in communist activities" (Ceplair and Englund 1980).

The announcement produced a cry of outrage from all quarters. Telegrams flooded the office of the president and members of Congress calling for the dissolution of the committee and protesting that Dies was out to destroy all progressive thought and action in the country. The chairman apparently got the message; the hearings were canceled (Ceplair and Englund 1980).

It was in Europe, however, in the last days of August 1939, that the tenuous respectability of American Communism was effectively quashed. Joseph Stalin of the Soviet Union entered into a nonaggression pact with his archenemy Adolf Hitler. Within a fortnight, Germany invaded Poland, later divided her up with Russia, and soon the Second World War had begun.

In anger and disappointment, artists and intellectuals across the country resigned from the party. They would continue their support of antifascism and the humanitarian ideals that drew them to communism in the first place, but by the early 1940s, many of the thousands who had gone in had come out again.

•

By 1947, the war had been fought and won. Our amicable partnership with the USSR, once she too had been invaded by Germany, was over. Now, with Stalin's ruthless acquisition of the Baltic states, anxieties over U.S. connections with the Kremlin and fears of a possible dreaded take-over here at home were rekindled. Then President Harry S Truman established a Loyalty Review Board, barring American Communists or their sympathizers from service in the executive branch. If there was any semblance of the old liberal-radical coalition, it had all but disappeared.

In the chill of the ensuing Cold War, the "partisan war cry" of HUAC was heard once again. And on the morning of October 20, under the watchful eye of news and television cameras from around the world, then Chairman J. Parnell Thomas reconvened the committee in the nation's capital. Nine years after Dies' announcement, hearings on an alleged Communist infiltration in the motion picture industry got under way.

The investigation quickly turned into an aggressive assault on, among many others in the industry, nineteen of Hollywood's best-known screen writers and directors. All had had active political pasts, some originating with the Hollywood Popular Front. Unlike the committee's so-called friendly witnesses, however, the nineteen were not allowed to read statements, call their own witnesses, or cross-examine hostile witnesses. Despite relentless badgering, they stood on their First Amendment guarantee of freedom of speech and the right of peaceable assembly. They held that their political views were private and refused to reveal whether they, or their associates, were, or ever had been, members of the *still-legal* American Communist Party. The Screen Writers Guild, "fearful of the 'recklessness' of its left wing and the wrecking qualities of its right," showed no willingness to support them (Ceplair and Englund 1980).

There was an outpouring of anti-HUAC sentiment from all around the country, on radio and in the press. From Hollywood, the Committee for the First Amendment sent some of its members—writer Phil Dunne, director John Huston, and actors Humphrey Bogart, Lauren Bacall, Danny Kaye, June Havoc, and others—to protest HUAC's persecution of the witnesses, the assault on their civil liberties, and the slandering of the reputations of hundreds of others in the process. The flush of support soon faded, however. And despite earlier protestations by movie moguls that it would never happen in their studios, systematic discharge or suspension without pay of "uncooperative" witnesses began in earnest. In the so-called Waldorf Statement (made from the Waldorf Hotel, New York), only weeks after the hearings, the Association of Motion Picture

Producers issued a one-page affirmation of their new employment policy. The final lines of the statement read:

> We are frank to recognize that such a policy involves danger and risks . . . the danger of hurting innocent people . . . the risk of creating an atmosphere of fear. Creative work at its best cannot be carried on in an atmosphere of fear. We will guard against this danger, this risk, this fear. To this end we will invite the Hollywood talent guilds to work with us to eliminate any subversives, to protect the innocent, and to safeguard free speech and a free screen wherever threatened.

Of the nineteen writers and directors, ten were held in contempt and eventually imprisoned—not for injecting so-called Communist propaganda into their movie scripts, a charge the committee set out to prove and never did, but for their defiance of a congressional committee.

Most lost their jobs, many their marriages, homes, and savings. All lost their constitutional right to express their political minds. HUAC had won again. (Chairman J. Parnell Thomas was imprisoned the same year, convicted of defrauding the government. He had padded his payroll with persons unknown and pocketed their salaries.)

•

At the outset of the two-week-long HUAC interrogations, "friendly" witnesses presented their "evidence" of subversive activities within the motion picture industry. Among them were actors Adolphe Menjou, Robert Montgomery, Gary Cooper, George Murphy, and the president of SAG, Ronald Reagan, a liberal Democrat at the time and an admitted confidential informant for the Federal Bureau of Investigation (FBI). A portion of his testimony to Chief Investigator Robert E. Stripling follows.

> Q: Have you at any time observed or noted within the [guild] a clique of either Communists or Fascists who were attempting to exert influence or pressure on the guild?
> A: . . . There has been a small group within the Screen Actors Guild which has consistently opposed the policy of the guild board and officers of the guild, as evidenced by the vote on various issues. That small clique . . . has been suspected of more or less following the tactics that we associate with the Communist Party.
> Q: Would you refer to them as a disruptive influence within the guild?
> A: I would say that at times they have attempted to be a disruptive influence.

Q: You have no knowledge yourself as to whether or not any of them are members of the Communist Party?

A: No, sir; I have no investigative force, or anything, and I do not know.

Q: Has it ever been reported to you that certain members of the guild were Communists?

A: Yes, sir; I have heard different discussions and some of them tagged as Communists.

Q: Have you ever heard that from any reliable source?

A: Well, I considered the source as reliable at the time.

Reagan went on to say that as abhorrent as the Communist philosophy was, he would not want to see fear or resentment of the group compromise the country's democratic principles (Vaughn 1972).

So much for lively debate in the halls of the screen guild.

•

Albert Dekker, co-organizer of the old Actor's Forum, was the first of George Heller's intimates to feel the lash of the Hollywood witch-hunt.

Since the early 1930s when the two had met and worked together on Broadway, their relationship had deepened into a loving and joyous friendship. With George's trim five-foot-six and Van's broad six-foot-two—"When he remembered to stand up straight," his wife, Esther, said—they made an unlikely pair and had great fun playing up the differences. In their principles and convictions, however, their enthusiasms, love of life, and respect for one another, they measured the same.

In the spring of 1937, while Heller and Loeb were agitating on the Actors' Equity council for what would become AFRA, the "craggy, dark-voiced" Dekker gave up his career on the New York stage and headed for Hollywood and motion pictures.

"He soon became," according to friend Carey McWilliams, author and, for twenty years, editor of *The Nation* magazine, "a most popular figure in Hollywood circles [of the political] left, right, and center" (McWilliams 1978). Within a few years, Dekker built a thriving career playing character leads and heavies in dozens of films, including *The Man in the Iron Mask*, *Dr. Cyclops*, and *Beau Geste*.

With his robust personality, good looks, and outspoken liberal point of view, the Hollywood Democratic Committee induced him in 1944 to run for the California State Assembly. Too old for the army, Dekker put aside his lucrative career, happy to serve his country through politics. He was the first Hollywood actor to be voted into state office; Helen Gahagan Douglas (wife of Melvyn), whom Dekker vigorously supported, was sent to the U.S. Congress in the same election.

Once seated in the California Assembly, Dekker and Senator Jack Tenney, chairman of the Joint (upper and lower houses) Fact-Finding Committee on Un-American Activities, came head to head—often toe to toe—on a number of issues: capital punishment, fair employment policies, racial equality. (Of Tenney, the *San Francisco Chronicle*, a Republican newspaper, would write that people who wanted to overthrow him were "likely to be hauled up and smeared by inquisition and innuendo. His methods have done more damage to the cause of intelligently combating communism than almost any other influence in California.")

His term over, Dekker returned to Hollywood. "He soon found, however, that he was not getting the number and kind of roles he had formerly been pressed to accept" (McWilliams 1978). Why was this so? He had never been called before un-American activities committees, nor had he been named in testimony by others. It was found that he (with a number of other film celebrities) was cited in the 1947 Tenney Committee Report as having so-called links with Communist fronts. He became a target of the newly aroused ultraright and the conservative press. Within one year, he was virtually unemployable.

Esther Dekker, a onetime leader of the California Parent-Teacher Association and the League of Women Voters, explained, "Van was *never* a Communist and in no way a 'subversive.' He was a Roosevelt Democrat—an open-hearted, public-spirited, righter-of-wrongs." It was, he was told, his association with certain "suspected" friends and his positions on right-wing politics and politicians that placed him on a so-called graylist—a blacklist with no specific charges—rendering him jobless in the industry.

Not a man to apologize for his convictions, as many in the film industry were doing, he got little help from those who might have influenced the people responsible. "Fuck 'em!" Dekker said. "I *won't* compromise. . . . I won't crawl to those bastards. Never" (McWilliams 1978).

George Heller was in Hollywood for a meeting with Jack Dales and Ronald Reagan about their ongoing jurisdictional problems and, as he would whenever he went West, he visited the Dekkers. As Heller had once urged his friend to quit New York and the Red-baiting in Actors' Equity for job offers in Hollywood, he now urged him to return to New York and the theater, where his talents would be better served, where artists were hired on merit alone. "You've got to get out of here, Van," Heller argued, "there's no future for you here."

When, some months later, the role of Willy Loman in Arthur Miller's *Death of a Salesman* was unexpectedly vacated by Lee J. Cobb, Heller took the initiative, immediately phoning his old friends, producer Kermit Bloomgarden and director Elia Kazan. "Look," he said, "Van needs a job, and he's right for the part."

Following years of lost opportunity, Dekker's aborted acting career resumed in 1950 when he joined the *Death of a Salesman* company on Broadway and later toured in it for several seasons. But the loathsome, elusive graylist, with its consequent harassment and public boycott, followed him, Miller, and Bloomgarden to Peoria, Illinois, and on other occasions to Syracuse, New York, and to Dallas. The three wired the *Peoria Journal Star*:

> Any allegation that any part of the income of the play has gone, is going, or will go to the Communist Party or its affiliates is an outright and preposterous lie. Nor is the producer, author, or star a 'front' for any political theory or organization.

Dekker would work intermittently over the next years in supporting roles on the New York stage—*The Andersonville Trial* and *A Man for All Seasons*—and later in Hollywood—*East of Eden* (Kazan brought him back to film in the mid 1950s as well) and *Suddenly Last Summer*. But the impetus of his once-busy career had been lost.

Esther Dekker remembered, "He did what needed to be done to support his family." He reactivated his literary tours, which, when he was unemployed in the late 1940s, gained him some celebrity. He read Mark Twain, Edgar Allan Poe, and Langston Hughes to the B'nai B'rith and other willing organizations; he told tales from American folklore and Indian legend, researched and written by himself.

To cheer the family through it all, he cited the motto *Illegitimati non carborundum*, or "Don't let the bastards grind you down." But the indelible stigma of the graylist, of the earlier loss of his sixteen-year-old son by a self-inflicted gunshot wound, of his own personal and private demons, however, did. *The Wild Bunch*, filmed in 1968, would be Albert Dekker's last work. That same year, his body would be found in the bathroom of his Hollywood apartment. His death was ruled an "accidental strangulation." He was sixty-two.

•

The New York Times, October 22, 1949, reported that, following a seven-month-long trial, "Ten of eleven top American Communist leaders, convicted earlier for criminal conspiracy under the Smith Act, were fined $10,000 each and sentenced to five years in federal prison." The eleventh was sentenced to only three years due to his outstanding war record. Bail was denied pending appeal.

Defense counsels had argued to Federal Judge Harold R. Medina that the rarely used 1940 Smith Act—which punishes persons who "knowingly or willfully advocate, abet, advise, or teach the duty, necessity, desirability, or propriety of overthrowing or destroying any government of the United Sates by force or violence; or publish or distribute printed matter advocating violent overthrow; or organize any society with such a purpose; or knowingly join in such a society"—was unconstitutional.

No clear and present danger existed, counsels maintained, to justify the abridgment of the defendants' right to free speech. Nothing more blatantly violated the First Amendment than making advocacy a crime.

•

7

~~~~~~~

The Four-Bit "Bible" and the Muir Matter

It was, in the end, Joseph R. McCarthy, the lackluster junior senator from Wisconsin, who elevated the growing anticommunism paranoia into a national, bipartisan hysteria. On February 9, 1950, he launched his modern-day inquisition: "I have here in my hand a list of 205 [the number changed with subsequent tellings] State Department employees known to be card-carrying Communists."

On June 22 of the same year, the American Business Consultants of New York—Ken Bierly, John Keenan, and Ted Kirkpatrick—convinced that "efforts of government to expose and combat Communist activities have failed," published a 213-page paperback entitled *Red Channels: The Report of Communist Influence in Radio and Television*, at one dollar per copy.

The consultants, former temporary FBI agents and researchers for various anti-Communist publications, had turned out a weekly newsletter, *Counterattack*, for the prior three years. From its pages they fired regular volleys at government officials, television networks, newspapers, and the American Civil Liberties Union (ACLU), calling them Communists or supporters of communism. They occasionally targeted individual performers, but it was *Red Channels*—a special report aimed specifically at creative artists in broadcasting—that exploded on Madison Avenue and burned out of control like some timeless incendiary bomb.

FBI Director J. Edgar Hoover warned menacingly from page one: "The Communist Party has departed from depending upon the printed word . . . and has taken to the air."

One Vincent Hartnett, a former radio production company employee and collaborator on the book, wrote its chilling introduction. It read, in part,

Programs produced by one network . . . have faithfully followed the
Party line. Several . . . sponsored dramatic series are used as sounding boards, particularly with reference to . . . issues in which the
Party is critically interested: "academic freedom," "civil rights,"
"peace," "the H-Bomb, etc." These and other subjects . . . legitimate
in themselves, are . . . exploited in dramatic treatments which point
up current Communist goals.

There then appeared the names of 151 actors, musicians, dancers, writers, announcers, directors, producers, and news commentators, most of
whom were well-known and highly respected in their fields, a number of
whom had been publicly commended for outstanding service in wartime.

Many were close friends of George and Clara Heller, including Henry
Jaffe's wife, Jean Muir, a 1930s Warner Brothers' star in more than
twenty-five films and the newly hired Mother on the television version of
The Aldrich Family; Sam Jaffe, a cofounder with Heller of the Actors'
Forum and just named Best Actor in the Venice Film Festival for his role
as the leader of the jewel heist in *The Asphalt Jungle*; and Philip Loeb,
another cofounder of the Actors' Forum, a TvA board member, and currently the husband, Jake, on television's *The Goldbergs*.

Others from the TvA board were Mady Christians, who played Mama
in the Broadway production of John Van Druten's *I Remember Mama*;
Mildred Dunnock, Willy Loman's wife in *Death of a Salesman*; as well as
Gypsy Rose Lee, Ben Grauer, Margaret Webster, and Kenneth Roberts.
Also named were Heller's old colleagues Will Geer, Burgess Meredith,
Will Lee, Morris Carnovsky, John Garfield, and Elia Kazan; writers Ar-
naud d'Usseau and James Gow, and, and . . .

Beneath each name were citings of reported political activities—not, as
one actress said, the facts of your past but what others said were the
facts—such as membership in or appearances on behalf of the labor
movement, world peace, antiracism, and antifascism. Some were named
for their support of a political candidate on the left or far left. The majority of the reported activities dated from years earlier; a number of the
organizations had been defunct since the late 1930s.

The citations were culled by *Red Channels* from many sources, primarily Attorney General Tom Clark's list, a reference of suspect organizations compiled for use when hiring Federal employees; the Tenney Committee's reports, which were criticized even by the American Business
Consultants for their inaccuracies; "Appendix IX," a supplementary
HUAC report naming over one hundred thousand Americans and their
so-called front connections ("Appendix IX" was suppressed following
publication because of its indiscriminate, often incorrect use of names);
the Massachusetts Committee on Un-American Activities reports; the

Daily Worker, a New York–based Communist newspaper whose reliability was often called into question; and the opinions or conjectures of the consultants themselves.

A disclaimer in Hartnett's introduction, that these persons may well have been innocents or genuine liberals, did nothing to soften the blow, nor was that its intent. Rather, it made it virtually impossible for a listed person to obtain legal satisfaction for any damages suffered (Cogley 1956).

The sobering news of the invasion of South Korea by Communist North Korea and the large number of Americans destined to be sent there as part of the United Nations (UN) resistance forces served to heighten the impact of *Red Channels*. It took no time for the networks and ad agencies to read its political significance and to adopt its point of view. It became, as Jack Gould of *The New York Times* wrote, "the bible of Madison Avenue," *the* employment manual for the television industry and all other interested parties.

In the melee that followed, the questions of truth or lies, guilt or innocence, loyalty or acts of subversion were lost or forgotten. No need for a hearing; no need to confront your accuser. The so-called evidence was proof perfect. Soon, reputations, careers, even lives would be destroyed.

•

Henry Jaffe reported to the TvA Board of Directors:

> Jean Muir has had a long record of anti-Communism, including unpaid performances on anti-Communist radio programs. Of the seven so-called subversive organizations of which she was to have been a member, she didn't know of four, had resigned from one soon after a question of possible Communist connections was raised, and had no apologies for the sixth, the Southern Conference for Human Welfare, of which Eleanor Roosevelt was also a member.

As for the seventh citation—yes, Muir, a longtime student of the Stanislavski method of acting, *had* sent a cable to the Moscow Art Theater congratulating them on their fiftieth anniversary. This and other links to subversive organizations were, as many in *Red Channels* proved to be, so faulty—even silly—that one must laugh. Some did, in disbelief; but not for long.

In his investigative report on blacklisting in broadcasting (prepared for the ACLU), former magazine editor and correspondent Merle Miller traced the behind-the-scenes events that led, weeks later, not to the first but to the most publicized casualty of *Red Channels*: the firing of Jean Muir. It happened during the last lazy weekend of August (Miller 1952, with the uncredited assistance of Alan Reitman).

Early Saturday morning, Ted Kirkpatrick, of American Business Consultants, was alerted to a press release concerning Jean Muir's television debut the following day on *The Aldrich Family*. Surprised and annoyed that *Counterattack* was scooped by the traditional press, he contacted a Mrs. Hester McCullough, of Greenwich, Connecticut, an anti-Communist committee of one. Mrs. McCullough had gained some fame a year earlier fighting a two-hundred-thousand-dollar libel suit brought against her by dancer Paul Draper and harmonicist Larry Adler; she and several other women had publicly accused the two of being pro-Communist. The Hartford jury was unable to reach a verdict, and the case was dropped.

Mrs. McCullough, in turn, activated twenty or so more persons, among them the Queens, New York, commander of the Catholic War Veterans, the Americanism Committee of the Connecticut American Legion, Rabbi Benjamin Schultz of the American Jewish League Against Communism (repudiated earlier by both his own temple and the New York Board of Rabbis for besmirching the reputations of a number of honored clergymen), plus several women on Long Island.

McCullough made two more calls: one to a neighbor, an executive of Young and Rubicam (Y & R), the ad agency that handled *The Aldrich Family*; the other to NBC, the show's network. She asked: "Did you know about Jean Muir's 'record'?"

Although officials were reluctant to discuss what happened next, the result was that Muir was dismissed and the show postponed until she could be replaced. During that entire weekend, the agency, the network, and the sponsor did not afford the actress an opportunity to speak for herself.

Recently, Muir told me: "I was in dress rehearsal when an announcement came through that the show wasn't going on the air. I tried getting more information but I couldn't; no one was talking. When I got home, Henry phoned Jack Gould at *The Times* and *he* told us what had happened. Early Monday, we called Y & R to check if what Gould said was correct. At first, they wouldn't accept our calls. When they finally did, it was all over but the shouting."

The event made headlines in the national and international press and was the subject of hundreds of editorials, the majority of which supported Muir. NBC and the show's sponsor, General Foods (GF), while receiving only eighteen telephone calls precipitating the dismissal, later received thousands upon thousands of letters. Excepting those from organized pressure groups, three to one were against her dismissal. Nonetheless, an earlier statement from GF would stand:

The use of controversial personalities . . . may provide unfavorable criticism and even antagonism among sizable groups of customers. General Foods . . . therefore, avoids the use of . . . personalities [who], in its judgment, are controversial.

There it was. Business, after all, was business, businessmen rationalized. And unlike other fields of entertainment, radio and television existed because of and on behalf of business. In the coming decade, it would be the exceptional sponsor, agency, or producer who would not succumb to the pressure of the almighty dollar. The Celanese Corporation, the Alcoa Company, the Ellington agency, Tom Murray of Grey Advertising, Robert Kintner of ABC and, to a large extent, Mrs. Gertrude Berg of television's *The Goldbergs* were six of the exceptions.

In early September 1950, Jean Muir and Henry Jaffe met with Chairman Clarence Francis and others of GF. There, GF officials deplored the unfair treatment accorded her, claiming no knowledge of *Red Channels* at the time of its publication. The validity of the charges against her seemed of little concern to the company, but the fact that she had been *listed* was; and were she to appear on *The Aldrich Family*, it might prove detrimental to the sale of Jello.

And so, with regret and sympathy and despite Chairman Francis' comment, "I wouldn't be sitting here with you if I thought these charges were true," GF officially rid themselves of Jean Muir. Her thirteen-week contract was bought out—much against her better judgment, she said—and with that, all responsibility of the company ended. Ended too was her decades-long acting career, soon her health and well-being, and the well-being of her three young children. She turned for a number of years, as she phrased it, to the "solace" of alcohol.

•

Ken Bierly of *Red Channels* later told *Sponsor* magazine:

When we devised [it] we made two mistakes. . . . One, no genuine investigation was made of the people listed. Second, the book didn't attempt to categorize whether the performers were innocents, dupes or Reds. It just listed all the people, as reported by the public records, under one cover.

And in another interview, Bierly added: "It was immaterial whether they were Communists or not, entirely immaterial to what we were trying to do. . . . In the first place, we don't know who is a Communist. In the second place, we couldn't find out if we asked" (Miller 1952).

At no time during the preparation of *Red Channels* or its subsequent editions did the editors bother to try.

•

"Henry would never say it, of course," Jean Muir told me, "but he suffered terribly through my blacklisting. He was married to a woman who was on the front page of every paper in the country, a woman who was being named a Communist. He had to defend me and, at the same time, he had to conduct a law practice. He couldn't risk being called left wing; he had to protect himself some way. I imagine it was the most—well, certainly one of the most—difficult times of his life.

"I was never able to tell him how I appreciated it because I went into alcohol pretty soon after that. And he was away a lot—traveling back and forth to LA, establishing business contacts there. So, for the last eight or nine years of our marriage, there was no real communication between us. And I'd go to bed at night crying and repeating the first lines I'd ever learned when I was nine years old:

> The quality of mercy is not strain'd,
> It droppeth as the gentle rain from heaven
> Upon the place beneath . . .

Attorney General J. Howard McGrath declared before the American Bar Association in September 1950:

> We seem to be going through a period of public hysteria . . . in which many varieties of self-appointed policemen and alleged guardians of Americanism would have us fight subversion by . . . stigmatizing as disloyal all those who disagree with or oppose them. This hysteria appears in vigilante groups who decree . . . beatings of purported Communist sympathizers; or who, in more polite circles, intimidate radio advertisers into silencing performers who they say have Communist leanings. (Miller 1952)

"George Heller was in private agony," Gene Francis said. "We talked about it endlessly. What was happening ran against all his personal principles. He must speak out!"

But the TvA was barely one year old and, with the jurisdictional, organizational, and contractual problems before it, it had not yet established its anti-Communist credentials. To urge the board to come out against *Red Channels* now was sure to be twisted by the right-wing press—George Sokolsky, Leon Racht, Jack O'Brian, and the others—as a pro-Communist statement. Dare Heller run that risk for the TvA? For himself? Or could he, in fact, persuade the board (he knew the political biases of many of the directors) to issue such a condemnation? All the while, beleaguered members were knocking at the door—needing, demanding help.

"If one member is forced off the air," said Henry Jaffe at the September membership meeting,

> the livelihood of all members is endangered. This is not a case which threatens Jean Muir, but every member . . . no matter what his be-

ginnings and associations. . . . The union must take a stand, either supporting its members or determining not to support them.

Following board approval by deferred agenda, Heller issued this statement, in part:

> TvA, representing more than 25,000 persons in television, views with alarm the tendency on the part of sponsors and advertising agencies of succumbing to self-appointed pressure groups. TvA condemns Communism and abhors this vicious and ungodly ideology . . . nevertheless, Americans must resist efforts of individuals or groups who, in their zeal, destroy basic individual rights. . . . Certain of the groups have recklessly ignored these rights and . . . irreparably harmed the reputations and livelihoods of many loyal Americans.
>
> The United States Government is the only body capable of determining who is and who is not a loyal American and TvA stands ready and willing to assist our government is ferreting out disloyal Americans . . . TvA stands ready to join the broadcasting industry to correct this evil and calls upon the American Bar Association and the Bar of New York to appoint a committee for this purpose.

Easier said than done.

Noting that dismissals without trial or redress could be imminent in radio as well as television, AFRA called for a conference of networks, sponsors, and ad agencies. Its purpose, "to explore methods or working out an intelligent solution to the problem posed by the Muir and similar cases which will be consistent with traditional American practices." Heller and Jaffe were invited to join.

The "intelligent solution" was a procedure wherein a statement of innocence by an accused person would be taken down by his or her union and held there, in confidence, until called for by an ad agency wanting to hire that person. It would, in turn, be presented to the sponsor.

The conferees noted, however, "If the performer, by his own actions, has made himself harmful to the best interests of broadcasters, it was his or her own personal responsibility and could not be shifted to the union." The report concluded, "Nor would the conference be expected to stand behind the veracity or validity of any such statement of innocence."

Both the TvA and AFRA boards acknowledged that, while the solution was not perfect, it was a step forward; perhaps it would end the kind of damaging notoriety that had been suffered by Muir and others. When one member queried, "Why doesn't the ad agency deal directly with the performer?" the answer was, "Because it's embarrassing for an employer to have to ask such questions."

The procedure, however, was doomed from the start, rarely used during its two-year existence, and even then returned only three—possibly four—persons to work. But it did give the sponsors and the ad agencies what they wanted most: anonymity.

At the same time that AFRA was instituting its imperfect, quasi due process for the "innocent" in radio, it took steps to deny that same protection to others. The board did a little "listing" of its own. The names of seven members "observed" marching in the 1951 May Day Parade—a celebration of the American labor movement that included all workers, Socialists and Communists alike—were entered (but did not appear) in the record.

•

In March 1951, HUAC, which had yet to prove infiltration of Communist ideology into American film, undertook a mammoth new round of hearings. They would alternate between the nation's capital and the city of Los Angeles for the next twenty-odd months.

"As severe as it was, the fate of the 'Hollywood Ten' turned out to be only a small foretaste of the political, professional and human destruction that was to occur. . . . This time there was no outcry of the liberal-radical tribes (Ceplair and Englund 1980).

Recantations for past party or so-called front activities (HUAC's list of such organizations had grown to more than six hundred) were not enough for then Chairman John S. Wood. What he would have now were the *names* of former "comrades" or 'fellow travelers," names HUAC had been unable to extract in the 1947 hearings. An agonizing, isolating fear gripped the liberal community. Some hid under pseudonyms, some fled the country, some made private deals.

Most, however, stayed and testified and, believing it a despicable act to inform on one's old associates, refused to do so despite citings of contempt. They invoked the Fifth Amendment as protection against self-incrimination and the incrimination of others. These were the government's so-called unfriendly witnesses—Victor Kilian, of the old Actors' Forum, among them—the sacrificial lambs of a punitive right wing. These were the ones left to suffer the now-familiar, dreadful consequences.

There were others, some thirty-two of them, who "named the names" the committee sought. Among these informers were Heller's old colleagues Clifford Odets and Elia Kazan (both had themselves been named earlier by Jack Warner of Warner Brothers). Each confessed, in executive session, that he had been a member of a Communist group within the Group Theatre during the years 1934–36. Each then obliged the chair with the identity of the others. In a later statement, Kazan outlined the party's main purposes: to become educated in Marxism; to support various front organizations by providing entertainment for meetings and rallies; to capture the Group Theatre as a whole and make it a Communist mouthpiece, an effort, he admitted, that failed; and to gain a foothold in the Actors' Equity Association.

"The tactics and sincere effort of many individuals was to raise a demand that actors receive pay during the weeks when they rehearsed for shows." Kazan testified that, "by leading a fight for a reasonable gain," the party and "individual Communists and sympathizers" would gain prestige and would, the party hoped, "then run the union." That plan too, he added, was unsuccessful.

Kazan had served the committee and, in doing so, had cast a new shadow on the sincere efforts of the Actors' Forum. As had been understood would happen, he was reemployed within days. His first film, *The Man on a Tightrope*, would—not surprisingly—have a clear anti-Communist theme.

In June 1951, the U.S. Supreme Court affirmed the 1949 convictions under the Smith Act of the eleven top Communist leaders, allying the Court, it was written, with anti-Communist Cold War sentiments and opening the door to a wave of arrests of party leaders in more than a dozen states across the country. Membership in the American Communist Party was now all but illegal, its ability to operate effectively destroyed.

•

No Communist infiltration was to be allowed in the radio federation. Where it did exist, the board would root it out. To that end, a debate was begun on an anti-Communist amendment to the AFRA Constitution. Proposals of varying degrees of severity emanated from both the eastern and the western sections. They triggered weeks of acrimonious debate, heavy with insinuations and allegations concerning directors' personal allegiances. They succeeded, finally, in tearing the board apart—to the extent that actress Anne Seymour, who like many other Chicagoans had transferred along with their shows to New York, handed in her resignation.

I have seen what happens to members listed in *Red Channels* and *Counterattack*. I cannot afford professionally or financially to be on those blacklists and there is no reason for me to be—but these are unreasonable times. Serving on the National Board in 1951 is a most unpleasant obligation . . . [The] unending friction between the two factions promulgates fear, lack of faith and lack of cooperation.

I believe we could work together . . . if we stop doubting one another. It's absurd to ask us to share exactly the same opinions—religious, social, professional or political. . . . We should be working on behalf of AFRA, not jeopardizing good unionism or Americanism for a "personal cause."

Anne Seymour was speaking for others like herself—decent, patriotic, fair-minded citizens. Who, then, was this other faction to which she referred? What was their personal cause?

•

8

~~~~~~

The Artists' Committee

As we entered the 1940s, fascism rather than communism was the greater threat to Europe, and to America as well. While much of the Continent was already engaged in a struggle against Hitler and Benito Mussolini, here at home Nazi agents carried out their campaigns of espionage and political disruption. From street corners everywhere, fascists and their supporters hawked anti-Semitic, anti-Roosevelt literature—Father Charles E. Coughlin's magazine, *Social Justice* and the *Christian Front* among them—and preachings of religious and racial bigotry sped over the airwaves into every home in the nation. Yet in official, isolationist America, it was the Communists who were perceived as the greater threat to our way of life, and all efforts to expose the Reds and their fellow travelers, and to extract them from our institutions, continued apace.

From the U.S. *Congressional Record*, July 4, 1940: "Deserving actors and actresses all over the country" are being deprived of federal relief because Communists have "taken over key positions in theater in New York." Thus spoke Congressman William P. Lambertson of Kansas, a member of the House Appropriations Committee, who one year before had so shockingly attacked Hallie Flanagan, closed the Federal Theater Project, and cut off aid to thousands of indigent artists.

"When the . . . project was killed," Lambertson went on, "Congress assumed . . . the profession would undertake a house-cleaning. Instead, there has been a growing rather than diminishing trend of Communist influence. As recently as last May 14, in preference to an outstanding American actress, Tallulah Bankhead," Sam Jaffe, whom Lambertson described as an "an avowed Communist," was elected to the governing council of Actors' Equity. (William B. Bankhead, Tallulah's father, was then Speaker of the House and Lambertson's colleague.) "There will be no W.P.A. Theater Project as long as this condition is permitted to exist" (*The New York Times*, July 9, 1940).

Lambertson named six others on the council as being Communists or Communist sympathizers: Philip Loeb, Emily Marsh, Hiram Sherman, Edith Van Cleve, Leroy MacLean, and the apolitical Alan Hewitt. Also named were George Heller of AFRA and former CIO organizer Hoyt Haddock, the new executive of AGVA. Heller shot back a wire:

> This is untrue. The plain facts are that I am not now and never have been a Communist. [It] was evidently instigated . . . by a crank or some one with a selfish, personal motive. . . . In times such as these one would think that men who hold high positions in our democracy would be doubly bound to act with scrupulous responsibility and regard for the truth. In this spirit I ask you to issue a public retraction of your completely unfounded charge. (*The New York Times*, July 10, 1940)

The others also wired their repudiations, demanding to know the congressman's sources and evidence. The head of an organization that Loeb was charged with belonging to stated that Loeb was not a member, but he had signed a protest with others of "all shades of political opinion" against continuance of the Dies Committee (*The New York Times*, July 14, 1940).

Equity President Bert Lytell, then starring with Gertrude Lawrence in Weill's and Hart's *Lady in the Dark*, emphatically denied that either the council or the membership was or ever had been controlled by communism or by any other un-American beliefs. He demanded tangible proof, if any, to the contrary. He called for an official investigation and journeyed to Washington to plead with Chairman Dies for an early hearing. HUAC took little notice of the case, however, claiming more urgent business elsewhere.

The charges stood, unsubstantiated, for nearly a year while right-wing reactionaries, led by Florence Reed and Peggy Wood, longtime Equity vice presidents, continued to feed the fire. The eye of the storm centered on incumbent Alan Hewitt and his pending renomination.

Apart from Lambertson's charge (which was eventually withdrawn), the chief evidence of Hewitt's communism was that he had voted with some fifty-six others to overrule President Lytell's "out of order" on a proposed antiwar resolution. The question of how a congressman seated 233 miles south of the Astor Hotel was privy to the goings-on in the association, complete with names and votes of its members, was never fully answered.

The Nominating Committee, chaired by Vice President Reed, eventually chose to bypass Hewitt. Lambertson hailed the chairwoman "for performing a truly patriotic duty."

Hewitt and several others then formed an independent ticket, a move rare in the history of Equity and not used since the days of the Actors' Forum. At the election meeting, Lambertson intervened again. He wrote and Lytell read—while balloting was still in progress, it was charged—an open letter to the electorate, repeating his threat concerning federal funds and urging Hewitt's defeat.

Despite this outrageous act of impropriety, Hewitt was reelected by a comfortable margin, along with independents Myron McCormick and Mady Christians (she was denied official nomination because she was a naturalized citizen). Eight from the regular ticket were also elected, including Cornelia Otis Skinner, Louis Calhern, Lillian Gish, Margaret Webster (who supported the independents), and Ethel Waters, the first black artist to sit on the Equity council.

Hewitt's victory was devastating to the right. When the moment arrived for the induction of the new officers, Reed, Wood, and eight other council members rose from the table and, in a grand gesture, handed in a mass resignation. Before the visibly shaken Lytell could open the document, the group had turned and walked out. The letter read,

> For years we have struggled against an influence in our association which seemed to us subversive of American ideals and institutions. We have seen this element change Equity . . . from a Guild of Professionals, working for the best interests of the theater as a whole, to a labor union of different objectives.
>
> In this long and hard-fought battle we believed we represented the vast majority of our fellow actors. The results of the last election prove conclusively that that majority . . . are not in agreement with our ideas and ideals. . . . The new order now controls . . . [the] council.

The departed officers would return only "if the seven named [by Lambertson] resigned until cleared by a governmental agency."

Edith Van Cleve responded, "I am not a Communist and never have been one, and I see no reason to resign because I am accused of being one." Sam Jaffe answered, "Nobody who has the interests of Equity at heart resigns." The others could not comment, being out of town at the time or in the army (*The New York Times*, June 12, 1941).

All efforts for the councilors' return, including a plea from Alan Hewitt himself, failed. Lytell was distraught; he was left with a skeleton council. Replacements were culled from a list of those "who were not outstandingly violent on either side"—Raymond Massey and Jose Ferrer among them. Executive Secretary Dullzell commented to the press:

> It is ridiculous for these people to say a "new order" controls . . . council. They did not name them and they cannot name them. . . .

[The] resignations were as unnecessary as they were unwise. . . . [Had they given it] more consideration they would have recognized that [many things] contributed to Hewitt's election . . . his record on council, his lack of affiliations, Lambertson's retraction, and the feeling that he had been discriminated against. (*The New York Times*, June 12, 1941)

From Washington, D.C., Lambertson expressed his "personal sorrow" at the departure of Reed and Wood. A member of the rank and file, however, wrote:

Accept [the] resignations, gratefully; if they are unwilling to fight fairly for their convictions, they are not worthy of representing us. . . . Let us have a Council who respect each other even in disagreement and who are capable of intelligent and unemotional cooperation.

The current witch-hunt was nearly over. Officials said it had been "the most serious breach Equity had suffered since the actors' strike of 1919."

On March 21, 1942, after a tumultuous effort spanning six months and involving two referendums, the Equity membership approved, 552 to 288, a constitutional amendment barring members of (or those who aided or abetted) the Communist Party of the Soviet Union and of the United States, as well as the National Fascist Party of Italy, or any subdivision thereof, from holding office or from being employed by the association.

President Lytell told *The New York Times*:

I hope it will end for all time this controversy. [I do not] think for one moment that those who voted against [led by Boris Karloff, Walter Hampden, Augustin Duncan, and others] . . . are by any means sympathizers. . . . They felt we had enough machinery in our [present] by-laws . . . to dispose of any undesirable council member.

The work of the organization was now free to proceed.

•

In George Heller's AFRA as well, right-wing reactionaries rose to prominence on both the New York local board and the eastern section of the national board. While somewhat more discreet than their counterparts at Actors' Equity, they too were driven with an immoderate fear of "Communist infiltration" into the union and, like their counterparts, perceived all left-wing, liberal, or progressive thought as being communistic. The group was known as the Artists' Committee.

Among their leaders were some of radio's busiest: Clayton "Bud" Collyer, lead actor on *Kitty Foyle* and *The Man I Married*; Alan Bunce, Albert on the *Ethel and Albert* comedy series and Doctor Jerry on *Young Doctor Malone*; Ned Wever, lead on *Dick Tracy* and *Bulldog Drummond*; Jack Arthur, narrator on *Grand Central Station*; Walter Greaza, the editor on *Big Town*; and William P. "Bill" Adams, then president of the New York local and a specialist in the voice of Franklin D. Roosevelt.

The committee was supported on the West Coast by the avowed conservatives of the Los Angeles local board and the western section of the national board. There, it was Frank Nelson, a founding member of the local and prominent union activist, who reigned as the right's undisputed and most venerable spokesman; and there, said director Tyler McVey, incumbents were rarely challenged and, when they were, defended their positions openly, without the secrecy and vilification that came to mark the Artists' Committee in the East.

In the fall of 1944, amidst the beginnings of a new national antiunionism and anticommunism, the Artists' Committee took steps to end what they perceived as left-leaning, expansionist efforts within the New York local. The committee proposed (the board approved, and the membership adopted) a highly controversial rule called the Arthur-Collyer Resolution, which essentially disallowed "all discussions, motions [or] endorsements . . . of any matter: religious, political, social or economic," other than wages and working conditions, on the floor of membership meetings. Further, all motions were to be submitted two weeks prior to board meetings for classification as to their "admissibility." If deemed inadmissible, the motion could be resubmitted (within seven days) but only with a supporting petition signed by one hundred members in good standing. Voting would be by referendum only.

The Artists' Committee underestimated many in the rank and file and their insistence on an open partnership with their elected leaders; they underestimated too their dedication to debating any item, at any length, that would strengthen the union—make it more effective in its dealings with the powerful radio managements. The Actors' Forum had been the training ground for most of them.

Following months of heated opposition, coauthor and newly elected President Bud Collyer was obliged to announce that, upon further review by legal counsel, the rule had been found to be invalid, that it would require several constitutional amendments, and it would, therefore, be withdrawn.

With the coming of the Cold War, however, the Artists' Committee's anti-Communist obsession became their badge and their banner. They grew even more contentious, more factional; they started using highhanded tactics at meetings and conventions; they managed elections by way of anonymous, insinuating literature. It was not long before these methods—which many perceived as antiunion—became, for most, their defeat.

In December 1947, in the New York local's first hotly contested election, a slate of "clear-thinking Independents" (some, breakaway members of the original Artists' Committee) emerged. With the motto "Let's Give AFRA Back to the Membership" and the promise to disband the slate immediately after balloting, they swept into office. Collyer and Bunce retained their seats.

The independents included Anne Seymour and Virginia Payne (former first president of the Chicago local); Les Damon, who played Nick Charles on *The Thin Man*; Carl Eastman, the lead on *Life Can Be Beautiful*; Arnold Moss, lead on *The Guiding Light*; Karl Swenson, Lorenzo on *Lorenzo Jones*; announcers Nelson Case, Richard Stark, Ben Grauer, and Dan Seymour; singers Julie Conway, John Neher, and Genevieve Rowe; and sound-effects man Robert Prescott, to name a few.

•

Peg Lynch, creator-writer and leading lady of the hit comedy series *Ethel and Albert*, told me: "Alan Bunce, Bud Collyer, and Ned Wever saw Communists under every bush. They believed the country was in mortal danger, and they were forever identifying others as either being on or not being on somebody's list. Alan, I know, was genuinely frightened. He felt he was doing something patriotic; he always was a flag-waver. Although he never pressured me about casting, there's no doubt that they were busy bees behind the scenes of many a show.

"It didn't matter that jobs and reputations would fall by the wayside; as long as they kept control of the union and made sure the 'Reds' didn't take over. Perhaps that's the key to it: Power. Control.

"If they weren't meeting somewhere, they were on the phone together—constantly, endlessly. These were the days of radio, remember—no lines to memorize; they just had to show up and read the script. Not like writers—they don't mingle. They just sit home alone writing, day after day after day. What's that quotation about 'idle hands?'

"Alan and I did two shows a day in the mid forties, one was a West Coast repeat, and sometimes after the 6:45, we'd go out for dinner together. I remember once we went to Danny's Hideaway. We ordered; Alan excused himself saying he had to call Bud. The shrimp cocktail came; I waited, then ate. The dinner arrived; I waited, then ate. Ditto dessert and coffee. I asked for the bill, walked to the phone booth, opened the door, handed it to Alan and turned to leave. He just nodded, smiled, and kept right on talking. You can see how I was more than a little bored by the whole thing.

"In the same vein," Peg went on, "Alan's wife, Ruth, tells of how one night they were going to the Wevers' after dinner. They had their coats on, ready to leave, when the phone rang. It was Ned. Alan started talking, so Ruth sat down. After a while, she took her coat off and went into the kitchen. She tidied the dishes, then cleaned out a cupboard. Finally, she went upstairs, undressed, got into bed, and started reading a book.

"Then Alan came running up the stairs, yelling, 'Come on! Come on! What are you going? Let's go' as though *she'd* been holding *him* up. It was ten minutes to 10:00. He'd been on the phone three hours, still with his coat on. Ruth just said, 'Good night,' and rolled over. Sheepishly, Alan phoned Ned to say they weren't coming, then talked for another hour."

•

"Bud Collyer and I were great friends," Jackson Beck told me, "we'd worked together on *Superman* since 1939. He was a marvelous guy and smart as hell; one of the few authentic geniuses I ever knew. We had an understanding about union politics, though. I told him, 'Look, we don't agree. I'll oppose you on the floor and you'll oppose me. But let's leave it outside the studio.' And we did.

"The first I heard about the Artists' Committee was sometime around 1947. I was crossing Sixth Avenue at Forty-second Street when Staats Cotsworth—he was Casey on radio's *Casey, Crime Photographer*—caught up with me. He looked real worried—said we had to talk. He told me about this anti-Communist group in AFRA headed by Collyer and Bunce, that they held regular meetings and made up lists, which they took to advertisers saying that these people shouldn't be allowed to work in the business. 'I'm fighting like hell,' Staats said, 'to keep you off that list, but you're gonna have to defend yourself.'

"I answered, 'Staats, I'm no Communist; I have never signed anything. And I'm not afraid.' "

•

By late 1949, American had been drawn deeper into the Cold War. The threat of communism was the fear and preoccupation of the entire country. A new, expanded Artists' Committee prepared to run for the New York board. Superpatriots all and fueled by a renewed dedication to protect their union, they won enthusiastic support from the troubled majority. And, once again, they became the dominant voice of AFRA. Not just anti-Red, several made little attempt at meetings to conceal their anti-semitism as well.

In addition to Collyer, Bunce, Arthur, Wever, and others, the committee now boasted Vinton Hayworth of radio's *Myrt and Marge*; Vicki Cummings, stage and television actress; Vicki Vola, Miss Miller on *Mr. District Attorney*; Anne Elstner, who for eighteen years played Stella on *Stella Dallas*; Elizabeth Morgan of the *Stella Dallas* company; former silent film star Conrad Nagel, host of the *Silver Theater*; and Walter Kiernan, commentator and quiz show panelist, among others.

This, then, was the other "faction" Anne Seymour referred to in her letter of resignation to the AFRA board. Rabid anticommunism was their "personal cause."

●

AFRA's national executive secretary, A. Frank Reel, who was the young army captain appointed in 1946 to defend General Tomoyuki Yamashita at his war crimes trial, remembered: "Personally, it was very distressing for me with my civil libertarian background. It was a constant, *constant* battle trying to make sense with the Artists' Committee people. None of them had too many brains, you know. Except for Collyer, the intelligence was all over on the other side. They [the independents] were the acknowledged brains and heart and guts of the union. And they were outraged by this bigoted attitude.

"Ned Wever was an extreme right-winger," Reel said, "and Vinton Hayworth was a child; he had the most immature childlike attitude. A lot of the others had it too, but with Vinnie it was dangerous. I'll tell you an incident.

"One member of our board was Minerva Pious, Mrs. Pansy Nussbaum on the *Fred Allen Show*. Pious had been 'named' in *Red Channels* and was out of work for months; she was falling into big financial troubles. We discussed it before a meeting one night. Later, Vinnie expressed his delight to me as we waited together on a subway platform. 'You don't want the woman to starve to death, do you?' I asked. He answered, 'Yes.'

"Alan Bunce wasn't the smartest guy in the world," Reel continued, "but he was a sentimental, sweet-natured guy, who'd cry real tears when someone he considered a friend was blacklisted—he mellowed when the tragedies started. You couldn't hate him. You couldn't hate Collyer, either. Bud was a brilliant guy. He like to present himself as a peacemaker, a great mediator. I had my difficulties with him, of course, and one day while we were having 'words' about *Red Channels*, he said to me, 'Frank, this thing will only get worse. It's unfortunate, but a lot of innocent people are going to be hurt.'

"I was stopped for a second. Then I answered something about, 'The protection of the innocent is one of the most important things in the Bill of Rights.'

"He said, somberly, 'Yes. I know.' But his attitude and his actions remained, 'Whatever happened couldn't be helped. We have to protect America.' "

•

"My father's politics," said Michael Collyer, New York theatrical attorney and then the chairman of the board of the National Academy of Arts and Sciences (purveyor of the Emmy Awards), "were sort of early Rooseveltian New Dealer into Eisenhower 'middle-of-the-roader.' He was a moderate; he did everything in moderation.

"Originally, dad was a lawyer, but times were hard for young attorneys in the early 1930s. He turned, instead, to his musical and acting talents to make a living. He and Alan Bunce were active in George Heller's AFRA from the very first days the union was founded. He soon became determined that AFRA must be kept an open and democratic union. It's so easy, you know, for any small, outside force to dominate the majority if they put the time and effort into it.

"America had just been through an era," Michael went on, "where we saw—but didn't see—a small group, the Nazi Party, come to dominate Europe and what it took to finally rid ourselves of them. After the war, the moderates saw the rise of another small group, this time the Communist Party, trying to obtain political power. People like my father knew they must apply force against it. 'Harsh treatment requires the use of harsh medicine.' "

"Did your father know, as fact, that Communists were attempting to subvert the union?" I asked.

"I don't know that," Michael answered, "but he was convinced that a certain group wanted to bend the union to their point of view. And to him, that was tyranny. He believed the union should not be a forum for a single political issue.

"There was a surprisingly violent undertone to the early 1950s," Michael continued. "I remember, once, walking with dad through Rockefeller Center and someone yelling out at him, 'I hope I'm on the firing squad when they shoot you.' Most of today's depictions are totally sympathetic to the sufferings of only a few, gifted blacklisted artists—as am I, too—but they don't tell the whole story of the time. There was emotional frenzy on both sides."

"With George Heller and Bud Collyer at near-opposite ends of the political pole," I asked "how was their friendship able to survive?"

"Because they respected one another," Michael said, "and could allow each other their own viewpoints, and because they continued to share the same visions, the same goals for the union. The goals were much more important than the ideologies. I have to believe they talked about it all the time: How are we going to get through this difficult chapter in AFRA's, AFTRA's history?

"Ironically, because of my father's union activities, because he took a stand, he became a political hot potato. He began to lose work; his income plummeted—thank heavens, my mother's didn't." Michael's stepmother, Marion Shockley, played Ellery Queen's longtime assistant, Nikki, on radio.

It was that loss of work that brought Collyer over to infant television in July 1948. He became host on the first of his many game shows, *Winner Take All*, despite the advice of many radio friends who didn't make the leap. "Bud," they told him, "you're crazy! It'll never last."

"The generous, caring side of my father," Michael concluded, "was not generally known. The side that to my mother's dismay supported Lord knows how many down-on-their-luck actors, that pushed his producers, Mark Goodson and Bill Todman, to hire the blacklisted John Henry Faulk for a stint on *To Tell the Truth*, that moved us from our hometown of Pound Ridge, New York, because the country club there adopted a policy restricting Jews."

Mrs. Audrey Mason, a friend of the Collyer's in Greenwich, Connecticut, where the family next moved, continued the story: "When the Collyers first came here they had the choice of three churches they might attend, one not far from the other. Bud decided he'd try each one out for a period of one month. He finally chose our First Presbyterian over the others because, as he said, 'It was the most run down and needed the most work.' "

And work he did. Collyer became a highly effective fund-raiser, an elder of the church, and superintendent of the Sunday School. After his death in 1969, the building which housed the school was named the Collyer Center in his honor.

"Bud was a very charitable man," Audrey Mason said. "He had his head on straight and his heart in the right place."

Collyer had no apology for his somewhat less-than-charitable attitude towards his opposition in the union, however. For him, none was necessary; he was in the majority of American political opinion. In 1948, and again in 1949, the AFRA National Convention elected him president. He would not be deterred. He would put his house—soon, both his houses—in order.

"The power and function of the President is sometimes played down a little too much," Bud Collyer told Bill Lipton.

He has more power than most people have ever tried to use or think. He has a certain amount of control over the paid executives of the union. He can command them to move here and there, as I often did. . . . He's not just a figurehead nor should he be. He must be a leader and take the lead. (Lipton 1963)

•

In late November 1949, Collyer, Bunce, Wever, and Hayworth were appointed part of the AFRA delegation (ten, plus ten alternates) to serve on the national board of George Heller's new TvA. And to Heller's dismay, in matters political they came to dominate the five-branch board, as they had the local and national boards of AFRA, outtalking and outvoting the moderates and the left on most issues to come before them.

And like Senator Joseph McCarthy, who was destined to appear on the national scene in a matter of months, they too were experts in the game of political hardball. In some quarters, it was rumored that the Artists' Committee was somehow connected with the people responsible for *Red Channels* and its parent publication, *Counterattack*. No one knew for sure.

•

The mechanisms of the 1935 Wagner Act, or the National Labor Relations Act, so effective in governing collective bargaining for both labor and big business, stalled following World War II. Often unable to win their arguments at the bargaining table, except by militant shows of strength, unions were predictably cast as the villains, even though complaints of unfair labor practices had doubled, even tripled, in the ten years since the passage of the act. With the right's militant antiunion campaign and their success in equating all of organized labor with communistic positions, the popularity of the trade-union movement had sunk to a new low.

Not that labor was blameless. Frequent disputes over jurisdiction and irregularities in the internal affairs of some unions cleared the way not for amendments to the Wagner Act, which had been generally anticipated, but for a whole new act and a whole new era in collective bargaining (Cohen 1979).

The Labor Management Act of 1947, known as the Taft-Hartley Act, was the reward from the newly elected, pro-business Congress to the leaders of industry for their decade-long, generally unsuccessful battle against labor unions. It told them what they longed to hear: that labor, which had been allowed to rise up to a superior position in relation to business, would, from that point on, be restrained, even curtailed; that the years of vigorous growth of the trade-union movement were over.

The Taft-Hartley Act was a sprawling, often unclear, highly complicated piece of legislation and three and one-half times longer than the Wagner Act it replaced. Essentially, it reduced the legal limitations on employers while increasing their legal protections. It added a variety of restrictions on unions; abolishing the closed shop, regulating strikes with regard to national emergencies, and prohibiting certain types of secondary boycotts (Cohen 1979).

It provided nonunion workers with protection against unions and union workers with protection against their own leadership. It made organizing far more difficult and allowed the right-to-work states to enact legislation even more restrictive on union security than the act itself (Cohen 1979). And if a union were to violate any provision of the Taft-Hartley Act, the NLRB must seek an injunction. The Norris-La Guardia Anti-Injunction Act was effectively dead; the courts were back in the center of the management-labor arena.

Philip Taft wrote, in *The A.F. of L. from the Death of Gompers to the Merger* (1959), that for John L. Lewis, then president of the United Mine Workers Union, it was "a hateful, despicable Act contrary to our concept of American privileges and it makes second-class citizens out of every man around the Council table and every man he represents."

One of the less-harmful but more objectionable features, Lewis felt, was Item 9h—a provision requiring a non-Communist affidavit from all union officers as a condition of their continued use of the services of the NLRB; otherwise, decertification. There was a cry of outrage that 9h illegally abridged the rights guaranteed by the First and Fifth Amendments. Legal challenges were made and lost; CIO unions were thrown into disarray debating whether or not to follow the executive board directive telling them to comply. More than thirty unions did; eleven of them—the so-called soul of the CIO, including the electrical workers; the fur and leather workers; the mine, mill, and smelter workers; and the longshoremen—did not. For this and other irreconcilable political differences, they would later be expelled.

The American Communist Party was still not officially outlawed, but the Taft-Hartley Act's anti-Communist affidavit provision—upheld by a five to one vote of the U.S. Supreme Court—made membership in it, for union officials at least, very bad for their professional health. (Several years later, Congress would pass the Communist Control Act, doing away with the provision and, instead, making it a crime to hold union office while a member of the Communist Party or within five years of resigning.)

•

On June 4, 1951, the U.S. Supreme Court handed down its decision in *Dennis v. the United States*, the continuing case of the eleven Communist leaders convicted in 1949, fined and sentenced to five years in Federal prison. The Court ruled, 6–2, that the conviction under the 1940 Smith

Act for speaking and teaching Communist theory did not abridge First Amendment rights. In his dissenting opinion Justice Hugo Black wrote that the defendants

> were not charged with an attempt to overthrow the government. They were not charged with overt acts of any kind designed to overthrow the government. They were not even charged with saying . . . or writing anything designed to overthrow the government. The charge was that they agreed to assemble and to talk and publish certain ideas at a later date.

•

Let us remain with George Heller's first union a while longer. What happened there, as the Artists' Committee moved the radio federation further toward ultraconservatism, would directly and immediately affect Heller and the new TvA.

In late June 1951, the AFRA National Board finally emerged from weeks of rancorous, divisive debate with an anti-Communist amendment to the constitution, subject to approval by the AFRA convention. The proposed amendment ventured beyond Item 9h of the Taft-Hartley Act. It would bar from membership or employment in the union anyone who had been proved to have been a post-1945 member of the Communist Party; anyone who had been named or identified as a Communist by the U.S. State Department, the Justice Department, or the FBI; and anyone who, after adoption of the amendment, maintained membership in or rendered assistance to any organization listed by the U.S. Attorney General, or any other duly constituted government agency, as "subversive."

Board member Staats Cotsworth, former member of the Artists' Committee and a staunch supporter of the Bill of Rights, brought the proposed amendment to the attention of the ACLU in New York. The ACLU reacted with dismay. In a letter dated July 27, Executive Director Patrick Murphy Malin wrote AFRA that, while the union's past support of the principles of civil liberties was commendable, the ACLU urged the board to "immediately reconsider the manner in which they would deal with an undoubtedly real and perplexing problem." Director Malin continued:

> The ACLU recognizes the right of a labor union (under Taft-Hartley) to require its officers and key employees to be in accord with the purposes of the union and to disqualify them if they are members of the Communist party or other totalitarian groups. Nor does it oppose the expulsion of ordinary members for participation in acts tending to weaken or destroy the union. But the spirit of American constitutional freedoms is violated by the expulsion of persons from ordinary membership for political opinions alone.

Being "named" or identified as a Communist by the State Department, the Justice Department, the FBI or anyone else is simply an accusation, not proof, and taking accusation as proof is a shocking departure from the American due-process principle of holding a person innocent until he is proven guilty.

As has been repeatedly emphasized by officials in the Attorney General's office, mere membership in a listed organization does not in itself necessarily mean personal disloyalty; only a few organizations on the Attorney General's list appear under the "subversive" heading.

Labor organizations which have so severely suffered in the past from the denial of civil liberties . . . should be particularly scrupulous in observing the letter and the spirit of those guarantees, externally and internally.

The ACLU would later file a complaint with the FCC, based on evidence of political blacklisting in the broadcast industry, as gathered for them by reporter Merle Miller. Named as defendants were station WPIX, New York, for canceling Charlie Chaplin movie shorts; station KOWL, Santa Monica, California, for barring one Reverend Clayton Russell (named in *Red Channels*) from speaking on the station; NBC for canceling the singing group The Weavers and permitting the cancellation of Jean Muir; Dumont TV for canceling pianist Hazel Scott; and CBS for excising dancer Paul Draper from an Ed Sullivan kinescope—all for their real or alleged associations.

The ACLU asked that the defendants' licenses not be renewed until a promise was made by each to discontinue the discriminatory hiring practices. It further asked that the commission conduct a general investigation of these practices. The petition was denied on both counts (Foley 1979).

•

At the 1951 AFRA National Convention, delegates debated, modified, and eventually approved an anti-Communist amendment acceptable to the body. It would apply to membership under Article III and, in identical form, to employees under Article VII. In early September, the amendment was ratified by a national vote of 2,118 to 457. Article III, Section 4, of the AFRA Constitution now read:

No person shall remain a member of, or shall be eligible for membership in AFRA, who maintains membership in, knowingly promotes the special interests of, makes financial contributions to, or renders aid and assistance by lending his name or talents to the Communist party or any organization known to him to be a portion, branch or subdivision thereof, or any organization established by due Federal process, legal or judicial, to be subversive.

Later that month, the Los Angeles local instituted a non-Communist loyalty affidavit for board members and all employees, including legal counsel. Heller's TvA soon followed suit.

Years earlier, at the time of the first HUAC hearings into Communist infiltration of motion pictures, SAG had adopted provisions similar to those then in Actors' Equity, later in AFRA, and finally in the TvA. The guild's by-laws made an additional requirement, however, that of a signed non-Communist affidavit upon application for membership.

Caught in the new national rush for proof of fidelity to the government of the United States, by 1951 all four great entertainment unions had acceded to, or instituted on their own, tests of loyalty in one form or another.

•

9

~~~~~~

The Loyalty Questionnaire

The use of loyalty oaths, which historian Dr. Henry Steele Commager called "a rather fat-headed, feeble-minded, though not altogether depraved pattern peculiar to American life," proliferated across the country, in federal, state, and county governments, in schools, colleges, and unions. Not merely a phenomenon of the Cold War, oaths had been used throughout the ages, in every society and every country, wherever people were faced with a real or imagined danger. Dr. Commager continued in his speech at Barnard College,

> [It] has negligible value because Communists won't hesitate to perjure themselves if it suits their purpose and . . . persons who out of principle refuse to sign it, may just include the sort of dissenters and nonconformists who are the very kind of people we want to build loyalties around. (*The New York Times*, October 10, 1951)

One year earlier, CBS—long thought to be the most liberal of the networks—instituted a loyalty oath of its own. It, like the reported NBC oath before it, was devised as a condition of employment for staff people. In the summer of 1951, however, following a dynamic spurt of original programming requiring a large, new pool of creative talent, it was distributed (along with the W-4 form and an employment contract) to hundreds of New York freelancers as well.

CBS referred to it as a loyalty "questionnaire," justifying its use as protection against further attacks by vigilantes and the reactionary press; right-wing columnists had already dubbed the company "the Red network" and "the Communist Broadcasting System."

Jack Gould of *The Times* wrote: "By becoming panicky . . . [CBS] is adding to the negative hysteria which threatens to divert our attention from the important tasks ahead if we are to combat Communism successfully." Oscar Hammerstein II, then president of the Authors League of

America (he too was named in *Red Channels*), commented that the action was "more likely to condemn the loyal unjustly than to discover the unloyal" (Cogley 1956). The questionnaire read:

1. Are you now, or have you ever been, a member of the Communist Party, USA, or any Communist organization? [It was the same oath administered to employees of the U.S. government.]

2. Are you now, or have you ever been, a member of a Fascist group?

3. Are you now, or have you ever been, a member of any organization, association, movement, group or combination of persons which advocates the overthrow of our constitutional form of government, or of any organization, association, movement, group or combination of persons which has adopted a policy of advocating or approving the commission of acts of force or violence to deny other persons their rights under the Constitution of the United States or, of seeking to alter the form of the government of the United States by unconstitutional means?

If the answer was "yes" to any question, the signer was directed to state the names of all such organizations and give dates of membership and complete details of the activities, as well as any explanation he or she wished to make. On the reverse side of the sheet appeared the so-called Communist fronts and those "advocating overthrow." It was the all-inclusive Attorney General's list, the same unedited list used as source material for *Red Channels*.

Compiled under President Truman's loyalty investigations of federal employees at the outset of the Cold War, updated to October 1950, the Attorney General's list included the names of some 180 groups, twenty-one of which were, in fact, classified as "subversive." The validity of the Attorney General's list was being considered at that very moment by the U.S. Supreme Court.

Most performers signed and went on to their jobs uncaring or oblivious to the fact that a small piece of their guaranteed liberties, the freedom of political belief and discussion, had been chipped away. For others, it set off a wave of fear or righteous indignation or both. Who, they asked, is the Columbia Broadcasting System to question my allegiance to my country? Who is CBS to ask me to protest my innocence about something of which there is no reason to suspect me? for a one-shot on a television show? Particularly disturbing for those who had been or still were members of a listed organization was that CBS made no provision for a hearing on the matter or for the right of appeal.

William Paley would write in his autobiography, *As It Happened* (1979),

My own feelings for personal privacy are so strong that I am astonished that I could have tolerated the invasion of privacy that even our mild questionnaire required. Yet, the more I reflect on this, the more I see that CBS, too, was caught in the crosscurrents of fear that swept through the whole country.

•

On October 28, 1951, in Norwalk, Connecticut, Marguerita "Mady" Christians, distinguished actress and singer of the European theater and star of fifteen Broadway shows, was hospitalized and died, three hours later, of a cerebral hemorrhage. She had been in deteriorating health since her name appeared in *Red Channels* one year earlier. She was fifty-one.

Born in Vienna of a theatrical family, Christians was trained and managed abroad by the director Max Reinhardt and featured by him in scores of plays and motion pictures before coming to the United States to make her home in 1933. Leading roles in *Hamlet*, Lillian Hellman's *Watch on the Rhine*, and Van Druten's long-running *I Remember Mama* followed. All brought her acclaim. Ironically, it was Peggy Wood, Christians' political antithesis on the Equity council, and not she who was awarded the role when *Mama*, sponsored by GF, went to CBS TV.

During the war, Christians had been an activist for Russian war relief, for aid to refugees of fascism, for protection of the foreign-born living in America. These involvements earned her a listing in *Red Channels*. She soon was jobless. Her savings depleted, she grew despondent and complained of having high blood pressure. Only weeks before her death, she received a job call from NBC's Somerset Maugham Theater—her first in over a year. It turned out to be a mistake. The call was canceled.

•

Heller, the TvA board, and the entire theatrical community were stunned; their beloved, compassionate Mady, acting out of a sense of good citizenship, had become the blacklist's first fallen victim. Some panicked. Could they too become trapped in the same web of errors and false assumptions as had Mady, as had so many others? And, now, there was the CBS loyalty oath. Were they doomed either way—if they signed or if they refused to sign?

A group came before the board in November to report that, indeed, several members who had refused for various reasons were being blacklisted by the CBS. They argued that because the 1950 TvA Code of Fair Practice did not stipulate a performer's political point of view, the TvA should, as their petition read, "refuse to accede to conditions . . . less favorable than those set forth in the basic agreement, and demand of CBS that they cease to violate the agreement and withdraw their . . . 'loyalty questionnaire.' " The petition was signed by several hundred members and had earlier passed by an overwhelming vote at Actors' Equity.

Heller admonished the board: "We should not take this stand alone. In no way should we be allowed to become the 'guinea pig' in this matter. . . . Each of the five Branches . . . the Authors League and the Radio and TV Directors all should give expression to this stand together."

Longtime Heller supporters criticized him for not advocating immediate, independent action. "We do not shirk our responsibility," he answered. "Your Board is a trusteeship composed of appointed members from the five Branches. Until . . . they are properly elected, they are not in a position to speak for the collective memberships." He warned,

> As responsible leaders you must be very careful when these explosive matters come before us, otherwise you will split the union, ruin yourselves and do no one any good. . . . Unless you can get the support of conservative individuals and organizations on this demand, you will destroy the cause of this union and its performers, who are after all, here for protection.

Heller was seen now as fighting to hold on to the respect he had so recently won for the TvA—and for himself, its administrator and chief negotiator. Or was he, as some thought, simply stalling?

The board voted to refer the entire matter to the December convention in New York. There, it would be debated by the first duly elected body of the TvA. There, performers from all sections of the country would make their opinions known.

•

Four individual libel suits against *Red Channels* and American Business Consultants had been filed by late 1951—the last by popular radio actor Joe Julian for $150,000 in damages. The case would not come to trial until four years later. Although it was ultimately established that Julian had no relationship whatsoever with the Communist Party, the case was dismissed on a technicality. The other three suits were then dropped.

Film star Fredric March and his wife, actress Florence Eldridge (it was March who, with Dorothy Parker, Oscar Hammerstein, and Melvyn Douglas, organized the Hollywood Anti-Nazi League), brought a half-million-dollar suit against *Counterattack* in 1949. It ended in an out-of-court settlement, a printed denial, and an agreement by the consultants not to use the word *Communist* as a descriptive term except in the case of an actual party official (Miller 1952).

•

By the opening of the 1951 TvA National Convention, 648 New York members had signed the petition calling for withdrawal of the CBS loyalty oath. During the same interval, the U.S. Supreme Court handed down its hard-fought ruling concerning the Attorney's General's list. It stated that the office must desist from listing groups as "Communist front organizations" unless they had first proved them to be so.

The CBS matter came before the convention at the end of a long, wearying agenda, heavy with problems of jurisdiction and organization. The hotly argued, bitter debate, replete with amendments and substitutions to amendments, lasted through the night, till nearly 8:30 the next morning.

Counselor Henry Jaffe advised the delegates that TvA could not demand action of the kind called for: that CBS "cease" and "withdraw." In his view, the loyalty questionnaire was not in violation of the existing code. He asked: "If TvA ordered its members to refuse to sign, could or should the union then discipline the hundreds who had already signed and those who would want to sign in the future?"

Heller pleaded for calm and reason: "From a policy point of view," he said, "we simply cannot handle this matter alone. . . . We are a very new organization . . . in the process of gathering strength among ourselves so we may be united in our most principal objective—seeing to it that we get for the performer certain kinds of wages and working conditions." He told of how the television writers and the directors guilds were also split apart in their unsuccessful effort to remedy the blacklisting problems.

The New York local, Heller said,

> voted their support at a recent membership meeting, then overturned the vote by 5 to 3, in the subsequent referendum. It if turns up in the press that hundreds of TvA members want to eliminate the CBS loyalty oath, first SAG and SEG will come out with plenty of negative publicity and then Government agencies will want to know, "What's going on here?"
>
> It's all very well to say we must be against it, but . . . CBS has a right to know whether a performer is a proven Communist before they employ him. That part of the questionnaire should stand. The rest . . . should be eliminated. Then TvA would gain support from the majority of its members, the public and the press. Don't be anxious to just jump in head forward but take a little more time to make certain you do it the right way.

The petition failed. There would be no direct challenge, no official call for withdrawal. (Heller would meet informally with network officials.) The delegates voted a "condemnation of blacklisting" and directed

Heller to join with sister unions and others in an effort to end it. They voted unanimously "To aid members in their right to obtain a fair, impartial hearing of any charges brought against them."

Leon Janney, a TvA board member and future president of the New York local (1963), had been a radio, stage, television, and film actor since childhood, from the *Our Gang* series to the film *Charley*, starring Cliff Robertson. He had been named in *Red Channels* as being a member of the old Anti-Fascist Refugee Committee and had recently testified before a Senate subcommittee, revealing all pertinent information about himself. Now, he was being blacklisted at CBS. Janney rose in anger:

> I charge that George Heller has flatly refused to protect me and I am blaming him for what has happened here tonight. We could have had a great majority against this loyalty oath, and we could have had a blacklist resolution that would have had guts in it, but no, Mr. Heller filibustered it out of existence.
>
> And may I ask, who is it that is going to "hear" us? The Supreme Court? A committee of advertising executives? What makes them able to decide? . . . Or are we going to invite the House Un-American Activities Committee to hear us? And who is going to clear us? I'm not asking you to clear me . . . all I ask is, that if I am accused in any way, those charges should be proved!

Despite the efforts of an impassioned left and its moderate supporters, the first duly elected body of the TvA had spoken. They had chosen a cautious, studied approach. They understood that, although the assault on New York television artists was being made by but a handful of right-wing zealots, behind those zealots stood the weight of J. Edgar Hoover's FBI, John S. Wood's HUAC, Patrick A. McCarran's Senate Internal Security Subcommittee, the Hearst and other publications, and the vast majority of public opinion. They understood too that, while their union could be put in jeopardy, as on-the-air broadcasters and labor activists, any one of them could be as well.

●

In December 1951, character actor J. Edward Bromberg died of a heart attack while rehearsing at a West End theater in London. He was a veteran of more than fifty Hollywood films, including *Tangiers*, *The Mark of Zorro*, and Broadway plays *Jacobowsky and the Colonel* and *The Royal Family*. Bromberg's busy career had slowed to a near halt in the late 1940s when he was graylisted in Hollywood; he was later named in *Red Channels*.

Several months prior to his death, despite pleadings of recent heart failure, the Hungarian-born Bromberg was called to testify before HUAC.

He had been identified by "friendly" witnesses as having been a Communist while with the old Group Theatre. On the grounds of possible self-incrimination and wishing not to be a party to the incrimination of others, Bromerg remained silent on all questions. At the end, he struck out at the committee for conducting the hearings "in the nature of a witch-hunt calculated to scare a lot of people beyond those who are involved." He was forty-seven.

•

"The Hellers lived near us at the time," AFRA's Frank Reel told me, "up in Ossining, New York. Every morning, George and I would ride the train together down along the Hudson River into New York City. We'd discuss union matters and, of course, the blacklist situation. I knew his true feelings. George was adamantly opposed to blacklisting—as was I—as were others on our two boards. He was aware there was some, little communistic activity going on in the union, but he knew it wasn't serious—just stupid.

"But George was two people," Reel said, "the executive of a very new, very shaky operation that was trying to organize a messed-up industry, and the man who agreed with Leon Janney and the others but couldn't make his feelings known, not because he'd be labeled Communist—which he wasn't—and destroyed, but because the whole TvA would go down. He had to be very careful. He had to gain confidence from both sides."

•

Henry Jaffe decided that he also would make no demands, no direct challenge to the industry. He would not defend his wife, actress Jean Muir, in court against her listing in *Red Channels*.

"Why was that?" I asked Jaffe in an interview. "Was it the 'disclaimer' in the introduction that knocked the pins out from under a possible libel suit?"

"No," Jaffe answered. "Although I think Jean had a lot to atone for, I was anxious only that her name be cleared and that she get back to work. That was my purpose. It was not my purpose to prove she was a fine American."

Muir's appearance before HUAC in 1953 would be a giant step towards Jaffe's goal. There, she would testify that she had been associated, albeit briefly, with two of the organizations cited in *Red Channels*. But she flatly denied ever having been a Communist or having supported the party in any way.

"Jean was a militant liberal and a union activist," Clara Heller told me, "from her first days in Hollywood with the newly formed Screen Actors

Guild. She hated the idea of going before HUAC to plead for clearance, and she hated the committee—as we all did. She was an innocent. She didn't *need* to be cleared. She and Henry fought over it bitterly for months. Finally, he convinced her that it was of the utmost importance that she go."

The course Jaffe chose might have resulted in the protection of Muir—and thus himself—from further harassment but not from loss of esteem in the eyes of many of his colleagues, who began to describe him as "a turn-coat liberal." As Jaffe's personal course became more clear, he would be named "the defender of the Artists' Committee" and "the apologist for its blacklisting stand" as well.

•

Home from the tumultuous 1951 convention, Heller responded to two of many expressions of confidence.

Dear Ed,
Thank you for your note. Comments such as yours sustain me during these very difficult times. As you say, it's unfortunate that some of our younger element are so headstrong and ignore the grave responsibilities [that] we have to create and maintain a unified organization. You and I know that the performer will only be helped if he has a union that is not constantly beset and torn asunder by internal conflicts.

As for the extremists on both sides, I am realistic enough to know that they will not be satisfied with anything except a complete acceptance of their position, which to me is not only distasteful but detrimental to the best interests of our organization. If members like yourself are becoming aware of the necessity of rallying in the center . . . we will have taken a great step forward to fashion a union of which we can all be proud.

Dear Pete [Pryor, LA local general counsel],
Thank you for your note. . . . Friends do not need letters of appreciation, and you'll forgive me if I don't go into an Alphonse and Gaston routine.

You can, however, do one thing for me—for chrissake, work up that will and testament you promised to make. The way things were going in the last week or two, I was sure that I was going to drop dead during the Convention, and I will hold you responsible if Clara has to go through unnecessary and expensive procedures because you and I forgot about this.

•

10

The Loeb Matter

Heller was now convinced that, if he could create a tribunal made up of high-ranking, distinguished citizens from outside the union, a body to whom an accused person might present his case and be assured of a fair, impartial hearing, then the vigilantes would soon disappear. He tackled the mission with a burning commitment.

"Time is of the essence in this matter," he told associates. "[We] should not be in a position of protecting avowed Communists—they must be solely responsible for their own actions. But we do have the responsibility of defending innocent persons."

Veteran actor-director Philip Loeb, born in Philadelphia in 1894 and educated at the University of Pennsylvania, had served in the Great War and was currently an officer of Actors' Equity Association, a delegate to TvA, and one of the leading players on television's *The Goldbergs*. He had been harassed for months, ever since the publication of *Red Channels*. He appealed to the TvA board to move with all speed on Heller's plan, so that he could be cleared of the charges against him and allowed to continue peaceably on the show with which he had been so long and happily associated. He would sign an affidavit saying that he was not now and had never been a Communist. Loeb's enemies aside, no stage or television actor close to this free spirit believed him to be a Communist. He himself made no secret of his disrespect for those he knew who were.

Ezra Stone, Loeb's former student and longtime friend, told me, "I was taught to have an independent approach to my activism, to align myself with no person or organization unless I knew who my allies were. And I'm willing to swear that Phil was not a Communist—not even a 'fellow traveler.' He may have made some unwise decisions as a union leader, but no discipline in the world could have harnessed him except the discipline he imposed on himself. Communism was completely counter to his makeup and his philosophy."

In mid-January 1952, the matter came abruptly to a head when Gertrude Berg, owner, writer, and star of *The Goldbergs*—for years, one of CBS TV's top-rated shows—asked to appear before the TvA board. There, she told of how, when *Red Channels* was first published and it seemed possible that Loeb's career would be in jeopardy, she signed him to a run-of-the-play contract to give him every possible protection; how, for months, she had resisted the urging of both the network and GF, her sponsor, to remove him from the cast.

Loeb and Berg had been colleagues since the early 1930s, when he played supporting roles on her long-running radio series *The Rise of the Goldbergs*. In 1948, he was cast opposite her in her Broadway play *Me and Molly* (directed by Ezra Stone). When the radio show moved to television, Loeb went with it as the husband, Jake. "I have never believed Phil was a Communist," said Mrs. Berg. "It's un-American that his career should be so threatened on the basis of unproven charges. This is a clear case of blacklisting."

Merle Miller, in *The Judges and the Judged*, confirmed that Berg had saved Loeb from outright firing the previous spring, when she threatened GF that she would withdraw *The Goldbergs* from their sponsorship. She vowed to appear on every public platform available to her to denounce the company and to advise her listeners not to buy its products.

The confrontation triggered a reversal of the corporate policy established at the time of the Jean Muir firing. The next day, GF announced it would henceforth *not* drop performers merely because they were controversial. Further, all complaints regarding a performer's loyalty must be backed up by proof before the company would take any action.

Nevertheless, the inexorable blacklisting machinery, once activated, could not be stopped. It kept grinding out its letters of protest against Loeb—a total of 1,197 of them, a GF spokesman said. In late May 1951, the company announced that Sanka coffee would drop *The Goldbergs* for, as the company stated, "economy reasons." So too did the CBS network. Even when the show was picked up several weeks later by NBC, Loeb's presence remained anathema. Seven months passed, and *The Goldbergs* was still not back on the air.

So, on this bitter January night, Gertrude Berg had come to inform the TvA that she had succumbed to the economic pressure. She had regretfully reached the position that "the contract between Mr. Loeb and myself no longer exists." The role of Jake would be recast.

With Berg excused, the board considered their alternatives. There was currently a petition before them, signed by 255 members, requesting that *The Goldbergs* be placed on the "unfair list" (an official notice to members that they were not to work for any company that was violating a TvA contract) until such time that Loeb was reinstated. But to do so would put the entire twenty-odd-member cast in jeopardy, Berg included. Perhaps a better way would be to ask her to write Loeb's character out until the tribunal could be arranged. Failing that, the board concluded, "the practical solution is to authorize Heller to . . . secure as good a cash settlement for Loeb as possible."

Several directors protested that by setting up a hearing board, even though requested by Loeb, the TvA was giving validity to *Red Channels* to the extent that "we are trying to disprove their charges." Officer Bob Spiro pressed for direct action, "By going to outside sources we're throwing off our own responsibility in this."

Bill Ross of the Equity council, an intimate of Loeb's, was also dead-set against a tribunal. He challenged Heller, "You mean we are going to set up our own blacklisting procedure and make it official?"

Loeb had earlier held this same low opinion of a tribunal, while he and Berg met with executives of CBS, Y & R, and GF in their attempt to resolve the problem. But when Chairman Francis of GF asked him directly, "When are you going to clear yourself?" the independent, high-minded Loeb was forced to acknowledge that ignoring *Red Channels* as a matter of principle was not going to make it go away.

In the early morning hours of January 24, a settlement was reached in the Loeb matter. Heller said at the time, "And so a settlement was made, a financial settlement but not a settlement of the issue" (Cogley 1956).

"The issue," wrote Loeb in a subsequent letter to the board, "is my blacklisting. I did not come to you for a financial settlement. . . . I came for truth and justice. I am still seeking truth and justice. Although innocent, I am deprived of work and hounded from my profession by a cowardly, furtive smear campaign."

Gene Francis, who replaced Ralph Bellamy as the TvA vice president (Bellamy was then working in Hollywood), said, "George loved and revered Phil Loeb. It was breaking his heart that he couldn't get him back to work. He continued holding private meetings with the parties in hopes that he might yet, somehow, rescue the situation. He talked about it endlessly. What else could he do? What else could *we* do? I and others told him he should call a general strike.

" 'Strike? I can't call a strike!' Heller answered angrily. 'Who will strike?'

"As a servant of the board, George knew better than we did. Even if a strike was legal, which it wasn't under the provisions of the current code, on this issue he did not have the votes—not from the board, not from the members." Nor would he in his lifetime.

"George did whatever was possible for him to do under the circumstances," Francis went on. "He counseled, he suggested, he intervened behind the scenes. Hundreds came to George petrified that they were being blacklisted; often, he was able to assure them that they weren't. I was enlisted several times when he wasn't free to persuade this producer or that director to rehire an actor."

That Francis found himself in a position to help others—even himself in one instance—was all thanks to George Heller and that infamous Heller temper. One year before, while the two were having lunch one day, Gene mentioned in passing that he had decided not to extend his commission in the army. "I tossed the letter in the garbage—five years in World War II was enough military for me!" he joked.

Heller opened up at full throttle. "You go home immediately!" he ordered. "You fill out those documents and send them in. *Red Channels* is just the beginning, Gene. We're all vulnerable now. They'll be out to get you and anyone else who's active and outspoken in the union. They'll challenge your patriotism just like the others."

"But you've been handed a way to save yourself," he roared on. "You're a Captain in the U.S. Army Reserve. You have clearance to handle 'secret,' classified information. If you don't extend that commission, I never want to see you around here again. Ever!"

With his left-wing background, Heller fully expected to become a victim of the blacklist himself. Indeed, at that moment, Ronald Reagan and his Hollywood supporters were painting Heller with a Red brush, as part of their ongoing battle against joint television jurisdiction.

"That he survived while his friends and colleagues suffered was a constant embarrassment to him and cause for considerable guilt."

•

The January 24 membership meeting of the New York local was well attended. The details of Loeb's situation and the subsequent settlement were reported to an angry, restive crowd. Another of Loeb's good friends, Cliff Carpenter—Terry on radio's *Terry and the Pirates*—requested the floor. He wished to make a motion:

> Mr. Chairman, an actor should be paid to work, not paid not to work.
>
> *Therefore, be it resolved*: At the next contract negotiations TvA will demand that the "blacklisting" of any of its members will be deemed an unfair labor practice and a violation of the TvA code.
>
> *Further resolved*, that a National Anti-Blacklisting Committee be named to investigate any case reported to it by any member of TvA, and, where it finds "blacklisting" to have been practiced, shall rec-

ommend to the National Board that the blacklisters be placed on "unfair" status.

Carpenter told me, "I was so disturbed by what was happening to Phil that I had to do it—even though I knew it could take me down a treacherous road from which I might never return."

The debate was highly charged, complete with hoots and catcalls. Then came the vote. By 360 to 60, the motion passed. The body went wild. Eighteen months of seeming inaction by an uncaring, unapproachable board had been broken through by the members. The Anti-Blacklisting Committee was established on the spot. Members were nominated and elected to serve. Carpenter, having received the highest vote, was named chairman.

Within hours, Vincent Hartnett, contributor to *Red Channels*, appeared on Barry Gray's radio talk show to do his vigilante work. He named Cliff Carpenter as one of the marchers in the 1951 May Day parade.

●

"If Heller had taken decisive action at the outset," one member said, "the blacklist would have been blunted—as it had been in Equity." (Seen as a major deterrent was the strong, antiblacklist statement issued jointly by Equity and the League of New York Theatre Owners. But of equal importance was that legitimate theater was not beholden, as television was, to corporate sponsorship.)

"Heller understood the dangers of opposing the McCarthyites," said another. "It would have cost him his job, and the TvA was George's life. He'd be out and then what for the union? It could have been worse."

A third said, "When I berated him for not doing more, he snapped back, 'You get control of the board and I'll go along with you.' "

Henry Jaffe said, "George was a brilliant executive. In another time he could have been the head of some great corporation. But he didn't want to admit to his failings—that the TvA permitted *Red Channels*. He didn't want to get involved with the left-wingers and the Communists, either. Like what happened to Phil Loeb—that wonderful, very valuable union member—who got himself in too deep with the far left."

●

"The decision to settle destroyed Philip," Bill Ross said, "and he never would have agreed if George hadn't spent the night convincing him. Let me tell you how close those two were in the early days—you never saw Georgie that you didn't see Phil. They loved one another more than brothers. And it killed me that during his darkest times, Phil never once blamed George. He'd say to me, 'George is stuck with certain political needs and he's handling them as well as he can.'

"But I blame him," said Ross, "even though I understand the pressures he was under. Phil was the one man George should have gone all the way for—to every screaming extreme in his defense. He had the clout; he should have known how to use it."

Actress Madeline Lee blamed Heller as well. Her years of joy and pain—she and her husband, Jack Gilford, were both listed in *Red Channels* for having participated in fund-raising events for so-called front organizations—are well narrated in *170 Years of Show Business*, coauthored with Kate (Mrs. Zero) Mostel (see Mostel and Gilford 1978).

Madeline told me, "The process of blacklisting unfolded very slowly. It was almost impossible to grasp what was happening and what, or who, was behind it. I'd been in radio for years and was active on various committees in AFRA and the TvA. In the beginning, I'd go to George with reports of how this friend had lost a steady show, or that friend was mysteriously out of work.

"Even when it first happened to us—Jack was suddenly dropped from a Fred Allen show on NBC—George would listen and commiserate. 'It's terrible,' he'd say, 'I'll make some calls right away. But you've got to come in with some real evidence—names and dates.'

"Later, Jack was blacklisted off another NBC show. This time we had the evidence. We went before the Anti-Blacklisting Committee to officially press charges against the Kellogg Company and Pet Milk, the show's sponsors, and to give the names of those involved. Cliff Carpenter was there and Henry Jaffe, along with our dear friend Phil Loeb and others. We went through the formalities. We told how NBC, in an apparent attempt to make amends, had offered Jack a contract on another of their shows—local, this time, not network.

"George started to equivocate, 'If they offered you another show, then there's nothing more to be done. Listen, kids, don't make waves; even worse trouble can come down on your head. Besides, it'll blow over soon.' At that point Phil got up and ran over to Jack. He grabbed him by his lapels and, with tears in his eyes, pleaded, 'Don't let them do to you what they did to me.'

"In the end," said Madeline, "the charges came to nothing. George was just stringing us along." And in the indiscriminate sweep of the political witch-hunting madness, three other female actors—two bearing similar names to Madeline Lee and the third, a look-alike—would soon be blacklisted as well (The New York *Post*, January 26, 1953).

•

The Goldbergs, without Philip Loeb, returned to the airwaves in early

February 1952. Morton Edell, president of the Vitamin Corporation of America, the program's new sponsor, said that at the time he had not heard of the controversy. If Loeb had been a Communist, Edell would not have wanted him anywhere near the show, but he wished that there had been some way of finding out. The show, he felt, would have been a lot better with him in it.

"Phil's life was in total disarray," said Bill Ross. "He had had a son by an early marriage which ended in divorce. When his ex-wife died, he took the boy—then a bright seventeen-year-old—to live with him. Daniel (John, he liked to be called) had been raised to hate his father and, sometime after he arrived, there was an incident where he tried to murder Phil. The boy was eventually found to be mentally ill and was hospitalized in a private sanitarium outside of Washington, D.C. For years, Phil would return home after each visit shattered. And now this."

"Phil was left with so few resources," said Gene Francis, "and there was so little work. Bill Ross hired him, he hired Jack Gilford too, for *Where's Charley?* in summer stock. But it shamed Phil to have to rely so heavily on George. I often found myself in the middle. 'Gene,' he'd say, 'I don't want to bother George again. Please, you ask him for me.'"

•

As hard as Heller worked to establish the high-ranking tribunal, he was unable to find prominent persons—lawyers, judges, or theologians—willing to serve. His appeals to the American Arbitration Association, the Bar Association of New York, and the New York County Lawyers Association met with interest but polite refusals. The tribunal, one said, was not an adversarial matter but rather a fact-finding commission. Attorneys would not be interested in participating unless there were two parties in the proceedings and they, the lawyers, had power of subpoena.

The Ford Foundation likewise turned Heller down on his request for a study to "measure loss of purchasing power as a result of pressure tactics," a study he hoped would encourage sponsors to resist the maneuverings of the vigilante groups. A petition to the FCC, supporting the Authors League request for an official hearing on blacklisting in television, was also denied. The request was deemed "not a proper subject within the Commission's jurisdiction."

The Artists' Committee continued to hold him on a tight rein. Heller proposed a meeting of joint union memberships—the TvA and the writers' and directors' guilds—in order to dramatize the dangers of blacklisting and to develop greater public support to help end it. The TvA voted to allow him to meet and exchange information with the guilds but not to take action without further board approval. The joint meeting was not held.

•

A member of the TvA board remembered, "The settlement George worked out for Phil—it was around forty thousand dollars—went only so far in meeting expenses at his son's private institution. He'd fallen heavily into debt. Several of us got together and agreed to help support him while he continued the fight to clear his name.

"Suddenly, and without any explanation, those who had just said 'yes' to the plan backed out. At the same time, Henry Jaffe came to me.

" 'You have got to stop defending these people,' he said. 'If you don't, they'll get your husband' [who was a well-established actor popular in all media].

"But, of course," she went on, "I didn't stop and wouldn't stop; nor would my husband have allowed me to."

Jaffe's words turned out to be fair warning. Within weeks, the husband's work fell off sharply, both on television and in film. Later, the couple found his name on a list being circulated in Hollywood—a "private list"—attributed to actors Ward Bond and John Wayne, the president of the Alliance for Preservation of American Ideals.

•

Loeb appealed in a second letter to the TvA board:

I know it is not through fault or lack of diligence that a hearing has not yet been set, but I ask you, if in two weeks you still have no success, find a group within your own ranks—presidents, executives, counsel—to hear the evidence, including the editors of *Red Channels* if they will come. And if the findings are negative, issue a statement of clearance: that I was found to be a loyal American and entitled to employment.

The board voted to defer the request: "The governing body of a labor organization acting as a loyalty board is an abhorrent principle," said ranking member Nelson Case.

The pressure was unrelenting. An officer demanded that Heller fire Mary Sagarin, his right hand, for having been seen talking with Loeb outside the union. Loeb's beloved American Academy of Dramatic Arts, where he had once been a student, then an honored teacher for more than a generation (Garson Kanin, Hume Cronyn, and Jason Robards were among his students), summarily relieved him as codirector of the Executive Committee. Even later, when he went to Chicago with the national company of Ron Alexander's *Time Out for Ginger*, the American Legion would throw up a picket line, protesting his appearance.

It was no longer possible for Loeb to keep his son in a private hospital. The hope for a cure with the specialists there had to be abandoned. The young man would have to be moved to a federal facility.

•

Heller succeeded in regenerating the industry's interest in finding a way to reemploy controversial actors. To that end, he was authorized to engage the services of Robert E. Cushman, twenty-seven years a professor of government at Cornell University.

In late June 1952, Professor Cushman presented his report. In it, he recommended a plan that "would protect the industry, the advertisers, and the union from infiltration by Communists or other disloyal persons while protecting the individual artist from damage by irresponsible and ill-supported accusations." Months would go by before the Cushman plan was seriously dealt with. Meanwhile, there would be no tribunal.

A CBS executive commented at the time:

Kirkpatrick, Keenan and Bierly [publishers of *Red Channels*] have created what eventually may cost the industry fifty, maybe a hundred million dollars, and God knows how many ulcers and gray hairs and broken hearts. . . . Plus a lot of public respect—and good shows.

The trouble with people who've never joined anything and are therefore "safe" for us to use is that they usually aren't very good writers or actors or producers or, hell, human beings. . . . My God, it's straight out of Kafka, isn't it? These three gents have the whole industry stymied—three guys, count them. (Miller 1952)

•

11

~~~~~~~~

Hartnett's AWARE and the Prockter "Three"

For years preceding Loeb's cancellation, the buying public participated in a great national debate over employment policies of the sponsors and ad agencies by way of sensational front-page stories. Whether in fact or in error, the political preferences of and consequences to performers Ireene Wicker "the Singing Lady," Gypsy Rose Lee, Lucille Ball, Hazel Scott, Paul Draper, and other were spelled out regularly in the press. Distinguished writers, directors, and news commentators—Alexander Kendrick, William L. Shirer, and Howard K. Smith among them—received somewhat less notoriety, but they too suffered major crises in their careers: some with devastating results.

Protests were made; sides were drawn; boycotts were threatened by the right and counterthreatened by the left. The Kellogg Company, GF, Pepsi-Cola, Lever Brothers, and by 1952 the entire industry had resolved that steps must be taken to protect themselves and their products from any further damage by all this public scrutiny.

If a political check were to be made *before* performers were hired, then the American Legion, the Catholic War Veterans, the readers of *Counterattack*, and so forth would have no cause to charge sponsors with indifference to national security. And since there would be no public firings, liberals would not denounce them for violating due process and the American tradition of fair play (Cogley 1956).

"There was no conspiratorial decision on the part of radio-tv management," Cogley wrote, "there was simply a Gentlemen's Agreement to keep silent. . . . Blacklisting became institutionalized behind closed doors." For companies that did not have a clearance officer or lacked a legal department to do so, an outside consultant was hired.

Reenter—through the back door—lecturer, researcher, and self-named "top authority on Communism and communications," Vincent W. Hartnett and his newly established organization, AWARE. In a January 1952 advertisement in the *Brooklyn Tablet* promoting his appearance there, Hartnett proclaimed: "*Red Channels Was a Piker*—It only scratched the surface of Communist influence in Radio and TV. . . . Now, hear a full, documented exposé!"

Operating out of his East Twentieth Street apartment in New York, Hartnett, a Master of Arts graduate of Notre Dame and former naval intelligence officer (with the rank of lieutenant commander), collected and codified all existing data and hearsay gathered by other "authorities" into his now infamous *File 13*. He solicited networks, sponsors, and ad agencies who sought such a resource, offering himself as a "permanent consultant." Soon he was established as one of the key players in the industry's new employment policy, a judge and jury on the so-called Americanism of performing artists, a supreme arbiter on the "employability" of members of George Heller's TvA. His first corporate client was the Borden Company.

•

In May 1952, John Garfield, "tough-guy" actor, star of films *The Postman Always Rings Twice*, *Four Daughters*, and *Body and Soul*, was found dead of a heart attack in a New York apartment. His once-luminous career had stalled in the late 1940s, the result of accusations of earlier left-wing involvement. He appeared before the 1951 Hollywood HUAC hearings as a cooperative witness: "I have nothing to be ashamed of and nothing to hide. I am no Red. I am no 'pink.' I am no fellow traveler. I am a Democrat by politics, a liberal by inclination, and a loyal citizen of this country by every act of my life" (Vaughn 1972).

There was sporadic work for Garfield on Broadway: he starred in the 1952 revival of Odets' *Golden Boy*. At the time of his death, he was working around the clock on a lengthy magazine article, attempting to explain away his former political activities. He was thirty-nine.

•

In May 1952, Canada Lee, star of Broadway's *Anna Lucasta*, *Native Son*, and the film *Lifeboat*, costarring Tallulah Bankhead, died in New York following two years of failing health.

Lee was never a subject of an investigation, but his name was mentioned in a "confidential" report by a federal employee as a probable Communist sympathizer. The information lay unseen in a file inside a government office for some time. In 1949, however, that file became evidence in the Judith Coplon treason trial. The "mention" became "fact" and made its way into *Red Channels*. By this convoluted act of fate, Lee's career was ruined. Banned from television—roles were sometimes offered then withdrawn—there would be one last film, *Cry the Beloved Country*; then poverty, illness, and finally death. He was forty-five.

•

Heller was in despair over the death of his old compatriots, over his own loss of control. It was, simply, "eating him up alive." The great persuader, who only months before had TvA members on their feet, cheering wildly in support, the spellbinder, who could change the minds of the toughest adversaries and made seemingly impossible things happen for the union, would not, *could not* quell the growing destruction wrought by the blacklist.

Late in June 1952, George Heller entered the hospital for the first of what would be two major operations. Henry Jaffe informed the TvA that the surgery was for the successful removal of a stomach ulcer. George, Clara, and he were told it was for the removal of a cancer, which had already eaten away three-quarters of Heller's stomach.

•

The work of the Anti-Blacklisting Committee was bearing bitter fruit. "While George was surely not antagonistic to our efforts," one committee member said, "it was clear that he was holding us at arm's length." Mary Sagarin countered, "He was trying to keep a divided union from breaking apart; it was impossible for him to appear to be taking sides."

Cliff Carpenter told me, "It became apparent shortly into our work that one committeeman was particularly anxious to have everything documented. 'Where's the secretary? Where's Mary Sagarin?' he'd say, 'We've got to have these names and places taken down!'

"George would dismiss it, 'She's too busy; I can't spare her.' I realize now that he was protecting us and the witnesses and all those other persons being talked about."

Scores of actors, writers, and directors came to be interviewed; certain patterns began to emerge. Of the many courageous witnesses, three came forward who, until recently, had been employees of Prockter Productions, Inc., the producers of *Big Story*, *Treasury Men in Action*, and other successful television and radio series.

The evidence given by "the three," director David Pressman and writers Abram Ginnes and Dapne Elliott, was so startling, so specific, that Chairman Carpenter asked that they reappear before the TvA board the following week, July 24. Heller, though not yet fully recovered, was expected back in the office at that time.

There, the three told how they had been dismissed after refusing "to comply with their employer's demands to blacklist 43 of the company's regularly used actors"—the list of so-called questionable people on all Prockter shows numbered 138. They explained that, on numerous occasions in the recent past, their casting sheets had been sent out to some unidentified source. When they came back, every name was marked either "cleared" or "uncleared."

"We'd been checking against *Red Channels* and *Counterattack* for two years," they explained, "but now the list goes beyond a performer's political activities. Now they are being blacklisted for union activities as well—such as making speeches on the floor of a membership meeting."

There it was. No longer a horrifying, unverifiable whisper from some caring soul (followed by, "If you say it was me who told you, I'll deny it"), there now was solid evidence that a blacklist, a *tangible* blacklist, did exist. Moreover, a whole new category of performer was inadvertently falling into its web: those who disagreed with the officers of their union and said so publicly.

This was apparently fact, and it had been so not just in 1952 but in earlier years as well. Indeed, the well-known Broadway character actor Joe De Santis, long missing from radio and television, had only recently reappeared on CBS TV's *Studio One*. When his career came to an abrupt halt in 1948, De Santis set out on a desperate, dead-end search, countrywide, to find out why he was so unexplainably blacked out of radio. His name had never appeared in *Counterattack* or any other sheet that he knew of.

Not until he located an officer at CBS willing to show him would he know the reason. In an old, loosely bound volume of the American Legion's *Firing Line* (precursor of *Counterattack* by several years) his name appeared, underlined in red, with the description "leftist." "This is why, my son," the executive confided, "this is why." De Santis would find his name in the files of Hoover's FBI as well. There, the allegation read "the head of the Communist faction in AFRA."

Joe De Santis, in 1946, was the first of several AFRA members to question the constitutionality of the Jack Arthur–Bud Collyer Resolution and to speak out against it at membership meetings.

Only after a government security check, an FBI full field investigation (De Santis found work at United Nations Radio, where an FBI check was a condition of employment), and more recently a rereading of his AFRA speeches by a panel of U.S. senators was De Santis' loyalty found to be without question. He had lost three years. It could have been more; it was for others.

And now, as the De Santis inquiry ended, Senator Albert Gore of Tennessee rose to shake his hand. "Mr. De Santis," said the senator, "I think you are a valuable member of our society. I'm sorry that we had to come up from Washington for this kind of nonsense" (excerpts from De Santis' speech at the 1974 AFTRA convention).

•

Copies of affidavits of the testimony of the Prockter three were sent by Heller to officers of Prockter, along with a notice of charges. They were directed to appear before the TvA board the first week of August. The evidence—a photostatic copy of the "secret list of 138"—was delivered by an attorney only moments before the hearing began. Instructions were that it be seen by four persons only: George Heller, Henry Jaffe, TvA Chairman Alan Bunce, and Cliff Carpenter of the Anti-Blacklisting Committee. "Thank God," Heller remarked to Gene Francis, one of Carpenter's committee, "at last we've got a handle on this!"

Three Prockter attorneys appeared, one of whom was the company's vice president; Carpenter also attended. The chief spokesman, Mr. Eugene Bondy, denied that Prockter "has now, or ever has practiced blacklisting" and insisted on the company's right not to use people who would "repel instead of attract." He commented, "Unless they have cast approval, they could not stay in business."

The attorneys did, however, admit that Prockter Productions had been told by several ad agencies and sponsors not to use certain controversial persons. It was also true that Mr. Bernard Prockter had been called to Washington and told—by a person or agency then unnamed—not to use two particular actors featured in the audition show of *Treasury Men in Action*, sponsored by the Borden Company.

The attorneys questioned the TvA's right to summon them to a hearing. They maintained that the company was not in violation of the code and wanted it known that they were "appearing voluntarily in a wish to solve the problem." Unaware of the impact of his next remark, the spokesman added, "And there is no reason for us to be singled out since we have the same list the networks and other producers use, and we all get the names from the same source." The hearing being over, the gentlemen were excused.

To this moment, the leaders of the Artists' Committee had claimed ignorance of a blacklist, as had the networks, sponsors, and advertising agencies—many good people believed what they said was true. Carpenter himself had been challenged when first appointed chair, "If you can prove there is a blacklist, we'll do something about it." Carpenter's committee had met the challenge. Blacklisting not only existed; it was rife throughout the industry and had been going on for years—as far back, perhaps, as 1946. Now, what would the Artist's Committee do?

A resolution, the same as was passed by membership in January, was reintroduced by actor Frank Maxwell, a recent board addition and member of the Anti-Blacklisting Committee. Were it approved, the committee felt, it could well signal the end of blacklisting. The motion asked that Prockter Productions be declared unfair. Counselor Jaffe again went into the legal aspects of taking action on an issue outside the provisions of the code. He spoke of the possible consequences of an injunction, were it to be brought against the TvA.

After lengthy deliberation, the board determined that no definitive action should be taken until the list was given more careful study. Based on a cursory reading by the four men, it seemed to contain the names of several children, as well as some apparent cases of mistaken identity. The board moved that "the investigation be continued in order to ascertain the origin of the list."

Heller met with Prockter officials to persuade them to rehire the actors in question. He asked to be released from his pledge of secrecy so that he could notify each person on the list. He offered to negotiate the return of the Prockter three so that, by rehiring them, Prockter could help "prove their innocence." The three stipulated, however, "We will not be a party to a settlement which fails to eliminate the practice of blacklisting."

•

"If the board wasn't going to act immediately," Gene Francis told me, "Phil, Frank, I, and others felt it essential that we inform the general membership—make them aware of the reasons why so many of them weren't being hired." On August 26, Maxwell made the following motion:

Whereas, evidence of blacklisting against a large number of TvA members has been presented . . . and

Whereas, the evidence has been substantiated . . . by the producers in question, and

Whereas, the evidence clearly indicates the employment of the blacklist by still other producers, agencies, and sponsors, and

Whereas, the withholding of this information from the membership would constitute a serious disservice . . .

Therefore be it resolved: that . . . the National Board call a special meeting of the N.Y. Local within three weeks so that the members may know the facts of the case.

In another of its rancorous, into-the-early-morning sessions, the board turned down the proposal, 11–8, with seven abstentions. The majority argued that a special meeting "would result in no definitive action," and "the evidence against Prockter is not yet conclusive." Further, if the membership were to demand that the company be declared unfair, could that action be taken without incurring serious legal liabilities? The board voted to "refer the entire matter to the 1952 Second TvA National Convention," scheduled for late September in New York.

In what would be the Anti-Blacklisting Committee's last official act, on September 11, Maxwell proposed:

> *Be it resolved*: that the TvA National Board recommend to the Convention that a contract clause declaring blacklisting an unfair labor practice and breach of contract be made a *primary demand* in the forthcoming negotiations [emphasis added].

The intent of the motion was, by now, familiar and no less controversial than when it had been debated and passed months earlier by the New York membership. But that it be made a "primary demand"—that all other proposals, including wages and working conditions, be of lesser importance—*should* have engendered a great, hot, midnight debate. Strangely, it did not; the motion passed unanimously.

Cliff Carpenter was elated when he heard the news. With the dominant eastern section behind it, the convention would surely vote to approve. It would then go to the bargaining table—to be hammered out by George Heller and the employers.

•

"Yeah, I knew Prockter Productions," Jackson Beck told me. "I knew them well. When I was growing up and still living with my family—my father, Max Beck, was a New York actor himself—we lived in a great big apartment building on the West Side. And I was madly in love with Ruth, the girl upstairs.

"One day, I remember, I drew up my courage and went up to have a serious talk with Ruth's father. 'Sir,' I said to him, 'I've come for permission to marry your daughter.'

" 'Well, now,' her father answered, 'that's all very nice, young man, but you're only twelve now, and there's a little question of who will support her—Ruth's shoes cost twenty-two dollars a pair, you know.' "

Jackson assured him that he would be able to do it *very soon*, so Ruth's father said, " 'All right then; we'll think it over. I'll give you my decision another time.' "

Well, everyone grew up, and Ruth eventually married a Bernie Prockter of Prockter and Lewis, predecessor of Prockter Productions. Through the years, Jackson Beck and his family, Ruth's family, and the new Prockter family, along with partner Richard Lewis, remained close friends. Beck remembers walking the Prockter's first baby.

"I was a regular on *Quick as a Flash*, a Prockter and Lewis quiz-type show. It was June 1950; I hadn't gotten my calls for the coming week, so I dropped in at Bernie's office on West Fifty-seventh Street to check it out. For a long time, no one would come out to see me. I knew Bernie was there; he just wouldn't come out. All of a sudden, a glass curtain had come down.

"Finally, Lewis appeared, and he informed me that I was through on the show. There was no other reason except he said that I'd been 'a bad boy.' I'd insulted the client's wife at a recent party (Helbros Watches was the show's sponsor). 'You've got to be kidding!' I said. 'I'd *never* do a thing like that!'

"I went to the ad agency. The account executive phoned around, then he said the same thing. 'That's the word, Jack; I'm sorry, you're out.' There was nothing I could do.

"Years later, I got a call from station WOR to come and bail somebody out for some radio commercials that had to be cut right away. Lewis was the director. When I saw him, it was all I could do to keep from walking out. I never would have gone if I'd known. To suspect me of something and not let me face my accuser. . . . Fine friends."

•

The stunning revelation concerning blacklisting by Prockter did not go unnoticed; it was, in fact, the talk of the street. But blacklisting was only one major issue among several destined for the 1952 convention.

The TvA's two-year trusteeship had lapsed months earlier. Who was going to negotiate the new network code? Merger, whether of five, three, or two branches, remained stalled in the Four A's. Should the TvA become a separate branch and stand alone? Should it demand an immediate merger with, at minimum, the radio federation? And what about the made-for-television-film dispute? It was crucial now for the rank and file to make themselves heard, that they organize and run for election, that they align themselves with the political right, left, or center.

The Artists' Committee mailing offered a slate of seventy-four candidates, notable among them were actors Walter Abel, Glenda Farrell, Marjorie Gateson, House Jameson, and Basil Rathbone; announcers Frank Gallop, Hugh James, and Dwight Weist; song-and-dance man Pat Rooney, Sr.; and dancer Butterfly McQueen. Their single claim was that they had "never given any support to Communist 'fronts,' either by contribution or by marching in May Day parades." They were not merely non-Communist, they were anti-Communist; and they had only one motive: "the welfare of the TV performer."

A second mailing offered nineteen performers, most of whom were incumbent or former TvA officers and board members, among them actors

Staats Cotsworth, Joe De Santis, Gene Francis, Virginia Payne, Anne Seymour, and Ezra Stone; and announcers Nelson Case, Ben Grauer, and Kenneth Roberts. They claimed, "No commitment to any party, faction or group—right, left or unidentified." They promised to uphold the anticommunism section of the TvA Constitution and to press for an immediate AFRA-TvA merger.

A third mailing promoted sixty-two performers. Their platform was, "Better working conditions, substantial pay increases in TV, a speedy and fully democratic five-branch merger, blacklisting to be declared a 'breach of contract,' and integration of the Negro and White performer." Along with Carpenter, Janney, Loeb, and Maxwell, the slate listed such notables as actors Alfred Drake, John Forsythe, Jack Gilford, Lee Grant, Walter Matthau, Darren McGavin, Leslie Nielsen, Frederick O'Neal, and Sidney Poitier; dancer Christine Karner; singer Juanita Hall; and puppeteer Bill Baird.

The opposition slates did not stand a chance, in more ways than one. When the votes were tallied, the Artists' Committee proved to have the majority still firmly on their side. And now there were dozens more names for Vincent Hartnett's burgeoning but somewhat-less-than-secret list, names to be marked "not cleared" for employment.

•

12

~~~~~~

The Hard-Fought Merger

Who would hold jurisdiction over film made for television? The TvA, SAG, and SEG were well positioned for this final, crucial test. SAG and SEG had, as promised, taken the battle out of the hands of the Four A's International Board and brought it, in the spring of 1950, to the agency that determines a proper bargaining unit: the NLRB. The guilds filed in Hollywood for a representation election and certification as exclusive bargaining agent for actors employed by motion picture producers to appear in films, irrespective of where those films might be exhibited. The TvA intervened.

Likewise, the TvA filed in New York City for election and certification as exclusive bargaining agent for *all* performers employed by the television networks and advertising agencies, whether appearing live or on film. SAG intervened.

"SAG will challenge our representation but it's not what we say or what SAG says," Heller advised the members. "It will be dependent on what the employees want, and if they want John Doe to represent them, they have that right under the law. The Guild won't be pleasant to us, but I'm not afraid of that." And while the process would take nearly a year to unfold, the issues—as far as the members were concerned—remained the hot topic of the day.

Were the TvA to win, Hollywood screen actors feared having to belong to two different unions, both covering film, one of which was and would continue to be headquartered in faraway New York, where only a small portion of film work was done. How would SAG officers sit with a superboard located in the East and have time to look for work? What would become of the all-important "conditions of employment," which had always meant additional pay, above and beyond basic minimum? Would the conditions of employment be sacrificed for merely higher minimums—the traditional focus of radio entertainers?

Were the guilds to win, television performers feared that the networks would transfer live work to film, where minimum fees were not yet established (SAG won its television agreement in 1952). And lacking uniformity of fees—Jack Dales had turned down Heller's requests that they meet and coordinate demands—the minimums that the TvA was proposing in its first contract could easily be undercut.

In February 1951, with the TvA Code of Fair Practice successfully concluded, the challenge to the guilds got under way. Chester L. Migden was the NLRB hearings officer in New York. His job was to supervise the proceedings, making sure that a complete record was developed for study and deliberation by the full Labor Board in Washington, D.C.

"The hearings," Migden told me, "were expertly contested by the extraordinary legal talents of Bill Berger for SAG, Bob Gilbert for SEG, and Henry Jaffe and Peter Pryor [of LA] for the TvA. Jaffe built a carefully detailed picture of television and its methods of production, likening them to methods used in radio for many years. It became clear that the hearings would have to be moved to Hollywood for testimony on how filmed work was done for television.

"The principal LA testimony," Migden continued, "came from a director of a filmed television program. Trained in the medium of film, that's how he did his show [except that he did it faster]. . . . The testimony adduced . . . that filmed television was a form of normal film production and used the same methods and working conditions as the making of motion pictures." Subsequently, in a very important first ruling, the NLRB named SAG and SEG as the proper bargaining units and ordered a representation election to follow; the TvA contested.

Now the performers themselves could choose "either" or "neither" as their bargaining agent; a simple majority would be conclusive. Balloting, as ordered by the NLRB, would not be of the entire memberships, instead it would be only of those working on filmed shows currently in production. There were two such shows, *The Groucho Marx Show* and *Amos 'n' Andy*. With a combined vote of only forty-six performers, SAG won by a margin of two to one (SEG did not vote), and their outlook for future elections was considerably brightened.

In late March, a second decision came down, this time on the petition for certification. The NLRB ruled against the TvA and upheld, in every particular, the guilds' position, stating:

[There is] no persuasive reason for disregarding a well-established unit merely because of the existence of a new outlet for the product. . . . The making of television motion pictures requires no change in the technical processes either in front or in back of the motion picture camera and the hiring of actors from the employment pool is the same for all types of productions.

It presented a huge victory for the guilds, and they celebrated it in the trade press. SAG president, Ronald Reagan, proclaimed: "The NLRB . . . demolished the entire basis on which the Four A's granted overall jurisdiction to TvA . . . the efforts of a little band of wilful men to disrupt [the guilds] have been frustrated." And from the extra players: "From now on, George Heller and his little power-grabbing clique of Television Authority promoters will have the federal government to contend with if they continue their attempts to split Screen Extras Guild."

In June 1951, nine separate and simultaneous elections were held in New York and Los Angeles. Three involved the large associations of motion picture producers and the independent movie studios—which were of no interest to Heller. The TvA did appear, however, on ballots in the remaining six: the independent associations of television film producers.

Early results made it painfully clear: the "one unit" idea was being rejected by the majority of film actors. Heller agreed to end the dispute. The TvA withdrew. The test was over, for now.

Jurisdiction was, at long last, established. It was split in two. Live performance and kinescope, "done in the live manner," remained with the TvA; performance on film, "done in the motion picture manner," stayed with the guilds. The inevitable gray areas that would develop in the mid 1950s, when tape and film technologies were combined, were left for the parties themselves to thrash out.

Screen actors, who worked primarily in feature films, were saved from having to join the TvA. Television performers—if they wanted continuity of employment—were obliged to join SAG. Most of the two memberships would shortly carry both cards and would shoulder the financial responsibilities of both organizations.

●

"George and I had our differences," said Jack Dales. "We'd been at odds for years. Even so, I felt—and said so to the Four A's—that in the event the NLRB ruled for one bargaining unit for both live and film, George should be the head of it, not I. The guild had no interest in live entertainment; we would have stayed off the ballot.

"Later, we got to know one another better and in a different way," Dales continued. "After George's cancer operation, he was a man with a changed demeanor. It seemed he wanted to be loved. My wife and I had him out to our house on several occasions when he was in California. He turned out to be a real nice guy."

Jack Dales reminisced further: "One day, Bill Berger and I were walking along together, talking about how the time had come for me to get some help at the guild. Bill said, 'Jack, you need someone like that tough, young NLRB hearings officer we had in New York back in '51.'

"And I said, 'We don't need someone *like* him; we need *him*.' "

Chester L. Migden would move to SAG as assistant executive in the mid 1960s; and, on Dales' retirement in 1972 (after thirty-five years of dedicated and outstanding service), Migden became the guild's national executive director.

•

The Four A's' long and formidable struggle was over. The screen actors and screen extra players returned to the now-foundering, financially strapped International Board of Directors. Legal and general expenses in seeking the television settlement had taken their toll. But by the beginning of 1952, the International Board was a family again and, as family members would, they resumed their fraternal relationships and confronted their next pressing task.

The time had come, as stipulated in the two-year TvA trusteeship agreement—it was, in fact, months overdue—for a decision to be made: Should the TvA continue to exist, or should it be merged with one or more of its five member branches?

It was George Heller's long-held dream that there be "one union, one card for all performers." With no hope of achieving it with the establishment of AFRA and, later, of the TvA, the trusteeship was a necessary, acceptable alternative. During its two-and-one-half-year existence, it had proved that five unique organizations could cooperate, albeit tumultuously, and negotiate and administer a major, national contract as if they were one. And once again, like the voice of the turtle, merger talk filled the spring air.

In April 1952, Georgie Price, the president of AGVA, presented the Four A's with a resolution calling for "a full five-branch merger." It was greeted with enthusiasm. Abolishing all jurisdictional lines would end, now and forever, what had become regular and crippling disputes.

Actors' Equity, pointing to earlier failures, recommended that professors from Cornell University and the University of California at Los Angeles be engaged to draft a merger plan. Gene Francis remembered, "In spring, full merger appeared all but certain; by summer, Equity and Chorus Equity began having second thoughts." They asked that certain revisions be made and that additional time be allowed for their study.

There was no question about the broadcasters' position. At both the AFRA and TvA 1951 conventions, delegates had overwhelmingly supported a full merger. With the exception of some "no" votes from LA, the

AFRA board had recently approved the professors' plan as offered and indicated its willingness to wait for a constitutional convention "to put flesh on the bones of it." An AFRA national referendum concurred (with 97 percent approval), urging adoption by the Four A's no later than July 1, 1952. Otherwise, a merger of AFRA and TvA alone should be effective on that date. A special convention for just that purpose was planned for August 23. "It was clear to me," said AFRA's A. Frank Reel, "that [our] union was the one geared to handle television. It was the only organization that had a national membership; it was the only organization that understood the economics of the industry" (Lipton 1963).

Reel, it should be noted, had not only achieved for AFRA a nearly 400 percent increase in the then heavily used commercials section of the radio transcription code but had successfully completed a first-ever Code of Fair Practice for Phonograph Recordings with the so-called shady side of the recording industry—the popular music side—parts of it still dominated by old-time gangster elements.

It was early radio, with its rich schedule of live orchestral music and singing artists, that all but killed off the pop record business. And it was radio as well that came to its rescue. With the "big band" remotes in the 1930s through the 1940s from ballrooms all across the country and the new radio "disc jockey" (Martin Block and his *Make-Believe Ballroom* from WNEW, New York, was one of the first), everyone wanted to own a copy of the latest Dorsey or Goodman hit they heard over the air the night before. Record sales were booming. When, in 1950, tastes changed from the big band sound to the more intimate strains of solo vocalists and small singing groups (the many sister and brother acts of radio fame), it was time for AFRA, bargaining agent for singing artists, to step in and organize this reputedly difficult field.

In August 1951, after months of friendly persuasion, Reel secured what promised to be "more stable, harmonious and ethical conditions" for its members. Solo singers, actors, and narrators too (plays and other recorded readings had become popular) were now assured a minimum of forty dollars per hour or per "side," whichever was greater; singing groups of two to five, seventeen dollars per hour (or per side); singing groups of six to sixteen, fourteen dollars per hour (or per side); on up to groups of twenty-five or more, nine dollars per hour (or per side). The minimum call would be two hours. Religious and educational groups, as well as persons of high reputation in fields outside of AFRA, were exempt.

•

The summer of 1952 dragged on; the July 1 merger deadline came and went. Performers in television grew more and more restive. They feared that their November negotiations would arrive, and they would again be in limbo with a board of random appointees, many of whom seldom worked in the medium, passing on their contract.

On August 7, a mass membership meeting was called at the newly air-conditioned Grand Ballroom of New York's Hotel Park Sheraton. Its purpose was to acquaint all performers with the Five-Branch Merger Plan and to discuss problems arising from it, particularly the structure of the merged locals and local autonomy. There, Equity appealed for an additional six months, so that differences with AFRA and TvA could be negotiated. Reel responded,

> Based on history, if we sit down now to negotiate . . . no five-Branch merger will ever come about. It's a simple question with us—three weak, financially embarrassed unions fighting rear-guard actions . . . or one financially strong union, able to meet industry on a basis of equality.

The musical artists too criticized any further delay, but it was the remarks by Georgie Price that brought the thespians to their feet with cries of "Apology!" and "Out of order!" Said Price:

> Dear, dear Fellow and Lady artists and sufferers in this union brawl. I am sick and tired of going up to the Four A's meetings and battling guys I love—such as George and Frank—over jurisdiction. We have wasted so much time, so much money. . . . AGVA had been killing itself trying to organize fields that belong to us. . . . If we had one card, one union—we could do it right away.
>
> The same thing happens with the others. AFRA hasn't scratched the surface of organizing radio. Equity—it's a joke. They have a little country club here in New York and a little bit of a place in Chicago, a little nothing.

After order was restored, Price continued:

> Another very, very important point[:] . . . there is such a thing as the Taft-Hartley Act. If AFRA gets into trouble with their negotiations, AGVA cannot walk out. . . . It is a secondary boycott. Equity can't do a thing to help them; none of us can do a thing to help each other. For that reason alone, if there were no other reason, we have to have one card and one union.

When Paul Dullzell, then chairman of the Four A's, introduced George Heller as "a man that has given the best years of his life . . . to do something for a lot of individuals who couldn't help themselves . . . a man who has been very often misunderstood . . . but has been carrying on in this thing now for over two years," the audience stood in a "rising vote" of appreciation. Heller spoke:

> Mr. Chairman . . . I am thankful for the gesture, but we are here to talk about the proposal by the universities; a proposal, not a blueprint. TvA was created over two years ago . . . no one worried about jurisdiction then. No one worried about Branch conflicts then, because too many performers were getting $5, $10, $25 for shows for which they now get from $75 to $350 to do.
>
> We are on record as advocating, in the strongest terms, a merger of the Five Branches, period . . . [but] TvA is the foundling, as Mr. Willard Swire [of Equity] perhaps ineptly remarked. We are the adopted child. We have no vote. We have no charter. We have [only] a trusteeship . . . but we cannot continue as a trusteeship; our members will not stand for it.

In early September, council members Margaret Webster and Bill Ross, who had always held "the theory of merger" close to their hearts, articulated Equity's now-firm conviction: that in a merger—"as Webster's Dictionary defined merger—theater would be swallowed up, immersed, sunk" by the new electronic medium. "The proposed use of existing AFRA Locals as the basis of operations," said Ross, "hands all the Branches over to AFRA—a complete surrendering of the democratic processes for which we have all fought for so long."

It was over. Equity and Chorus Equity withdrew their support and, with that, Heller's fifteen-year dream came undone. Interestingly, while the two vetoed a five-branch merger, having learned to live compatibly with one another under George Heller, several years later they voted to merge with one another.

On September 11, the long-awaited announcement arrived. The Four A's International Board of Directors granted approval by unanimous decision (SAG abstaining) of the immediate merger of the TvA with AFRA, provided "it take place under the AFRA Constitution, following which there would be discussion on changes and points of disagreement."

The boards immediately went into merger mode. They voted that both bodies would continue to serve jointly until a June 1953 election, bringing the national board to one hundred members, plus officers (the official title of *chairman* would be retained for the interim). All committees and personnel would remain in place. The TvA's highly anticipated convention—with its crucial antiblacklisting recommendation—would be canceled. New York delegates were instructed to join with the Wages and Working Conditions (W & W) Committee to formulate contract demands for the imminent negotiations.

The final motion before the TvA was made by "the great statesman" Nelson Case: "Our deepest gratitude to Heller and Jaffe, who carried TvA through its formative years and succeeded in obtaining the greatest first contract ever achieved by any union in the entertainment business."

On Saturday night, September 20, 1952, at 11:59 P.M.—with a combined national membership of more than twenty-five thousand actors, comedians, masters of ceremonies, quizmasters, disc jockeys, singers, dancers, freelance and staff announcers, sportscasters, specialty acts, sound-effects men, walk-ons, extras, puppeteers, reporters, news and policy analysts (other than government employees or other specialists), models, moderators, and members of panels with an entertainment format—the TvA and AFRA became one: the American Federation of Television and Radio Artists.

•

George Heller (seated left) with cast members of *Sailor Beware!*, 1933. Courtesy The Billy Rose Theatre Collection; The New York Public Library for the Performing Arts; Astor, Lenox and Tilden Foundations.

President Frank Gillmore of Actors' Equity Association, 1928–38. Courtesy *Equity* magazine.

Paul Dullzell, executive secretary of Actors' Equity Association, 1928–48. Courtesy *Equity* magazine.

Clara Mahr, Repertory Theater of Pecs, Hungary.
Courtesy Francesca Heller.

Sam Jaffe. Courtesy Bettye Ackerman Jaffe.

Actor-director Philip Loeb. Courtesy *Equity* magazine.

Albert Van Dekker as Baron von Geiger in *Grand Hotel*, 1931. Courtesy Jan Dekker.

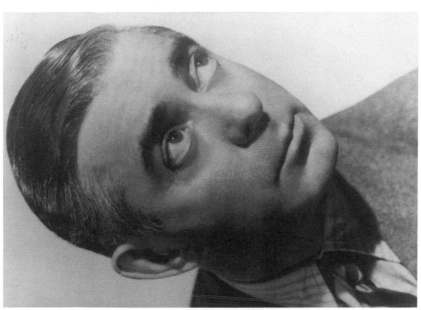

Eddie Cantor, the 1930s' most popular radio star and first president of AFRA. Courtesy *Stand By!.*

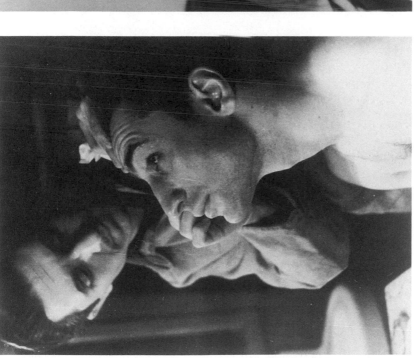

George Heller and Elia Kazan backstage before a performance of *Waiting for Lefty*, 1935. Courtesy Clara Heller.

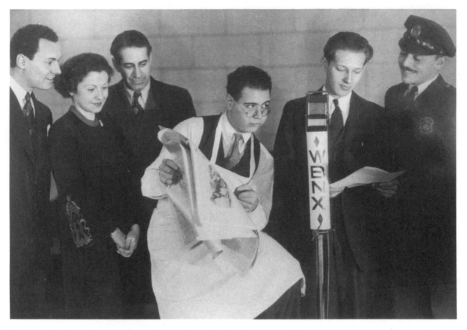

Jackson Beck as August (*seated center*) with the *Danny and August* company, radio station WBNX, the Bronx, New York, 1935. Courtesy Jackson Beck.

George Heller, AFRA Executive Secretary Emily Holt, Virginia Payne, first president of the Chicago local (Ma on *Ma Perkins*), and unidentified, at the 1944 AFRA National Convention in Cleveland. Courtesy AFTRA, New York local.

AFRA's first strike, 1941, against station WKRC, Cincinnati, Ohio. Courtesy *Stand By!*

AFRA Executive Secretary George Heller, NBC announcer and board member Ben Grauer, with Zack Becker, head of business affairs at CBS, 1946. Courtesy AFTRA, New York local.

AFRA General Counsel
Henry Jaffe, George Heller,
and Associate Executive
Secretary A. Frank Reel
(*at microphone*) at the 1948
convention, San Francisco.
Courtesy AFTRA, New York
local.

Alan Bunce and Peg Lynch of
ABC radio's *Ethel and Albert*.
Courtesy Peg Lynch.

Casey, Crime Photographer company, 1947: Lesley Woods (Ann), John Gibson (Ethelbert), Alan Devitt, Staats Cotsworth (Casey), director John Dietz, Abby Lewis, and Hester Sondergaard. Courtesy Abby Lewis Seymour, with permission of CBS News.

Milton Berle with Jackson Beck at Berle's radio show, mid-1940s. An NBC radio photograph, courtesy Jackson Beck.

Jean Muir, 1930s Warner Brothers' film star. Courtesy Margaret Bauer.

Kenneth Roberts, CBS staff announcer. Courtesy Kenneth Roberts.

Anne Seymour, Mary on NBC radio's *Story of Mary Marlin*, with her uncle, actor John D. Seymour. Courtesy Abby Lewis Seymour.

Fran Carlon, Lorelei Kilbourne on CBS Radio's *Big Town*. Courtesy Casey Allen, with permission of CBS News.

The Aldrich Family: Ann Lincoln, House Jameson, Katherine Raht, and Ezra Stone, 1939. An NBC Radio photograph, courtesy AFTRA, New York local.

Crime busters of radio: Basil Rathbone as Inspector Burke, NBC; James Meighan as The Falcon, Mutual Broadcasting System; Lon Clark as Nick Carter, Mutual; Brett Morrison as The Shadow, Mutual; and Richard Keith as the Editor on *True Detective*, CBS. A WOR Mutual Radio photograph, courtesy Anthony Tollin.

Americans at Work, with Luis Van Rooten, Jackson Beck, announcer Frank Gallup (*seated*), Carl Frank, and Santos Ortega. Courtesy Jackson Beck, with permission of CBS News.

Philip Loeb and Gertrude Berg on Broadway in Berg's *Me and Molly*, with Lester Carr and Joan Lazer, 1948. Courtesy The Billy Rose Theatre Colection; The New York Public Library for the Performing Arts; Astor, Lenox and Tilden Foundations.

TvA Vice President, actor Gene Francis.
Photograph by Talbot, courtesy Gene
Francis.

Singer and TvA Vice President Bob Spiro.
Courtesy Bob Spiro.

SAG President Ronald Reagan with SAG Executive Director Jack Dales, 1947.
Courtesy Screen Actors Guild.

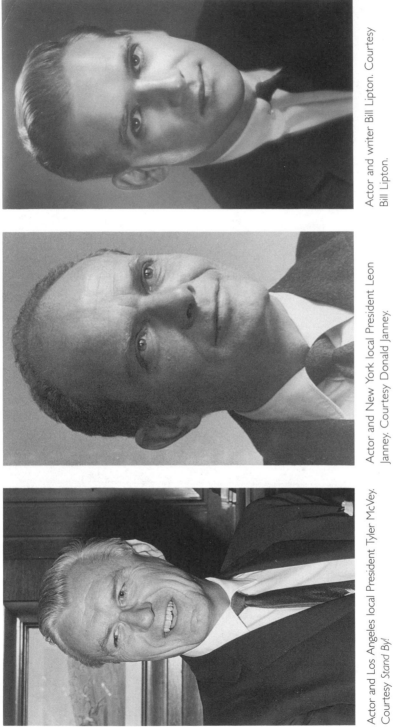

Actor and writer Bill Lipton. Courtesy Bill Lipton.

Actor and New York local President Leon Janney. Courtesy Donald Janney.

Actor and Los Angeles local President Tyler McVey. Courtesy *Stand By!*

Madeline Lee and Jack Gilford, June 1950, days before the publication of *Red Channels*. Courtesy Madeline Lee Gilford.

Henry Jaffe and his wife, Jean Muir. Courtesy David Jaffe.

The Heller family at Fire Island, 1953: George, Toni, Francesca, and Clara. Courtesy Clara Heller.

Actor Cliff Carpenter, chairman of the Anti-Blacklisting Committee. Courtesy Cliff Carpenter.

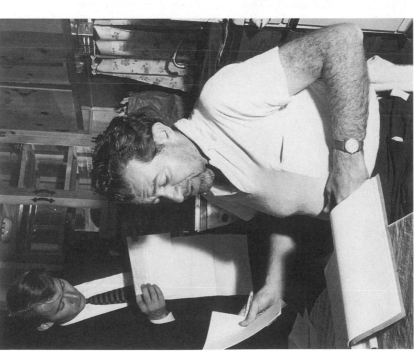

Director, production stage manager Bill Ross (*seated*) at work with an unidentified associate. Photograph by Chuck Meyer, courtesy Anita Ross-Fein.

Between scenes at a CBS TV *Studio One*. Extra player James Dean, with an unidentified cast member, 1952. Courtesy Casey Allen, copyright © Casey Allen, 1995.

Albert Dekker as Willy Loman, on tour in *Death of a Salesman*, with Paul Langton as Biff, 1951. Courtesy Jan Dekker.

Actor Leslie Barrett. Courtesy Leslie Barrett.

Actor Bert Cowlan. Courtesy Bert Cowlan.

Announcer Cy Harrice. Courtesy Cy Harrice.

Actor and AFTRA President Frank Nelson. Courtesy Stand By!

AFTRA Executive Secretary George Heller, Morris Novick, AFL President George Meany, and Bob Welch of NBC at an AFL Convention in Hollywood, 1954. Photograph by Ransdell, courtesy AFTRA, New York local.

A meeting of the Four A's International Board, mid-1950s: Vinton Hayworth, AFTRA; Ralph Bellamy, Actors' Equity Association; unidentified; Peggy Wood, Actors' Equity; unidentified; Lawrence Tibbett, AGMA; Georgie Price, AGVA; and Ray Cook, Chorus Equity. Courtesy *Equity* magazine.

Comedians Paul Winchell, Herb Shriner, Red Buttons, Sid Gould, Red Skelton, and Jack Carter at a Gould opening night. Author's photo.

The Hamilton Trio dancers: Bob Hamilton, Florence Baum, and Helena Seroy, of NBC's *Your Show of Shows*, starring Sid Caesar and Imogene Coca. Courtesy Helena Seroy Harrice

Singers Rae Whitney, Joyce De Young, Barbara Mach, and Joyce Ferrin on the Garry Moore show. Photograph by J. Peter Happel, courtesy Barbara Nelson Mach.

At Actors' Equity Association, mid-1950s: counselor Hiram Scherman, Executive Secretary Angus Duncan, President Ralph Bellamy, and counselor Frank Maxwell. Courtesy *Equity* magazine.

New York delegates at a 1960s convention: (*in forefront*) actors Sidney Blackmer and Conrad Nagel, (*at table behind Blackmer*) Rita Morley, Ken Harvey, Merrill E. Joels, and Elizabeth Morgan, (*over Nagel's raised arm*) Reginald Dowell, New York assistant executive. Courtesy *Stand By!*

AFTRA Presidents Bud Collyer and Virginia Payne at a convention in the 1960s.
Courtesy *Stand By!*

The Four A's delegation at an AFL-CIO Convention, mid-1960s. (At top) AFTRA executives Kenneth Groot, New York local; Claude McCue, Los Angeles local; and officer Conrad Nagel. (Below) President Frederick O'Neal of Actors' Equity Association; Chester Migden, assistant executive of SAG; SAG officers Walter Pidgeon and Whit Bissell, with SAG executive Jack Dales. Courtesy Equity magazine.

CBS news commentator Charles Collingwood, president of the AFTRA, New York local, with mentor and friend Edward R. Murrow. Courtesy Tatiana Jolin Collingwood, with permission of CBS News.

Former New York Vice President John Henry Faulk (*standing*) with attorney Louis Nizer, 1962. Courtesy of Faulk (John Henry) Papers, The Center for American History, The University of Texas at Austin, CNO 5709.

13

~~~~~~~~

The Immediate Fallout

The gavel came down on the first meeting of the eastern section of the AFTRA National Board on September 30, 1952. Heller was on familiar territory. With the exception of the newer members of the AFRA Artists' Committee or their supporters—among them actors Lee Tracy, Sidney Blackmer, Vaughn Taylor, Eric Dressler, Claudia Morgan, King Calder, Beverly Roberts, Peggy Wood; announcer Ed Herlihy; singers Dennis King, Travis Johnson, and Jean Tighe—he knew everyone on the merged board.

The first order of business would be the engagement of an executive and general counsel. The final vote, by deferred agenda, was, for executive secretary, George Heller, seventy-six, Frank Reel, fourteen; and for counsel, the law firm of Jaffe and Jaffe, fifty-nine, Frank Reel, forty.

Reel recalled, "Any support I got for executive came mainly from Chicago and the smaller locals, but I had no ambitions for that position. I felt George should have the job. I did hope, however, that I might stay on as general counsel. I knew that Henry Jaffe was on very shaky ground; he was opposed by a lot of people, both here in New York and on the West Coast."

The less-than-unanimous vote that reappointed Heller to the top position had a profound effect on him. While the count represented an approximate 80 percent approval, he experienced it as a serious and irreversible loss of confidence. Clara Heller told me, "Those lost votes seemed to trigger him into a kind of depression—no, a despair, really. For days, he'd pace the house repeating over and over again, 'I can't do what I need to do; I can't do what I need to do.'"

Could anyone fault Heller's devotion? "Around the clock with AFTRA," one member phrased it; "consumed with it," said another. Heller founded the unions; he successfully merged them. All his genius, all his nurturing had been poured into this dream, a dream that in two short, agonizing weeks would become his unbeatable nightmare.

•

With the predominance of the Artists' Committee on the augmented W & W Committee, one might have anticipated Chairman Ned Wever's final report. It came late in the October 9 board meeting. After a reading of the approved network contract demands, Wever stated, "The package of proposals contains a final recommendation. Blacklisting is not to be an issue in the forthcoming negotiations. Move to accept."

The boardroom erupted. Chairman Alan Bunce ruled a fifteen-minute limit on debate. Nelson Case declared that a matter of such importance should not be limited to fifteen minutes.

Kenneth Roberts moved to postpone approval to the next meeting: motion defeated, twenty-one to thirteen.

Leon Janney moved to include the essence of the Radio and Television Directors Guild–Industry statement, that management agrees not to establish political criteria as a basis of employment and will participate in efforts to prevent injury to persons where charges are based on surmise, rumor, or hearsay: motion defeated, seventeen to twelve.

Phil Loeb moved, by substitution, to adopt the essence of the joint Equity–League of Theatre Owners agreement; that is, to take all lawful means to remedy and to actively to resist blacklisting: motion defeated, twenty-nine to four.

The minority had fought and lost. Wever moved the original motion. It was approved by the eastern section twenty to thirteen and, several days later, by the entire board.

If, in fact, the old TvA had given Heller the motion he needed to challenge industry at the bargaining table, the new AFTRA had taken it away.

•

Certified social worker and private practitioner Toni Heller Hall, the Hellers' eldest daughter, told me, "I remember my father as an exuberant, outgoing, zany kind of guy. Constantly reassuring and easy to talk to, he was always—well, *almost* always—great fun to be with. My memories of growing up and of our times together are rich and very happy ones." All of that would change in the first weeks of October 1952.

Toni had just turned thirteen; the Hellers had moved south across Westchester County from the quiet, country setting of Ossining to a new home in suburban Harrison, a home about which Heller wrote a friend, "It's one of those Blanding affairs, in reverse. . . . I'm hooked up to my ears with a house we don't think particularly reflects our 'personality.'" It was then that the "awful telephone calls" began.

Toni remembered, "Dad took the calls on his bedroom phone and then the screaming would start—one four-letter word after another; my mother would quickly close the door so we shouldn't hear. Whoever was on the other end didn't have a chance to say a word. My father just screamed; he screamed and screamed. Then there'd be quiet. He'd come out all flushed, and that would be the end of it. We didn't know what it was about."

"Why do you even deal with these guys?" Clara demanded after a particularly explosive session.

"I *have* to deal with them," George spit back. "Those bastards'd tear the union apart!"

"Who was it that provoked the fury?" I asked. Clara did not know for sure. "George kept it, like he kept all his union business, separate from the family. Perhaps it was Henry—I don't know."

It was all coming together now: Heller's fear for the union, his own career, and now his own mortality; his guilt at having escaped the vigilante attacks himself; his shame at being party to a process in which blacklisting was, in fact, condoned; and, with the board's dramatic reversal on the antiblacklisting demand, his sense of helplessness—and his rage.

•

Late afternoon a week later, there was a telephone call from AFTRA. Mary Sagarin was on the line. "Hello, Mrs. Heller? I don't want to alarm you, but Mr. Heller was to have been at a meeting this afternoon, and he hasn't shown up. I thought perhaps he might have felt ill and gone home."

"No, he's not here. Call me the minute he comes in."

In a few hours, Jean Muir, from neighboring White Plains, was unexpectedly at the front door. "Your mother is on the way, Clara; she'll look after the children. Come with me." And then the two were in the car together, racing south to New York City, to a midtown hospital, to George's bedside.

"I never drove so fast in my life!" Jean Muir told me. "I kept thinking of the pain in Henry's voice when he phoned me—George was one of Henry's few close friends—and of Clara, next to me, so self-controlled, so brave; I wouldn't have been so brave; and of their marriage—how wonderful the two of them were together, how much in love—and my own marriage, falling apart."

Mary Sagarin remembered, "I called every place Mr. Heller might have gone, then every hospital, then every hotel in the area." Heller was found, registered under his own name, at a small, second-rate hotel off

Broadway—a nearly empty bottle of sleeping pills at his side. He was rushed to a local hospital.

"George was conscious when we came in the room," Clara said. Our dear friend, Dr. Sydney Bassin was there. And another doctor, a psychiatrist, whom George consulted with after his cancer surgery, was standing over him, his awful voice deriding him, 'You couldn't stand the gaff, George. You couldn't stand the gaff.' "

Then they were alone. George had Clara's hand. "I've done a terrible thing to you, my darling. Please forgive me."

•

No one was to know. Jaffe reported to the board, October 16: "George returned to work too soon after his operation; he's been hospitalized as a result of exhaustion from the strenuous activities of the past few months." Heller was voted a vacation with pay, "the length of which to be determined by his doctors." He would spend that vacation in Florida. The meeting proceeded.

Conrad Nagel, having voted to accept Wever's W & W report, moved to reconsider the action taken on the blacklisting proposal. The motion passed, nineteen to seven.

Then, the unlikely duo of Nagel and Leon Janney moved that, in order for a member who believes he is unjustly accused to have a place and the means to clear himself, Heller negotiate the formation of a review board—a fact-finding impartial review board—similar to the one outlined earlier by Professor Robert Cushman of Cornell. The motion carried nineteen to seven and was added to the package of proposals slated for approval at the coming membership meeting.

Heller returned from his board-approved vacation within only two days. But he returned apparently a changed man, with a new and better sense of how to cope with his political realities. Said Clara, "There was a marked difference in George's attitude towards life in general and specifically towards his job at AFTRA."

He wrote to Margot Stevenson, an old colleague from the *You Can't Take It with You* days who was then appearing in George Axelrod's *Seven Year Itch* in London:

After fifteen years of aggravation, my stomach acted up on me, so I had to have it removed. Then, like a damn fool, I came back to work too soon and I was near wrapped up and buried. But now I am all right again and just as mean as ever.

On October 27, 1952, National Executive Secretary George Heller was back on the dais at the New York membership meeting, back in his place at the head of AFTRA, and more determined than ever to hold the organization together, despite the opposing views that had threatened to tear him and that still threatened to tear it apart.

Following presentation of the contract proposals, Cliff Carpenter, chair of the Anti-Blacklisting Committee, reintroduced his committee's resolution—that blacklisting be considered an unfair labor practice and breach of contract—as a substitute to the Nagel-Janney review board proposal. The debate was on.

Ed Sullivan spoke:

> Some of you may feel that history has reached a point where nothing can be done once a person is accused, but . . . in the cases of both Lena Horne and Katherine Dunham, where pressure was brought on me . . . to take them off the show, I looked into the facts myself and found the accusations to be false . . . and the ladies appeared.
>
> The picture painted of ad agencies, sponsors and producers as ogres is untrue. They are completely hogtied; they do not know what to do. They will be delighted with . . . a Review Board that can say with authority that "this performer is cleared." I beg of you to support Nagel-Janney because the method is practical.

However he made it sound, not until Horne threatened to sue and AGVA, her union, told Sullivan that they were ready to remove their other performers was her appearance on *Toast of the Town* made certain (Miller 1952).

One Godfrey P. Schmidt, an unknown to the general performing community and a new associate (nonvoting) member who earned his AFTRA card by briefly reading children's stories on local radio, added his voice in favor of the review board: "Any actor who feels his reputation has been besmirched can go to this tribunal, lay the facts on the table and 'the truth shall make you free.' "

George Heller spoke:

> I, too, do not like what has been happening in the last two years, particularly in the performers' unions. I feel that any member should be free to get up . . . and say whatever he wants to say without having to worry about whether it would put him on a blacklist.
>
> We know that many persons are circulating lists—we know that. But to simply penalize a sponsor or producer, or put him in a position where his show might be cancelled, does not get to the heart of the question. What you have to do is offset these self-appointed, so-called "investigators" by providing a place for the unjustly accused to go.
>
> The substitute resolution makes no distinctions. If a Communist is blacklisted, then presumably this union would have to declare the

employer "unfair." This is totally unrealistic as far as the current complexion, the policy and the Constitution of this union is concerned.

We have to come down to earth on this. If it did become a strike issue, there would be no chance whatsoever to win it, and if you think that the employers are not out there waiting for us, waiting to get their claws into us this year, you are living in a dream world.

Heller's appeal hit home. Could or should this controversial issue—this essentially New York issue—which had been turned down by New York delegates and was unsupported in either LA or Chicago, be made a part of a national package of proposals? Would it, in fact, cause even greater apprehension in the industry, perhaps hurting even greater numbers of performers as a result?

The Anti-Blacklisting Committee's substitute motion was defeated two and one-half to one. The package with the fact-finding impartial review board proposal would go to the bargaining table. Not one word, only a great shrug of shoulders, passed from Heller to Carpenter at meeting's end.

•

Through the magic of the coaxial cable, network o & o's in New York and the East were linked to sister stations in Chicago and the Midwest in 1949. Two years later, all were linked to California and the rest of the country. Hundreds of independent stations, newly licensed by the FCC, joined the networks as affiliates. There were many worthwhile things to see and affordable sets on which to see them. By 1952, television was in more than twenty million homes across America.

Black-and-white television was dazzling and fast replacing radio in popularity. Most top entertainers had joined the intrepid radio-into-television pioneers. Now there were Eddie Cantor, Red Skelton, Lucille Ball, Jack Benny, George Burns and Gracie Allen, Ed Wynn, Ken Murray, Red Buttons, and Dean Martin and Jerry Lewis, all to be enjoyed regularly in your own living room. And there were great pop musicians too: Paul Whiteman, Fred Waring, Perry Como, Frank Sinatra, Kate Smith, and Sammy Kaye. There were *Your Hit Parade*, *Behulah*, and *Kukla, Fran and Ollie*.

There were new dramas: *Robert Montgomery Presents* and the *Lux Video*, *Celanese*, *Schlitz*, *Goodyear*, *Armstrong Circle*, and *Somerset Maugham* theaters; and mysteries: *Dragnet*, *Suspense*, and *Danger*. There were more than a half dozen weekly crime fighters and that many quizmasters. And there was Edward R. Murrow's *See It Now*.

•

Most AFTRAns were working. Nearly every show was sponsored and under the direct control of the advertising agencies. SAG had recently completed its first television contract, and a number of new, filmed-for-television shows were hitting the airwaves out of LA. There was tremendous excitement throughout the industry. The four networks, ABC, CBS, NBC, and Dumont TV (along with the New York independent WOR TV), were now showing good profits, and each was being careful about how, or if, they allocated those profits.

The 1952 negotiations were, as predicted, a bitter fight. Heller took the position that no national agreement would be concluded unless and until all network o & o contracts were signed as well. It created a stalemate; the December board meetings recessed in preparation for possible strike action. But with the holidays fast approaching, the parties worked diligently and with relative good cheer to cut through the differences. A good and fair settlement was reached on the first AFTRA Code of Fair Practice for Network Television Broadcasting on Christmas Eve day.

With the merger of the TvA and AFRA, the Artists' Committee consolidated under one roof and entered the year 1953 more powerful than ever before. No longer the dominant faction in the two unions, now, in AFTRA, they *were* the union. And Heller, more than at any time since the founding of the radio federation, was an employee of the union.

Despite protestations from the still-vocal minority on the old TvA side, that "no cognizance was taken of an opposing opinion," the AFTRA board voted that all committees be dissolved. The Anti-Blacklisting Committee, generator of the threatening antiblacklist proposals, was out; sister unions would be notified that the federation would no longer participate in what had been regular, joint meetings on the subject. Henceforth, the issue would be addressed through the soon-to-be-formed fact-finding impartial review board.

The disgruntled Committee to Further Employment Opportunities for Negro Artists, viewed as politically suspect, would also go. Its gains, in any event, were hardly measurable during its brief, volatile existence. With it would go Heller's plan to hire an executive to implement the TvA's policy of racial integration on television. "Appreciating that serious efforts to increase employment opportunities must be made," the board recommended that, "where the problem has arisen," locals should establish committees of their own. Gene Francis, former chair of that committee told me, "George's efforts to make the 1951 Industry Statement of Policy work, only cracked the door of opportunity. Madison Avenue did not want to use blacks in their commercials, afraid that the product would become identified as 'a nigger product.' Yes," said Francis, "that's what they called it."

To counter their resistance, Heller was able to get industry to agree to a convention of advertisers and agencies. The single topic for discussion would be the integration of Negroes into television commercials. Ralph Bunche of the UN accepted Heller's invitation to serve as chair.

"The convention was scheduled for late 1952," said Francis, "but after the merger, and with the clear disinterest on the old AFRA side, it never did come about." Heller was able, however, to negotiate the first No Discrimination Clause, pertaining to race, sex, creed, color, and national origin, in the 1952 code. Not until 1967 would AFTRA resume its efforts for greater employment opportunities for minority artists through the work of the New York–based Joint Equality Committee—a delegation of officials and members from SAG; the Writers Guild of America, East; and the Directors Guild of America—cochaired by Ernest Kinoy, then president of the Writers Guild, and Rita Morley of SAG.

Within one month's time, the Artists' Committee had redefined Heller's fifteen-year-old union of broadcasters. Accomplishing what they had been thwarted in doing under the old Arthur-Collyer Resolution eight years earlier, the Artists' Committee established a policy that rejected all participation, including financial contributions, in "outside organizations." They ended board involvement, whether through debate or by direct action, in what they deemed political and societal issues—issues in which Heller and others of the old AFRA and the old TvA so fervently believed.

•

14

The *Post* Articles and the Los Angeles "Three"

"Panic over blacklisting is stealthily spreading through the TV-radio world," read the opening line in the first of six consecutive articles that ran in the New York *Post* from January 26 to February 2, 1953. Gene Francis explained, "With the AFTRA National Board sitting for nearly four months on testimony given the old Anti-Blacklisting Committee, I took it upon myself, with George's OK, of course, to go to the newspapers—to try to get them to do a story on it. *The Times* and *The Tribune* showed no interest, but Jimmy Wechsler at the *Post* assigned an investigative reporter in fifteen minutes flat."

The Oliver Pilat article continued:

The facts are more alarming than the rumors. It is possible now to be blacklisted on the basis of a speech or a vote at a union meeting, an offhand telephone comment. . . . Everybody in the industry which has an unusually high quota of intelligent, sensitive, well-meaning individuals whispers over one phase or another of the situation without daring to bring it out into the open. *Variety*, one of the bibles of radio and TV, issued an anniversary edition recently, hundreds of pages of copy and ads, without a single reference to the blacklist. . . . Although a few corporations and *Sponsor* magazine had resisted from time to time, and radio-TV newspaper editors John Crosby and Jack Gould [fight back] month after month, it is the blacklisters who carry the day.

Why has this situation been allowed to degenerate so badly . . . one [reason] is that nothing acts so frightened as a million dollars. . . . The Communists themselves want no precise analysis . . . lest it end the present turmoil from which they are profiting. And some conservative union leaders . . . feel that blacklisting must run its course, and will solve itself in the end. . . . Meanwhile, there are more than enough rightist members anxious for the available jobs.

Who is being blacklisted? Scores of the busiest, most talented and respected performers on the air today . . . [and] there is no way to grapple with [it]. . . . Where there is no formal accusation, formal clearance becomes impossible. (New York *Post*, January 26, 1953)

A casting director says . . . "I have to settle for second-rate talent." . . . "Think of the irony of it," moans an ad man, . . . "think of all the whodunits on TV and all the sleuths on radio outwitting viciousness and helping virtue. What is truth in our life? —slander in its heyday and gossipmongers cowing decent people (like me) into burying their heads in their desks." (New York *Post*, February 1, 1953)

The chief "bogeyman," is one Laurence A. Johnson, a grocer from Syracuse, New York [a name presented in evidence by Madeline Lee and Jack Gilford to the Anti-Blacklisting Committee]. . . . In the case of the Borden Company, for example, Johnson had their radio-TV producers, Prockter Productions, so intimidated that they turned over their list of some 600 regularly used actors for his personal screening and approval. When he returned it to them, 138 names had been crossed off. . . . A former collector of . . . cigar-store Indians, mechanical toys and piggy banks, you might say he now collects human scalps. (New York *Post*, January 27, 1953)

Laurence A. Johnson was a man unknown to the general public and, it appeared, little admired by intellectuals and civic leaders in his own hometown. Yet this stocky, eccentric, sixty-three-year-old with a spastic condition of the esophagus, reigned alone as the great facilitator in the process of blacklisting. As spokesman for the upper New York State Association of Supermarkets, he singlehandedly exercised veto power over the entire two-billion-dollar broadcasting industry. His threat to advertisers—one they were apparently loathe to test—was a customer boycott of their clients' products were they to employ, as he phrased it, "one of Stalin's little creatures." Reporter Pilat continued,

Johnson and his cohorts, the Veterans Action Committee of Syracuse Super Markets, and the Committee on Un-American Activities of the American Legion Post 41, continued to hammer. Prockter Productions, in panic, felt obliged to show its super-patriotism and drew up a "white list" of 83 persons guaranteed to have no political background at all from which hiring, henceforth, would be done. (New York *Post*, January 27, 1953)

War was hell but was not without its triumphs. The fellowship of blacklisters rejoiced at monthly postings of those ousted from entertainment. The February 1952 "Box Score Outs," as reported in the *Post*, read, in part, "The Weavers—Fineto; Jack Gilford—He and *Fledermaus* Struck Out." Wrong. While production stage manager Bill Ross kept calm within the Metropolitan Opera's ninety-member touring company, an emissary from the Met's Rudolf Bing and the mayor of Syracuse intervened. "If you picket here," said the mayor, "there'll be no more parade permits." The legion was stymied, performances continued, and Gilford went on to win ovations in his nonsinging role of the drunken jailer. "Box Score Outs" continued, "Phillip Loeb (Jake on *Goldbergs*)—Done for good we hope; Artie Shaw—station W.O.L.F. still using his records—How Come?; Jose Ferrer—Maybe we should not see his new Motion Picture. . . . Judy Holliday—Ditto."

Johnson's evidence of so-called subversive activities was based on citings by the Boy Scouts of America, the publication *Counterattack*, the American Legion's *Firing Line*, and various un-American activities committees. And, reporter Pilat went on,

> according to friends, [Johnson] also draws on advice from . . . film actor Adolphe Menjou, who considers himself an authority on Communists; Harvey Matusow, 26-year-old ex-Communist [who admitted to giving false testimony against hundreds in congressional investigations and was later jailed for obstructing justice in the 1949 Smith Act trial]; Paul R. Milton of the Radio Writers Guild; and Vinton Hayworth and Ned Wever of the American Federation of Television and Radio Artists. (New York *Post*, January 27, 1953)

AFTRAns were sent reeling. "There had been, of course, vague rumors and suspicions," Cliff Carpenter told me. "Everyone knew the Artists' Committee was heavily *pro*-blacklisting. But the fact that these people, whom we'd elected to serve in high office, were blacklisting their own fellow performers came as horrifying news."

At the subsequent board meeting, a motion that the *Post* articles be dealt with immediately as a special item of business was made and defeated. Chairman Bunce placed the matter last, under new business. The agenda, heavy with proposed amendments to the new AFTRA Constitution, was not completed that evening. New business was held over for the next meeting, two weeks hence, allowing time to set up one of the smoothest double-play combinations outside of baseball history—from Vinnie to Neddy to Bud.

At an intervening New York local board meeting, where the players also held high office, President Vinton Hayworth categorically denied "any statements, implications or inferences about himself or Mr. Wever in the *Post* articles, or that the two influenced or directed Laurence Johnson's activities in any way.

"Inasmuch as AFTRA's Constitution bars Communists from membership, we conceived it our duty to keep ourselves well-informed on the subject of public opinion," said Hayworth. "We have met with Mr. Johnson, who, at various times, has discussed with us the entire problem of Communist infiltration in the broadcast industry."

The board moved for a unanimous expression of "full confidence in the two officials." It directed Executive Secretary Kenneth Groot to send Hayworth's statement to the *Post*, together with a letter expressing "regret that a major New York paper chooses to discuss so difficult a subject without full verification of the facts." (Heller's assistant since 1938, Ken Groot was then, and would be until his death in 1983, the executive of the New York local and, as Jackson Beck said of him, "The best damned negotiator we ever had there.")

The players next attended the resumed meeting of the national board, where Ned Wever presented Hayworth's statement with the subsequent vote of confidence. And, lest there be a lingering doubt, mediator Bud Collyer drove it home: "I had a long conference with both gentlemen, and I have satisfied myself that there is no truth whatsoever . . . in the article. The two have my unqualified support." The AFTRA National Board resolved, therefore, to approve and heartily endorse the action of the local.

Heller read the more than one dozen telegrams from individuals seeking, some demanding, an explanation of the *Post*'s assertions. Leon Janney spoke:

> The membership is entitled to a detailed summary of those talks. . . . Any information "the two" have that a member is a Communist should be the property of the National Board or the U.S. Government or both, but should certainly not be a matter of discussion by Board members with a person . . . representing outside pressure groups.

Janney's argument was lost on the poorly attended meeting. The players had touched all bases. With twenty-four proxies tucked in their pockets, the vote to "approve and heartily endorse" was easily won; thirty-one in favor, five against, and two abstentions.

Actor William "Billy" Redfield, a formerly outspoken board member, now mysteriously out of work, voiced the fear that immobilized so many in AFTRA—indeed, in the country: "Since this is a recorded vote, my vote, either way, may cause me to be discriminated against in the industry. I therefore abstain."

•

The proposed fact-finding impartial review board was having a hard time getting off the ground. For some ten months, before any procedural matters could be dealt with, the conference remained stuck on the question: Whose problem is blacklisting anyway? The Association of National Advertisers insisted that it was the responsibility of the union and the networks to resolve not of the advertisers, who, they were quick to remind members, had other media to which they could turn.

Kenneth Roberts, an AFTRA delegate to the conference, told me, "I remember one very moving moment. It came at the height of a big argument over who should be allowed to appear on television and who shouldn't. A Mr. Isaac Digges, legal counsel for the association of advertisers, a fine, old gentleman, born and raised in New England, rose and said, 'A man's right to work is God given and no one can deprive him of that God-given right.' And having said so, walked out."

Despite the controversy and personal discomfiture, an outline of the review board was developed. It would not be considered a "clearance" or "loyalty board," nor would it attempt to help those who were avowed Communists. It would provide support for the falsely accused and for those who had participated in so-called Communist front activities at some time in the past. The board would have no power of subpoena but would employ investigators and hold hearings in advance of rendering a report—not a decision—to the advertisers.

Then press generally approved: "The spreading panic requires quick, practical countermeasures of some sort," one paper wrote. And, "While the plan is not perfect, it has the advantage of dealing with blacklisting in terms of fact instead of propaganda and counter-propaganda."

According to a February 1 Pilat article in the *Post*, Robert J. Landry, editor of the ad newsletter *Space and Time*, however, wrote: "It is not by any means certain that the cure for private judges of political sin is a private court of appeal."

•

HUAC announced a new round of hearings in its ongoing investigation of communist activities in entertainment. They would open in Los Angeles on March 21, 1953, and continue intermittently—sometimes in Washington, sometimes in New York—for the next five years.

The Los Angeles local board moved quickly to adopt a rule allowing for disciplinary action against members who were in violation of the 1951 anticommunism amendment to the AFTRA Constitution.

Resolved, any member . . . who is asked by the HUAC or any other duly constituted committee, to state whether or not he is or ever has been a member of the Communist Party, is hereby instructed to so state. Failure to answer such question shall be deemed . . . conduct prejudicial to the welfare of AFTRA, and

Further resolved, any member who declines to answer . . . shall be summoned before the Los Angeles Board . . . who shall then interrogate such member as to whether or not he maintains membership in, knowingly promotes the special interests of, makes financial contributions to, or renders aid and assistance by lending his name or talents to the Communist Party or any organization known to him to be a portion, branch or subdivision thereof.

Failure to answer such questions shall be deemed . . . conduct prejudicial to the welfare of AFTRA. Violations of this rule . . . shall be prosecuted pursuant to the Constitution and By-laws of the L.A. Local and the AFTRA National Constitution. The effective date of this rule shall be March 20, 1953.

The proposed rule passed unanimously, subject to ratification, and came before the national board in New York on March 11, for approval. One director commented that the rule seemed questionable because it would penalize a member if he asserted his rights under the Constitution of the United States.

Legal counsel Henry Jaffe responded, "Our members possess no privilege so far as their personal and business life is concerned; they are subject to whatever frustration or embarrassment may be caused them by their refusal to answer."

Jaffe also said that LA had a problem affecting its welfare. Although a member may be exercising his privilege by being an "uncooperative" witness, he is also throwing discredit on his union. This would be solved by the LA proposal, and "I see no reason to deny them the benefits of their solution." Jaffe did not believe the rule would be applied "in a manner contrary to the law of the land."

He pointed out that expulsion would not be automatic, that there would be the right of appeal—to the membership, to the national board, and ultimately to the convention. Jaffe further urged that the proposal not be amended because "it would delay passage beyond the crucial date of the hearings. The rule may, in fact, have the effect of persuading some members to answer the '$64 question.' "

The Los Angeles membership ratified it, 831 to 72. The rule was now in place and just in time. (It would not be long before the AFTRA leadership would see the need for its "benefits" in all other locals as well.) Within weeks, three LA members who had refused to answer questions put to them by HUAC received a "notice of charges." The three also maintained their silence at the local's interrogation. Subsequently, a "notice of punishment" was issued: "Suspension for one year until they shall voluntarily appear before HUAC and freely testify. Failure to comply before June 23, 1954, shall result in automatic expulsion."

An appeal for reinstatement was denied. Immediately, locals throughout the country were admonished not to admit the three without Los Angeles' prior approval.

•

Ten weeks into the new round of hearings, actor Lee J. Cobb of the old Group Theatre privately went before a HUAC investigator to admit his "sins" and "name names" of old colleagues active in the party. All had already been named; all were known to the committee. But in his anxiety to oblige, Cobb offered up this bit of extraneous information: "Phil Loeb and Sam Jaffe were active in a far-left caucus in Actors' Equity, though I never knew them to be Communists. And I don't mean by mentioning their names to suggest that they were" (Kanfer 1973). Cobb's private testimony was later released to the press. No more harm could be done to Phil Loeb, but additional harm to Sam Jaffe was another matter.

Born in 1898 on the Lower East Side of Manhattan, Jaffe, who was fluent in seven languages, earned his Bachelor of Science in engineering at City College and attended Columbia University. He taught mathematics at the Bronx Cultural Institute for several years before going into the performing arts. A veteran of World War I and cofounder, with George Heller, of the old Actors' Forum, he was elected to the Equity council in 1940, the year he played King Lear in New York.

For years, Jaffe held a special niche on stage and in motion pictures with his portrayals of eccentric or unusual parts: the 250-year-old High Lama in the film *Lost Horizons* and the title role in *Gunga Din*. He and George Freedley of the New York Public Library arranged a coalition in 1944 for the use of free performance space for young professionals. There are few actors today who do not know of, or have not benefited from, the still-lively Equity Library Theater.

From the time of his listing in *Red Channels* in 1950, coincident with his nomination for an Academy Award for his performance in *The Asphalt Jungle*, Jaffe's film opportunities began to dry up. "But," said his wife, actress Bettye Ackerman Jaffe, "the 'total eclipse' came a few months later when an article appeared on the front page of Hollywood *Variety* quoting academy member Ward Bond as saying, 'We will not vote for that Red.' "

Two years passed with no work. His savings spent, he relied more and more on his sisters and friends. When in 1953 Lee J. Cobb made him suspect once again, his career was clearly finished.

•

Speaking at a New York meeting on behalf of a small slate of independents, Bert Cowlan, formerly of radio's *Stella Dallas*, declared:

> We are "at war," here and now! "At war" against the fear and smear and impugning of names in a business that so depends on the value of one's name. "At war" for our economic lives against those, who out of their own fears and insecurity, have determined to destroy us.

The race for seats on the first member-elected AFTRA National Board and for delegates to the First AFTRA National Convention had officially begun.

One young actor reported to the rank and file that members were "refusing to run for office . . . refusing to sign petitions, even though they endorse the candidates. Fear and hysteria has taken the place of logic and reason." But no matter the fears, no matter the determination by a courageous few to defeat "those blacklisting bastards," the Artists' Committee unsurprisingly swept clean.

Relieved of office were all the old TvA moderates and the left. Actors Gene Francis, Frank Maxwell, Karl Swenson, John Larkin, and Leon Janney were out; announcers Nelson Case, Richard Stark, and Ben Grauer were out; singers Bob Spiro, Jerry Wayne, and Leon Bibb were out; dancers Chris Karner and Frances Rainer were out. AFRA founders and longtime vice presidents—the beloved Virginia Payne and Anne Seymour—were out as well. Payne would return to be elected the first woman president of both the New York local and national AFTRA, but not until 1958.

Vinton Hayworth offered a perfunctory but polite farewell to the outgoing directors: "My thanks to all retiring members, who, regardless of any differences of opinion, have worked for the good of the union in their respective ways."

•

In Los Angeles at the Hollywood-Roosevelt Hotel, Thursday, July 23, 1953, the opening session of the First AFTRA National Convention was held. Admonishing the delegates in his state of the union address, George Heller said:

> Ours is a strongly anti-Communist union. We want no part of Communists, subversives or others of like nature. But in our zeal . . . we must be on guard not, by excess, to destroy the very pattern which is the basis of democracy.
>
> Snap judgements, careless deductions are dangerous companions which help, rather than hurt the Communists. An ancient philoso-

pher once said: "Blame no man before you have inquired into the matter: understand first and reform righteously." Rumor is without witness, without judge, malicious and deceiving. We must become inured to the doctrine of requiring facts to substantiate our judgements.

Saturday afternoon at 2:30 P.M., the LA "three"—the suspended members of the LA local, a female dancer and two male actor-announcers—went before the convention to appeal their punishment. Their attorney, Robert Shutan, asked the body:

> Can any organization, in which membership is a requisite to hold a job, require something of its members, on pain of expulsion, which the United States Constitution says they cannot be required to do? This is what is happening to these members.

Newsman Averill Burman, then preparing for his master's degree in American constitutional history, spoke in their defense. Counsel David Ziskind presented the position of the LA local. Rebuttals were made, and the arguments continued throughout the long afternoon.

Mary Sagarin remembered, "Mr. Heller—always so buoyant, so energized—went through the convention speaking barely a word to anyone. He sat silent throughout the appeal, his head down, chin to chest; he displayed no emotion."

The ordeal was over by 6:15 P.M. By secret ballot, those assembled voted "To affirm, in all respects, the decision of the Los Angeles board" (151 in favor, 16 against, 2 abstentions). The U.S. Constitution be damned; the AFTRA convention had spoken. The body adjourned for dinner.

At the 10:00 P.M. election of officers—those hours when delegates take a breather from the day's labors to enjoy a scathing, often riotously funny roast-lovefest and to select the next year's leaders—the convention reaffirmed the union's political tilt.

Ranking officers Alan Bunce and LA's Frank Nelson of the old AFRA were reelected president and first vice president of AFTRA. Also elected were Vice Presidents Vinton Hayworth of New York; Donald Hirsch of Pittsburgh; Jack Gannon of Chicago; Janet Baumhover of Portland; Ernie Winstanley of Detroit; and Bob Bruce of Los Angeles. Conrad Nagel of New York was elected treasurer, and Bruce Grant of Kansas City, became recording secretary. AFTRA's national policy was now officially in the hands of the right and the ultraright and would remain so for the foreseeable future.

In New York, at a subsequent membership meeting, blacklisted actor

Stanley Prager—who would later direct television's *Car 54, Where Are You?* and *The Patty Duke Show*—rose to say:

> It appears to me that it is not this union or any other union's job to make conformity in the political arena a condition of membership. What AFTRA members think and say, what they read, with whom they meet and where they worship is not the rightful field of either government or union investigation.
>
> The right to work should be without exception to the color of a man's skin or to the shade of his political opinion and this right is fundamental to the existence of this union and of this country. Curtailment or denial of this right must seriously endanger the freedom of us all and cannot safely be ignored.

•

15

~~~~~~

The Impossible Plan and
AWARE Incorporates

As black a time as it had been for George Heller, he returned from
the 1953 convention with a prize he had been working toward for
years—instructions to "negotiate a Pension and Welfare Plan, national in
scope, with benefits applicable to all members working in television." Always a dreamer ahead of his time, Heller had nurtured the idea of "a
means of protection for members from old age and illness" since he had
introduced it, fifteen years earlier, at the first AFRA convention. "I remember," Mary Sagarin said, "when Mr. Heller spoke of it . . . and how
everyone gasped—a pension for radio actors, who were referred to, only
recently in the press as 'vagabonds'?"

In six successive bargaining rounds, Heller had asked for a pension
and welfare plan as one demand among many. Management regularly
shunted it aside. Unions that had achieved such a plan were the more traditional trade unions, those in which there was a single employer, in
which the work force remained relatively constant, and in which the
workers were regularly employed.

While staffers at television and radio stations could benefit from the
company's plan, the largest segment of AFTRA was (and still is) freelance
artists. They worked a number of jobs within a given year and, most often, each job was for a different employer; the duration of employment
varied as well. Most freelancers moved in and out of the broadcast jurisdiction. Others came in, stayed for a while, then disappeared. Only a
small portion of the population was what one might consider regularly
employed. No plan covering this set of circumstances had ever
existed—it was, in fact, unheard of. Gene Francis recalled, "I was there
the day Jack Dales said to George, flat out, 'You're wasting your time on
this; it can't work. These people are transients.' "

Earlier in 1953, Heller initiated a meeting with Martin E. Segal and Co., the oldest and largest firm involved in establishing and administrating pension and welfare programs, to attempt to develop a plan involving multiple employers. Segal was doubtful at first that such a plan could be made, but Heller was determined to find a solution. He told Segal to proceed with a first study.

Throughout the following months, everyone was hard at work: Heller and Segal, collecting and correlating voluminous data, weighing the methods of funding, the size of the contributions; the AFTRA Study Committee, debating the members' needs, the eligibilities, and the possible benefits. Thousands of member hours went into the preparation of that one proposal.

It was soon apparent that pension and welfare would be an enormous demand on management and would have many ramifications. Clearly, it could not go to the table as only one part of a larger package. Heller must persuade the board and the membership that, if it were to succeed, the plan would have to be presented as a "single demand" in the 1954 negotiations.

Not everyone loved the idea of sacrificing the "cold, hard cash" of immediate pay increases for some vague benefits in the far distant future, and they made their voices heard from coast to coast. It was going to be a long, hard sell.

•

In December 1953, under the laws of the State of New York, Vincent Hartnett's AWARE, "An organization to combat the Communist Conspiracy in the Entertainment World," legally incorporated. One immediate benefit was the removal of possible liability from individual officers and members of the board.

Godfrey P. Schmidt, associate member of AFTRA, former assistant professor of law at Fordham University, and newly elected president of AWARE, Inc., announced the roster of officers: actor Ned Wever of AFTRA, first vice president; writer Paul R. Milton of the Radio Writers Guild, second vice president; actor Richard Keith of AFTRA, treasurer; and Jeanne Somerville, secretary. The new board included founder Hartnett; radio director Wynn Wright; AFTRA actors William "Bill" Keene, William M. Neil, Leigh Whipper, and Vinton Hayworth, president of the AFTRA New York local. Among those stepping down after a first term in office were actress Jean Owens, wife of Vinton Hayworth; Newton Fulbright, *New York Herald Tribune* reporter; and J. B. Matthews, former staff director of the Senate Permanent Subcommittee on Investigations, Senator Joseph R. McCarthy's committee.

AWARE had grown by leaps and bounds in its nearly two-year existence.

In addition to the Borden Company, Hartnett was now "consultant" for numerous clients of the Y & R and Kudner advertising agencies, Lever Brothers, and ABC. Its mailings—regular bulletins and various news supplements—were circulated to more than a thousand persons, to networks, sponsors, ad agencies, and independent television producers, as well as to state and federal agencies. Membership stood at 350 and would grow in the next few years to more than six hundred; nearly one-third of those, it would develop, were AFTRA members. And, at one time or another, Bud Collyer and Alan Bunce were among those members (Faulk 1983).

Though it would be years before it became public knowledge, Laurence Johnson and his Syracuse coconspirators, John Dungey of American Legion Post 41 and Francis Neuser of the Veterans Action Committee of Syracuse Super Markets, were also AWARE members and attended meetings in New York. Even preceding AWARE, Johnson enjoyed a working relationship with Vice President Paul Milton, in furtherance of Milton's blacklisting activities at the Radio Writers Guild (Nizer 1966).

•

With the revelation that leaders of AFTRA were conferring with vigilante Laurence Johnson, the number of candidates for the New York local board decreased markedly in the December 1953 elections. Still, a challenge was made by a small band of independents. They too lost, joining the hundreds of others on Hartnett's closely guarded list of unemployables. The campaign against the contenders followed the customary smear attacks: the "party boys," under the guise of fighting the blacklist, were trying to "infiltrate the union," and under the pretext of fighting for jobs for Negroes, they were actually working "to plant only Negro party-members and sympathizers," while "blacklisting out of jobs the *anti-*Communist Negroes."

Actor-singer Ken Harvey responded from the floor of a membership meeting, "If wanting this platform results in our being called 'subversive,' then this is a slander which honors us and dishonors our accusers." (After a long, self-imposed absence from union activities—not unusual for those damaged by the Artists' Committee group—Ken Harvey would return to be elected president of the New York local, 1968–71; national first vice president, 1970–73; and president of AFTRA, 1973–76.)

David Susskind, producer of many top-rated shows, including the *Philco Television Playhouse* and the *DuPont Show of the Week*, would testify at the John Henry Faulk libel trial (see chapter 18) about the secrecy that surrounded the practice of blacklisting. He told of how one-third of the names he presented for clearance on a particular series came back rejected, including that of an eight-year-old child, the daughter of a controversial actor. But like all producers in television, Susskind was under strict instructions not to let on to the talent or to their agents that the turndowns were for political reasons. Susskind testified:

> I told the vice president at Young and Rubicam in charge of the Reynolds tobacco account how difficult it was to find the right actor, the right writer, the right director for each project and that Y & R was making production . . . unworkable and artistically impossible.
>
> "I know many of the people you're rejecting. I know them socially and professionally—and there is no question about their political reliability or good citizenship or loyalty to the country. I beg you to let me confront them with the charges, or whatever you have on them, and let them answer."
>
> "I can't give [it] to you," the ad man answered. "I deplore the practice as much as you do, but we're caught in a trap; there's no alternative. . . . And we have to pay $5 for each one of these clearances and $2 for every recheck—it's costing us a bloody fortune. Cut down on your submissions." (Faulk 1983)

Actor-announcer Casey Allen told me, "It was Susskind who took to adding phony names to his lists for clearance, and when an actor he wanted got rejected, he gave him one of the phony cleared names to use on the show."

•

The industry conference to establish the fact-finding impartial review board was dying of its own skittishness and lack of commitment. Even while Heller reported that the number of unemployables had grown to nearly five hundred, including cases of mistaken identity and similarity of name, there was still no plan that the conference could agree was advisable, effective, or practicable.

Heller submitted yet another proposal, this time for a "politically mixed" board, one that would hold interviews with accused persons and evaluate the charges against them. Those evaluations would be available to interested ad agencies. "Unless we convince certain organizations to come into the clearing process, the work of the Review Board will be of little value." He suggested several individuals who might be willing to serve: labor columnist Victor Riesel and Eugene Lyons of the *Readers Digest*, both knowledgeable anti-Communists and both known to be fair; the well-known labor leader Richard Walsh, president of the International Alliance of Theatrical Stage Employees; and a Catholic priest, possibly Father Benjamin Massey or Father Philip Carey.

He met with James O'Neil, past commander of the American Legion, then in charge of publications, who had been on a similar West Coast board for the film industry "where the problems were far less complicated." Heller reported, "O'Neil was cooperative and even willing to serve. But, he stressed, 'Were I to serve, the board must be 'unofficial.' '" In a meeting for the same purpose with the New York Archdiocese of the Catholic Church, it was concluded that they, on the other hand, would not be interested in participating if the board were unofficial.

Conference delegates continued to find fault. Some now felt the review board should be eliminated entirely. The networks raised fears that it could become an antitrust matter. Advertisers worried that, if they re-hired a controversial performer, even more damaging pressure would be mounted against them. They worried too that Communists might attempt "to take over" the hearings. Finally, the advertisers reverted to their original position: that it was a union-network problem and they, alone, should find the solution.

None of the twenty-five conferees—excepting George Heller and Robert Dreyer, legal counsel for Metromedia / Channel 5—were willing to present ideas for, or commit themselves to, action of any kind. After fifteen months of wrangling, AFTRA delegates Vinton Hayworth and Ned Wever too announced their opposition to any and all plans for "they would not afford equal opportunity to persons blacklisted because of their anti-Communist activities." Here was a familiar and oft-repeated charge by AWARE, the Artists' Committee, and others. John Cogley (1956) would write,

> It is practically impossible to find specific, incontrovertible evidence . . . and this point is agreed to by both liberal and right-wing anti-Communists. . . . It can be established beyond question, though, that there was never any network-wide or agency-wide blacklisting of anti-Communists.

Cogley's report on blacklisting in broadcasting was soundly criticized by the right for not making a more thorough investigation of this complaint. Only weeks after its publication, he was subpoenaed by HUAC and interrogated as to the patriotism of his researchers and the "true purpose" of the report. But Ralph S. Brown, Jr. (1958), would write as well: "It seems unlikely . . . that any blacklisting of anti-Communists ever approached the pervasiveness of the recent blacklisting of pro-Communists."

It has been documented, however, that due to other factors, certain individuals were not employed. Vinton Hayworth, for example, worked regularly throughout the early 1950s for producers outspoken on the left as well as on the right. But by the mid 1950s, more than one right-leaning producer would no longer hire him because he "was a divisive element" or because he "caused trouble" in the studio (Cogley 1956). Hayworth had become an unemployable, a controversial person, only one more in that vast company he had helped to create and he so reviled.

When the industry conference died out in early 1954, Heller's last hope for a reasoned, joint solution to the problem of blacklisting died with it. During his brilliant career, he made few mistakes in judgment. Trusting the industry, shackled as it was by self-serving interests, to rid itself of a practice it embraced for its own protection was, clearly, one of them.

•

The 1954 AFTRA National Convention rewarded Heller's long, careful campaign for a pension and welfare plan; it gave him a mandate and a go-ahead for his single-demand strategy. At the Saturday night election of officers, the delegates gave him a new president as well: a brilliant unionist, the leader of the movement for mandate, the moody, ultraconservative "dictator of the LA local" Frank Nelson (so named by members of his own board); and a new, national first vice president: New York's own Vinton Hayworth.

Negotiations for the AFTRA Code of Fair Practice for Network Television Broadcasting were at hand. If any pessimism was being expressed, and it was, it was not to be heard in the offices of the newly energized George Heller. Sharpened by intimations of his own mortality and a resolve, perhaps, to make up for what he was unable to do in relation to blacklisting, Heller prophetically vowed to Mary Sagarin on the eve of the sessions, "I will get this if I never get anything else in my life."

Industry learned quickly that Heller had come to the table this time around for one thing and one thing only: a pension and welfare plan for his members. "I made it clear," he reported, "that unless there's a commitment on the concept, it was useless to proceed further."

Heller was asking employers to fund the entire plan, and he wanted a contribution from them of 5 percent:

> We're not introducing a higher figure to negotiate down, and we're not saying five percent now for the purpose of settling at three percent. We've gone to considerable difficulty appraising what we need for a worthwhile program and what we need is five percent. (Lipton 1963)

Contributions would be based on the gross earnings of every performer, from those earning the basic minimums (the vast majority of AFTRAns) to those earning as much as the Jack Bennys and the Jimmy Durantes of television. And, in what NBC's chief negotiator, George Fuchs, later described as "Heller's most important concept," the larger contributions would help fund the plan for the many whose contributions were inadequate to meet the costs. The concept was known as the "Robin Hood theory."

Henry Jaffe recalled, "The concern of the networks was that if they gave AFTRA a plan, it would open the door to all the others. It seemed almost ridiculous to think the industry would ever abide such a thing. But, again, it was CBS's chief negotiator, Zack Becker, who said to George privately, 'Stay with it; I think you're going to win.' "

"But winning was slow going," said Jaffe, "and hard for George. We didn't talk about it, but I saw he was in big trouble. He and I were all over town on negotiations, and we'd stop at noon to grab a sandwich. He'd take one bite, then quit; he paid no attention to it."

There was little interest in contributions on "gross earnings" from most around the table. Not until several behind-the-scenes sessions, during which the networks helped persuade the agencies that "the people who supply the industry with entertainment must be made to feel as secure as possible," did the group express a readiness to negotiate. There were the expected counterdemands—calls for big cutbacks in the radio and transcription codes—but none would come about.

Accepting no concessions, Heller achieved his most spectacular triumph and his greatest legacy—the AFTRA Pension and Welfare Plan—the first of its kind among performers' unions. Within several years, the plan would apply to all AFTRA codes, radio, transcription, and phonograph recordings alike. Employer contributions have always varied with each local and national contract. The range in 1993 was between 9 percent, the lowest, and 12.65 percent, the highest.

Zack Becker said at the time: "George did a wonderful job in his own colorful way; he traded all other improvements against this plan which, I think, was proper because it represented an awful big slice of dough"—an estimated four to six million dollars in the first two years alone.

"It was clear to us that a system to take care of his performers was absolutely essential to George, and we in industry agreed among ourselves that its time had come," Becker continued. "The sessions were tough and exhausting, but George was indefatigable. When we reached a final agreement, I saw a momentary look of disbelief on his face" (Lipton 1963).

•

16

~~~~~~~~

McCarthy Falls While McCarthyism Prospers

An event of high drama got under way in the U.S. Senate on April 22, 1954: the Army-McCarthy hearings; Joseph McCarthy, chairman of the Permanent Subcommittee on Investigations versus Robert T. Stevens, secretary of the army. The charge: the secretary had concealed evidence of espionage at a New Jersey base.

How far had our proud and now-prosperous nation come since World War II? The Soviet Union, our former ally, was now our major competitor and, with their acquisition of an atomic bomb, our foremost threat. We had been thrust into the Cold War and, too soon, into a hot "police action" on Korean soil. In little more than a decade, we had battled both fascism and communism; an estimated 461,000 young American lives had been lost. Still, we felt no safer, no better off for any of it. How could things have gone so wrong?

According to the simplistic junior senator from Wisconsin, the fault lay with the Eastern intellectuals, the Washington policy makers, the twenty-five thousand American Communist traitors, and their numberless "liberal dupes" here at home. Unrestrained by either political party, McCarthy was left free to hurl his outrageous accusations, including that of "treason" against former President Truman and the sitting Dwight D. Eisenhower administration. Despite his earlier grandiose promises "to uncover massive infiltration into the State Department," by 1954 he had yet to produce a single Communist.

The Army-McCarthy hearings were carried in full by the ABC and Dumont television networks. It was this factor, the public's living-room view of the real McCarthy—the truculent, erratic, often inarticulate McCarthy—together with news analyst Edward R. Murrow's brilliant, albeit belated, commentaries on CBS, that signaled the end of his four-year-long witch-hunting madness and, finally, of the senator himself.

"We must not confuse dissent with disloyalty," spoke Murrow on the March 7 *See It Now*. "We must remember always that accusation is not proof, and that conviction depends upon evidence and due process of law." (Following the broadcast, Murrow too became a target of the vigilante publication *Counterattack*.)

Nine months later, at a special session of the Senate, McCarthy would be condemned by his peers for bringing the body into "dishonor and disrepute through his displays of contemptuous and insulting behavior" and "for obstructing its constitutional process." The vote to censure passed (67 to 22). Three years later, ravaged by alcohol he would be dead.

During his heyday, however, McCarthy and his vast army had victimized countless numbers of good, decent citizens. They included not only artists and unionists but librarians, college professors, public school teachers, journalists, and clergymen—anyone with political perceptions differing from theirs.

On June 22, 1954, CBS newsman Don Hollenbeck became the latest AFTRAn to fall. While anchoring the *Eleven O'Clock News*, immediately following the Murrow broadcast, Hollenbeck proffered a glowing, on-the-air tribute to his colleague. The result was a vitriolic blast from right-wing columnist Jack O'Brian in the *Journal-American* and others. There were demands from high places that he be fired.

Suffering from regular attacks on his liberally oriented *CBS Views the News*, plus a recent bitter divorce, Hollenbeck became a sick man. Twice in the preceding months he had been hospitalized with severe stomach ulcers. Now he was publicly smeared again and faced losing his job. Hollenbeck, father of two, ended his life alone in his New York apartment. The cause of death was gas asphyxiation. He was forty-nine.

•

Obtaining political clearance, establishing one's innocence through recantation (accompanied by "certifiable anti-Communist acts") or through "proved" denials to those responsible for one's blacklisting, was an excruciating, often expensive undertaking. Be it sought from HUAC or the Senate Internal Security Subcommittee; from columnists Jack O'Brian, George Sokolsky, or Frederick Woltman; from CBS "security officers" Joseph Ream, Alfred Berry, or Daniel T. O'Shea; from the Batten, Barton, Durstine and Osbourne (BBD & O) agency's Jack Wren; from the American Legion's James O'Neil or Laurence Johnson; or from a combination of any of those and more, there were precious few who could or would give that clearance.

The American Business Consultants, publishers of *Red Channels* and *Counterattack*, claimed that their door was always open. The New York *Post* quoted Ted Kirkpatrick as saying: "[Anyone] can feel free to come to me and my associates and convince us that a mistake has been made or give us reasons why they should not be listed."

Editor Francis McNamara drew an even sharper picture of the publisher's "open-door" policy: "You should see the big act some of them put on in this very office. It's a panic to hear them! Those acts that we consider obviously fake, without the people showing us proper affidavits, we don't print their statements" (Miller 1952). But for the few they did believe and ultimately print, the damage had already been done.

In what turned out to be a highly profitable spin-off from American Business Consultants, cofounder Ken Bierly established an auxiliary "clearance" service. *Sponsor* magazine commented that the consultants serve

> at one and the same time as disturber of the peace, prosecuting attorney, judge, jury and detective agency. That is to say, it publishes allegations in *Red Channels*; then follows them up by urging letter-writers to put pressure on sponsors in *Counterattack*; later holds hearings on the accused in its private offices; and personally solicits sponsors to hire its detective agency "research service." (Miller 1952)

Vincent Hartnett of AWARE, whose earnings would rise to approximately twenty-six thousand dollars a year, expanded into the clearance service as well. His standard fee for a political check had run a modest twenty dollars per head; five dollars per head for a long list, two dollars per head for a recheck. But for a clearance—with no guarantee, of course, that it would materialize—Hartnett could and did take in from between two hundred and three hundred dollars per person. To establish new clients, however, he first needed to establish new victims (or possible informants). Having long since run out of so-called subversives from public records, Hartnett now beat the television bushes, aided by members of AFTRA-AWARE, for more grist for his blacklisting mill.

Employing what he later described in court to attorney Louis Nizer as "a kind of trick used by interrogators. . . . You put it as fact and ask for affirmation or denial," Hartnett set up his contacts. Here are but a few of scores of examples of his brand of terrorism. The first came in a letter to actor Leslie Barrett, dated December 9, 1954.

> In preparing a book on the Left Theater I came across certain information regarding you. A photograph of the 1952 New York May Day Parade shows you marching next to _____ . It is always pos-

sible that people who have, in good faith, supported certain causes come to realize that their support was misplaced. Therefore, I am writing you to ascertain if there has been any change in your position. You are, of course, under no obligation to reply . . . [but] if I do not hear from you, I must conclude that your marching . . . is still an accurate index of your position and sympathies. . . . I am enclosing a three-cent stamp for a reply.

Barrett read the implicit threat. He knew the ramifications of being listed by AWARE. His lawyer (his uncle, a Mr. Harvey L. Klein) responded: "Mr. Barrett has never marched in a May Day Parade in his life, and has no Communist leanings or sympathies whatsoever." But another letter from inquisitor Hartnett arrived.

To my surprise I received a letter . . . from a Mr. Klein, a lawyer. I was according you a privilege of commenting on certain information in my possession . . . not Mr. Klein or any other member of your family. . . . Parenthetically, is this the same Harvey Klein who is listed as having signed Communist Party nominating petitions in 1939–40?

Frankly, I am disappointed. In my experience . . . people who had nothing to hide did not pull a lawyer into the discussion. They simply denied or affirmed the evidence. I hope you will be equally . . . direct.

Barrett's uncle was *not* the signer of the petitions. Barrett was *not* a marcher in the parade. An answer, written in his own hand, reiterating his absolute denial for himself and refuting the innuendo about lawyer Klein, was posted at once. Hartnett responded:

I appreciate your personal warranty. . . . I hope you incurred no expense by the unnecessary move of calling in a lawyer—this only muddied the waters. Frankly, two people, prominent in radio and TV who know you, thought the man pictured in the May Day Parade photo was you. . . . Research to establish positive identification . . . is continuing.

Barrett showed the correspondence to Gene Francis. Francis, in turn, told him to go see George Heller. Barrett remembered, "Heller scowled as he read the letters. Clearly, he was sickened by the man. 'Don't let this pass,' he said. 'Meet with Hartnett. It may not be right, but they are a powerful group. They can ruin your career.'

"Heller's advice that I cooperate with this horrible vigilante astounded me. For whatever his reasons, I saw he couldn't help me; he seemed shackled by his own board. I would have thought him a far more admirable person if he'd resigned. His advice that I go to the FBI made more sense. But all they could say was, 'You [meaning AFTRA] should never have cooperated with those people to begin with.' "

In a second example of Hartnett's methods, actor Frank Maxwell, a former independent candidate for the TvA board, a member of the old Anti-Blacklisting Committee, and a future president of AFTRA (1984–89), recalled his first encounter.

"My career was going full tilt in the early 1950s. Between radio, television, Broadway, and London's East End, I was working all the time. Then, one day," he told me, "I got a phone call from a Vincent Hartnett. 'Frank, there's a producer I know who'd like to use you on his show, but you have some things on your record. I'm looking at a statement here that you attended a caucus meeting at so-and-so's house on such-and-such date with so-and-so people.'

" 'Oh, that's not so strange. What else?'

" 'I also have it on reliable authority that a Frank Maxwell, who attended the University of Michigan on so-and-so date, was a member of the Young Communist League.'

" 'Oh? Were there any other Maxwells there at the time?'

" 'No, only one. Frank Maxwell.'

" 'But his name wasn't Frank, was it? His name was Charles.' I didn't use the name Frank until I came to New York. 'And Charles Maxwell was never a member of the Young Communist League!' " And in an aside to me he said, "even though I could sympathize with them."

Maxwell continued, "But facts didn't matter to Hartnett. From that phone call on, I was done in television. Washed up. Finished. My name wasn't on any other list but Hartnett's—the buddy of the Artists' Committee."

There are observers who, from the beginning of blacklisting, felt that it was more professional jealousy than superpatriotism motivating actors to name fellow actors—that, with so many talented performers home from the war and making their way back into radio—then dominated by the Artists' Committee's group—it was the committee's way of getting rid of some of the competition. Several asked me if I thought it merely coincidence that so many of those blacklisted were also Jewish. Frank Maxwell said, "I served as a gunner for my country, and with all their phony Americanism, not one of those AFRA bastards ever put on an army uniform.

In a third example of Hartnett's terrorism, actor Bert Cowlan told me, "The first thing I did after hearing from Hartnett was arrange to clear up the misinformation he had on me. I told him that I and another person would meet with him that week for lunch.

" 'You don't need to bring a lawyer,' Hartnett snapped.

" 'Who said it was a lawyer?' I answered. It was, in fact, my old naval commander. A former intelligence officer in the U.S. Navy—as Hartnett had been. He volunteered to stand up for me, in full uniform.

"But even after I proved I was only twelve at the time he had me listed as a member of a 'subversive' organization, even though I later sent him a copy of a letter from the (then) HUAC chairman, Harold H. Velde, stating, 'A thorough search of HUAC records had failed to reveal any information regarding [me],' I still wasn't taken off his list and allowed to go back to work."

Cowlan was offered a different road to clearance, however. Here is a portion of a Hartnett letter to him, dated October 1954:

> There is only one effective way of setting things right . . . and that is to stand shoulder to shoulder with all anti-Communists in AFTRA on clear-cut issues involving Communism . . . *when the chips are down*, there should be no factionalism.
>
> This is especially urgent in your case, because of your past close association with the Independent group. . . . Let me know what you do (though I'll probably hear of it anyway,) so I can 'update' the material on you and—I hope—offset it. I am happy to assist . . . anyone sincerely trying to avoid the pitfalls of the present and mend the mistakes of the past.

By 1954, the blacklisting machine was operating smoothly throughout the industry. The time had long gone—if, indeed, it had ever existed—when George Heller could have made a difference. It needed many George Hellers, each a leader in his own segment of the business, to end it. Heller knew that. He also knew that there was no such unity of purpose, no such desire for unified action. Still, he told Gene Francis, "In a dynamic democracy, corrupt behavior will ultimately be rejected." Four years had passed since the emergence of McCarthy. Now he was discredited and soon to leave public office. Surely, fair-minded AFTRAns would rally together in large enough numbers to clean their house as well.

The December local board elections brought together yet another independent slate—this time of twenty-six candidates. Despite the past and probable future damage to their careers, they mounted a vigorous campaign against the radical board, demanding, "Action, once and for all, by AFTRA on its ever-repeated opposition to the blacklist." And like the many independents who had gone before, they were soundly trounced.

Within weeks, AWARE, Inc., went public with a supplement to its privately disseminated bulletins. In a broad, general mailing, *Publication No. 12* hailed the victory of the New York incumbents and proclaimed: "AFTRA is one of the few unions in which flatly declared anti-Communism and anti-totalitarianism have won many clear victories." Wrong:

at the 1949 CIO National Convention, delegates voted out all unions with Communists or perceived Communists in leadership positions. The AFL board had had no Communists since the mid 1930s.

Publication No. 12 went on to besmirch the independents' names. Its evidence of their un-Americanism included working for former Vice President Henry A. Wallace's presidential candidacy; speaking out on behalf of Willie McGee, a wrongfully convicted southern black man; addressing a memorial meeting for the late J. Edward Bromberg; performing in a play produced by the Committee for the Negro in the Arts; supporting a recent coal miners' strike; and being praised for a performance by the *Daily Worker*. And there were those with but a single charge: that they spent time at the Actors' Lab, a professional acting company in Hollywood operated by members of the old Group Theatre, or that they belonged to the Actors' Studio, or that they studied at the Dramatic Workshop, or that they married a liberal television director.

"Thus, out of 26 candidates," *Publication No. 12* continued, "at least 13 have what are considered significant public records in connection with the Communist-front apparatus. Still others have what may be less significant records." The sheet concluded: "In the opinion of qualified observers, this year's Independent slate demonstrates the need for a full-fledged official investigation of the entertainment industry in New York City."

HUAC had not often appeared in the City; glamorous Hollywood held far more appeal. Since the Dies Committee's investigation of the Federal Theater Project in 1939 and the brief Velde hearings in 1953—neither of which noticeably aided the study of subversion in America—essentially all of HUAC's work had been done for it by the local vigilantes and the vigilante press. AWARE's call for "a full-fledged official investigation" was clearly intended to silence all spirited independents and end their opposition—now and in the future.

AFTRAns were appalled. AWARE's "proof of disloyalty" was out in the open now for all to see. The effect on many moderates, who formerly may have felt uncomfortable associating themselves with critics of their union's officers, was to unite them—not with the politics of the defeated candidates, necessarily, but against the tactics of Vincent Hartnett and members of AWARE, Inc.

•

"I was ten years old," said Francesca Heller, George and Clara's youngest daughter, now director of a child-care center in New York, "and my whole world was falling apart.

"My father looked so bad; he hardly ate. I was told he wasn't well but how serious it was I didn't know. My mother was under a tremendous strain, seeing the man she loved in such trouble and so desperately sick, and unable to help.

"I knew that many of our friends were also in trouble, that it had something to do with their being 'outspoken,' and something to do with the kind of work my father was in. And it all had to do with Senator Joseph McCarthy, whom I'd seen on television and knew a little about.

"I was told, 'If anyone asks about your dad—where he works or what he does for a living—don't tell them anything; just say you don't know.' It was all very scary. I withdrew from my friends; my father was my only playmate. Yet, in an odd sort of way, I had a feeling of importance—as if I was in the middle of an intrigue of sorts."

•

In early January 1955, trustees were appointed to the new, jointly administered AFTRA-Industry Pension and Welfare Fund. On the union side were George Heller, Frank Nelson, and Bud Collyer. Representing management were Zack Becker, then president of Air Features, Inc.; Emanuel "Manny" Sachs, vice president of RCA; and Edward G. Wilson, vice president of the J. Walter Thompson Advertising Agency. Martin E. Segal and Co. was the fund's administrator. Together, these men would launch a plan that was the pride of the union, the envy of the entire industry, and the forerunner of all such plans in the entertainment field to come.

Heller spoke to the New York members: "To you who feel it was a mistake not to also improve minimum wages we can go back 'to the table' in two years and correct that, but we and your Board felt it was extremely important to build a substantial fund at the outset, while the money is still being made in 'live' TV."

"George knew the day was coming fast," Gene Francis said, "when all entertainment would be 'in the can,' whether on tape or on film. With the established 'full original fee' for program repeats and now pension and welfare, he felt assured that AFTRA was in a good position to face the future."

Aside from the landmark Pension and Welfare Fund, however, 1955 would long be remembered by AFTRAns as the year their union was turned inside out—and nearly upside down.

•

The March 16 headline in *Variety* read: "SEVEN UP ON AFTRA CARPET." The article went on:

[The] New York local of AFTRA will be asked to vote on a resolution next Tuesday (22) condemning seven members. Latter are Jean Hayworth, Vinton Hayworth, William Keene, Richard Keith, William Neil, Ned Wever and Leigh Whipper. They are listed as board members of Aware, Inc., which . . . "attacked an entire (independent) slate of candidates for AFTRA office," accusing them of association with " 'the Communist front apparatus.' " . . .

A bulletin sent out . . . by Acting Executive Secretary Alex McKee, of N.Y. AFTRA, referred to the then proposed resolution as a violation of the Union's constitution. It suggested certain revisions to conform . . . and apparently these were made [enabling] the document to be presented at the [membership meeting] at the Astor Hotel at 8 P.M.

Modified by the deletion of the names of the seven, the resolution stated:

Whereas, in its News Supplement to the Membership Bulletin Aware No. 12, December 27, 1954, Aware, Inc. publicly and scandalously attacked an entire slate of candidates for AFTRA office accusing said candidates of associating with the 'Communist front apparatus' by the now familiar smear methods of inference and innuendo from alleged 'public records,' and

Whereas, it is now common knowledge that such attacks are calculated to, and have in fact served, to injure members in jobs and to deprive them of economic opportunity and security in their professional life, and

Whereas, AFTRA has in the past expressed a policy of opposition to the circulation of such inflammatory material or lists, and

Whereas, such attacks upon a slate of candidates undermine the democratic process of elections in the Union and has the decided tendency of discouraging the right or duty of members to take an active part in the election of officers to head our Union,

Now Therefore Be It Resolved: 1. That the membership deplores the circulation or promulgation of smear tracts or lists in general and the one published by Aware, Inc. in particular which seeks to condemn the entire "independent" slate which recently ran for office against our incumbent officers in order that we may

a. preserve and protect our democratic process and its effective operation, and

b. protect all of our membership from the harmful effects of such attacks which would undo the very point and purpose of our Union.

Be It Further Resolved: 2. That Aware, Inc. be condemned for interfering in the internal affairs of our Union.

The resolution was proposed by actor George Ives, who was then appearing on Broadway in *The Seven Year Itch*, and submitted by one hundred members in good standing, a number of whom had already been targeted by AWARE. A general mailing from the one hundred signers (plus many others) followed, outlining the action taken and calling for support.

AWARE countered menacingly:

> Members of AFTRA with *notorious* Communist-front records apparently succeeded in getting some unsuspecting AFTRAns to sign the letter with them so that all of the signers, *guilty and innocent alike*, would be in the same boat.

A palpable chill fell over the hundred; only fifty-eight names remained on the motion by the crucial March 22, 1955, meeting.

The resolution came up under new business. The visibly ailing George Heller was there but did not participate; it seemed, rather, that he was a spectator—observant, apathetic, separate. Members sat riveted to their seats as the pain, the hatred, the paranoia of the last few years was played out before them.

Leslie Barrett, a quiet man not given to speech making, rose in support. He read excerpts from Vincent Hartnett's letters.

> Since then, I've experienced nothing but grief and anxiety. . . . I can neither hold my food nor sleep. But few will speak out. Why? Because, "I've got a little list," as the saying goes, and if your name is on it you do not work. . . . One is afraid to look at anyone, to speak to anyone, to protest on the union floor. You come in silently; you leave silently.

Godfrey P. Schmidt, president of AWARE, smartly defended the organization. He denied that it was in any way involved in blacklisting. In a slip of the tongue, however, he quoted from the original motion to condemn—the one rejected by AFTRA as being unconstitutional.

He was challenged from the floor by an irate member, "How did you know of its contents, not being a board member and privy to internal board discussions?"

The motion was brought to him, Schmidt responded, "by the aggrieved board members, who found themselves the butts of a set of slanderous charges and aspersions." And as he, Schmidt, was an attorney, those same members requested that he "write a set of charges against the proponents," which he did. And as he was the president of AWARE, he "filed them" for release via *Publication No. 12*.

Schmidt pressed forward:

One thing should be clear . . . [that] criticism is part of the American tradition. It would be a sorry and sad day, ladies and gentlemen, if you as a union were to curtail criticism of a slate of candidates. . . . No matter who tells the story, these candidates' records should be laid bare . . . these people, who were foolish enough to be beguiled by Communist propaganda are precisely not the people to be entrusted to office.

A member answered angrily: "AWARE's criticism is not sent to AFTRA members, nor did Schmidt bring his criticisms to the floor of the union but, rather, he sends them to people who could have no interest in our union and who have no vote here."

Time limitations brought the fierce confrontation prematurely to an end. It would be resumed at the next regular AFTRA membership meeting in May, two months hence. In the interim, the matter was taken up by Actors' Equity Council, Ralph Bellamy presiding. There, a motion to condemn AWARE passed unanimously. "It is simple," said councilor Thomas Chalmers. "You are either for blacklisting or you are against it. It's time now to stand up and be counted!"

•

17

~~~~~

Membership Finds Its Voice

George Heller would not share in this climactic moment for his beloved union, so many years in the making. Seven weeks before, no longer able to dismiss his gnawing misery, he was hospitalized and scheduled for a second surgery. The cancer was found to be inoperable.

The board was still not to know the facts or the prognosis. Henry Jaffe advised, "It may be necessary for George to have medical attention for some time and, depending on the patient and his rate of recovery, expenses might run high." AFTRA voted to assume financial responsibility and directed acting executive Alex McKee, a former singer and early officer of the radio federation, to send "flowers or some other gift at frequent intervals during Heller's hospital stay."

As the May 24 New York local membership meeting was gaveled to order, Heller lay desperately ill and in agonizing pain. But his members were there, and through some of their speeches he would, at last, publicly speak his heart as well.

•

Ventilation in the crowded downstairs casino of the New York City Center was inadequate for the heat and passion that would be generated there. Members sat rigid, straining to read each face, grasp every word. The stakes were enormous for AFTRA—but even more so for hundreds of performers and their hard-earned, oh so vulnerable careers.

"Meetings had become literal battlegrounds between the two warring factions," said Mary Sagarin. This meeting would rise above the battleground; it would become a hall of justice. Singer Travis Johnson, then president of the local, announced a one-hour limit on debate, opposing sides to alternate, three minutes per speaker.

A telegram from blacklisted actress Kim Hunter, an Academy Award winner for her role as the wife in Tennessee Williams' *Streetcar Named*

Desire, was read. There was a murmur of disbelief from the liberal side; the telegram supported AWARE. Only later would we learn that the wire had been sent involuntarily. It, plus a two-hundred-dollar clearance fee, was the price she had to pay before Hartnett would allow her to work again in television.

Actor Harold Gary was given the floor.

> I have never been smeared or blacklisted; I have never joined any or-ganization other than AFTRA, the YMCA, and a couple of veteran's organizations. My interest . . . is motivated purely by an objective sense of justice and fair play, the welfare of this trade union and my fellow members. Mr. Schmidt presumed [earlier] to give us an edu-cation on American tradition. . . . I should like to presume to tell Mr. Schmidt something about actors.
>
> We are the representative cross-section of America . . . composed in part, of ex-ministers, ex-newspapermen, ex-college professors. Look around you . . . actors are tall and short, fat and thin, outgoing and reserved. . . . They are of every political persuasion, worship God in many different ways, some of them being atheists . . . among them are middle-of-the-roaders, some far to the right, some far to the left.
>
> But strangely enough, Mr. Schmidt, I like them all—or nearly all. The purchase price of my esteem . . . is not total agreement with my ideas and opinions. I think my fellow actors are entitled to their own ideas and opinions just so long as they don't try to use them to blud-geon, to intimidate, to blackmail, or to superimpose their beliefs on me. This, I will not stand for, neither will they.

Actor Bill Keene, board member of AWARE and the New York local, said that one aim of anticommunism "is to aid people who have been taken in, who have seen the error of their ways and want now to get off the Communist hook." He then recommended "for your consideration a pamphlet published by . . . AWARE called, *The Road Back.*" *The Road Back* outlined a twelve-step program that a person in trouble might use to achieve rehabilitation. First, one should ask, "Do I love my country?" Then, the following actions should be taken, in part: full public or private disclosure, with identification of those who "drew the subject in"; vol-untary interviews with the FBI; testimony and other cooperation with HUAC and all federal, state, and local un-American committees; public announcement of one's change of position about the union through speeches at AFTRA meetings and letters to the *Stand By!* editor; refusals to support the "crypto-Communist element" on any issue—"No matter how attractive it may then appear." The pamphlet made a final observation: "If the subject's new convictions draw him to, or back to religion, so much the better." Keene concluded,

> The faction that opposes those of us now in office . . . are urging you to take a step that would blacken this union's good name. Forever guilty of irresponsible thinking, they would besmirch our record of clean anti-Communist unionism; the first organization, ever to be condemned or censured by AFTRA, would be—if these people had their way—an anti-Communist group.

Actor Douglas Gordon asked,

> On whose authority have you taken such actions? By what right do you make political book on your fellow members? Did the membership vote that you were to be the political arbiters of this union? Are you duly elected members of the government engaged in official work?
>
> The question has been asked why the people involved didn't bother to answer the allegations against them. Why should they? Why should anyone have to answer to any organization which circulates miscellaneous derogatory information? —an organization working without the authorization of the union, and in no way connected with the state or federal government?
>
> Until a member has been proven guilty on specific charges and expelled . . . it is the union's job to guarantee his right to work. . . . To stop the destruction of the democratic processes within the union, AFTRA should forbid its members to cooperate in any way with such organizations; AFTRA should condemn AWARE, Inc.

Announcer Rex Marshall, a member of the local board, spoke:

> If the members indicated [by AWARE] feel that these accusations are not true . . . I am astonished that none have filed formal charges against the members of AWARE who they accuse of 'conduct unbecoming AFTRA members.' . . . We would welcome such charges if it would bring out anything which was unjust and slanderous. . . . It seems to me that adopting this resolution—which I hope won't happen—would be like . . . a group of accused criminals saying to a police department, "We can't refute the charges, but we certainly deplore the investigation." . . .
>
> We are indebted to a group which gives its time freely to expose elements that are dangerous to this country and to this union. . . . I don't think you can condemn a vigilante committee for being vigilant, but if it is accused of being a lynching committee, I think the accusations should be made by the persons who consider themselves in danger of being lynched.

Actress Nancy R. Pollack, who had not intended to speak, was none-theless compelled to because of the "flagrant lies." "I am one of the members 'indicted' and listed by Aware. I hereby deny those charges and call those who made them thieves and liars. . . . They are trying to steal my good name, and this is a very grave offense." Pollack continued,

> They have me down as being a teacher for the Arts and Professions. I have never taught there in my life, but that is not important. The fact is, that by association—and that is what they try to push down our throats—by association they will destroy us. And what is more important than Equity or AFTRA, they will destroy our nation. . . . I tell you these people are vicious, and must be scourged and taken out of circulation.

Actor Vinton Hayworth then spoke:

> During the past few days we have all received voluminous literature concerning the subjects of tonight's meeting. All I wish to do is put a few facts . . . into the record. . . . I want to impress upon you, I am not speaking on an emotional basis. I have the facts to prove whatever I say, and it is a principle of law in this country that facts are not libelous.
>
> The majority of you received this long white paper dated May 18, 1955, signed by some 176 people. It's headed, "I'm not interested in politics," the inference being that politics have no place on our union floor. I am in complete agreement with that statement, or would be, if it were based on the truth.
>
> In another piece, a long yellow paper, a cry was made for "Truth and Decency" in our union. I am in whole-hearted agreement with that principle. Now going back to the long white letter, there is a reference to Aware, Inc., as an "outside organization," and further on, it underscored the fact that "seven AFTRA members are on its Board." That is true. My wife and I are two of the seven. We have never denied it, rather we do proudly affirm it, as do the other five.
>
> Now we come to the cry of "Truth and Decency." Why didn't the proposers of that letter have the decency to tell you the truth in that letter? Why didn't they tell you that the alleged politics they refer to are, in reality, participation in such activities as May Day Parades, entertaining for Communist-front cultural groups, Communist training schools, signing petitions for convicted Communist leaders and spies? The authors of that letter may call it politics, but the truth is, it is aiding and abetting the Communist Party.
>
> Did they have the decency to tell you that seven other members who signed that letter were, according to sworn testimony, members of another outside organization? Yes, fellow members, an organiza-

tion outside of AFTRA, outside the bounds of honor; yes, outside the United States—the Communist Party. Did they have the decency to tell you that? You bet they didn't! And nowhere in the letter do you see a proposal to condemn those seven "identified members" of the Communist Party. Isn't that strange?

Actor Leslie Barrett said that there had been a

clear attempt to flout this country's laws of jurisprudence . . . to tear up the Bill of Rights. We do not need AWARE, Inc., to alert us to those vocal ones in our own house. . . . It is not the vocal ones we have to fear. . . . [but] those we can't see and hear, that only proper law enforcement agencies can find. . . .

I do not wish to convey the impression that I condemn the entire Board of AFTRA, or that they are all of a grand conspiracy. . . . Some will continue to serve well, as they have in the past, but there are those who should not be elected to office. The table of government is no place to seat a fanatic mind. Let them continue to compete in the marketplace of talent; deny that to no man, as they have denied it to others.

I have been called "fool" for having . . . spoken up for the principles I believe in. To those, I would . . . answer: when fear corrodes your brain, as it did mine, when you cannot speak your mind, when you cannot walk with your head up, then there are things more important than self. That is the line from which no man should retreat.

Television host Bud Collyer then spoke:

It is unfortunate that AFTRA's record in the struggle against Communism has been obscured because so much of our energy is consumed in fruitless internal warfare on the blacklisting issue. Individual cases of injustice have aroused our deepest emotions and have caused conflicts between two groups of our membership who should be serving this union by working together. The two are both outspoken enemies of Communism; they differ only in the quality and the depth of their anti-Communism.

By now it should be clear that the loss of job opportunities indiscriminately affects the so-called right as well as the so-called left. . . . Nevertheless, the hue and cry . . . has rarely, if ever, been raised in protest against the loss of work suffered by the militant anti-Communist. Why do we not dedicate ourselves to fight all injustice with equal fervor? . . . On what basis do we demand civil rights for Communist sympathizers but none for Fascist sympathizers?

Whether you agree with AWARE or not . . . I implore you to defeat this resolution. . . . It is not the intelligent way to attack the problem. . . . Merely because an evil exists, don't let us be stampeded into action that could conceivably threaten everything that we at AFTRA have strained and sweated to build. . . . Demonstrate your desire to have our problems faced, as in the past, by cool and tempered judgment rather than [this] ill-considered, inexpedient action. . . . I call upon every thinking member of AFTRA to join with me in the defeat of this resolution, not only those opposed to it, but also by the votes of each and every one of its proponents.

The debate had run out of time; the motion to condemn was declared in order. An angry skirmish broke out as former TvA officer Bob Spiro demanded a secret ballot. President Johnson refused, maintaining that the local had always enjoyed open voting; he saw no reason to change from the usual show of hands. Spiro prevailed, however. The vote was made, the ballots collected.

Speeches for national board and convention delegates followed. The acrimony persisted as the opposing slates continued in their blistering assaults on one another. Demands were made that Hayworth disclose the "facts" he claimed to have about certain members. "I am not free to reveal that information," he countered.

Then a call to order was made for the reading of the results. The members froze. In a startling reversal of the old political divisions, the vote was 197 in favor of condemnation, 149 against.

Immediately, incumbents granted themselves a referendum claiming that the count represented too small a segment of New York's five-thousand-plus voting membership. The Artists' Committee group was, in fact, banking on an overturn once the decision was in the hands of the larger, friendlier rank and file. Hadn't they won every other vote in recent years?

As the referendum deadline approached, newspaper columnists all over the City made comment. Among the pro-AWARE majority, Leon Racht in the *Journal-American* warned that a vote to condemn "would, in effect, poke the Communist camel's nose under the tent of the AFTRAns" (June 18, 1955). And on the eve of the count, Jack Gould of *The Times* wrote: "If AWARE is condemned, it will mark a major defeat for a group which uses methods that have come into increasing public disfavor. . . . How the actors vote this week will have great importance for people besides themselves" (June 26, 1955).

●

It was a sad irony that the lead story in the June 1955 edition of *Stand By!*—the same issue that carried the details of the historic May meeting—was the announcement of the death of George Heller. The article began: "AFTRA suffered the greatest loss of its eighteen-year history on

Memorial Day, May 30 just past." It ended: "George Heller leaves his widow, Mrs. Clara Heller; daughters Toni, 16, and Francesca Julia, 11; and sisters, Mrs. William Jacoby and Mrs. Samuel Lipman. He also leaves an organization of 33 locals and a national membership of over 18,000. He was 49." Jack Gould wrote,

> With the death of George Heller, labor has lost one of its most influential leaders. . . . He was fiercely devoted to the economic well-being of performers on the air; all are in his debt. His fairness, his patience and good humor won him the respect of network executives as well. Mr. Heller was an able labor leader; he was also a fine human being. (*The New York Times*, June 31, 1955)

Clara Heller told me, "Without Henry Jaffe and Jean Muir, I never would have made it. They were with us at the hospital night and day—and with me, for months afterward. Henry would consult with George on union matters for as long as was possible.

"Once, near the end, I asked Henry as he came out of the room, 'Did George say anything?' hoping, desperately, that he'd talked about me. Henry nodded, 'He said, at least we got Pension and Welfare.' Those were his last words."

In *Stand By!* Jaffe wrote,

> Little has been known about George's private world. The reason is that he felt ashamed and afraid, really, to show any weakness or indecision. He felt the security people placed in him would be threatened were he to lift the curtain; that his shoulders might not seem broad enough to absorb the attack we constantly made on him with our problems, our insecurities, our convictions, our politics, yes, even our denunciations.
>
> So he lived a schizophrenic life, one for us and one for himself and he kept this pretense up to the very end. In his last weeks, while his keen mind and wit were still with him, he said to me in the course of some discussion or other, "If there were no one else in the world but me, George Heller, George would still argue with Heller and Heller still argue with George.

•

18

~~~~~~

The Next Five Hundred Days

Throngs of mourners crowded into the Riverside Chapel on June 2, 1955, to share in the ringing tributes and sorrowful farewells. Henry Jaffe, having risen from a sickbed, was there in a wheelchair. Ralph Bellamy spoke, as did Peggy Wood, Zack Becker, and Albert Dekker. Like Heller's family and other intimates, Van too suffered what daughter Jan Dekker described as "a long and terrible grief at George's dying."

Barely noticed in the overflow crowd (and then by only a few in the immediate vicinity), in the middle of Bud Collyer's eulogy—"You will forgive me if I do not speak of my beloved George in the past tense" —Phil Loeb and actor John McGovern, rose abruptly. Choking back tears of grief and rage as they exited the chapel, Loeb was heard to say, "I can't stand this. That sonofabitch hated George's guts."

•

By a record 982 in favor and 514 against, the anti-AWARE referendum passed in the New York local. Gould in *The Times* wrote:

> The overwhelming decision of television and radio artists . . . is a forward step in liberating the broadcast industry from the influence of outside pressure groups . . . [It] by no means, however, wipes away the dark shadows . . . [as] there still are widely circulated lists—[not] limited to actors only. . . . But the significance . . . is that the responsible "middle" group . . . recognized that careless and over-zealous anti-communism can have its own dangers just as communism does. (July 11, 1955)

Only days later, the plenary session of the AFTRA National Board, convening at the convention in Seattle, Washington, approved a referendum authorizing all locals to take disciplinary action (ranging from fine to expulsion) against any member who did not cooperate with a congressional committee. The referendum mirrored the rule passed two years earlier by the Los Angeles local. And like the LA rule, it passed—3,967 in favor, 914 against—on the very eve of the scheduled HUAC hearings, this time in New York City.

The 1955 convention also reelected Frank Nelson as president and installed Budd Collyer as first vice president, replacing Vinton Hayworth. Following his humiliating double defeat, Hayworth tendered his resignation to the national and New York local boards and all committees on which he served, "effective upon receipt." He, and later colleague Ned Wever, would transfer membership to the Los Angeles local where, it was hoped, they might find a more hospitable climate.

•

The Investigation of Communist Activities in Entertainment in the New York Area opened in room 1703 of the United States Courthouse at Foley Square on August 15, 1955. It was seventeen years to the month since HUAC began its exhaustive trials, touching every "suspected Communist" or "fellow traveler" in the whole of show business, East Coast to West. The committee had become redundant—its celebrity and usefulness, if only as a political tool, was fast petering out.

Chairman Francis E. Walter called the three-man subcommittee to order with a tone that masked only briefly what would become a typically aggressive, arrogant interrogation. He began,

> The Congress of the United States has imposed on this committee the duty of investigating the extent, character, and objects of un-American propaganda that . . . attacks the principle of [our] form of government. . . . [It] is not being conducted because this subcommittee has any desire to do this work. . . .
>
> Witnesses will . . . accuse the committee of being a tool of this organization or that organization, or being an instrument of fear to be raised over the heads of the television and radio workers. . . . [But] the committee is interested in one thing . . . alone. That is to ascertain, and identify individuals who are or were members of the Communist Party and who are using or did use their influence to promote the objectives of the Communist Party within the entertainment field.

Notable during those four searing days in downtown Manhattan was HUAC Counsel Frank S. Tavenner, Jr.'s, line of questioning: Was the witness at any time a member of the Communist Party? Who were his or her associates? Did the witness know of a Communist caucus in Actor's Equity? In AFTRA? Notable too was that only one of the twenty-three performers subpoenaed would say that he did. Indeed, while supporting their unions and deploring outside interference, none but one would say anything of consequence to aid HUAC. With varying degrees of decorum, fervor, or cheek, and invoking the First or Fifth Amendment, they stated —as had scores of others before them—that the committee had no right to inquire into their conscience, their private beliefs, their past or present associations.

Stage actor George Hall was the sole cooperative witness. He reported becoming a Communist in 1946, when things that he had seen in certain parts of the country (while in the army) prompted him to rebel against the status quo. "My instincts were right," Hall said, "in the terms of my love for my fellow man and my desire to help those I considered less fortunate than myself." Hall's attendance at some dozen party meetings and his performance at five fund-raisers in private New York apartments constituted his entire contribution to communism. He quit the party soon after because, as he said, he found it to be "a one-party dictatorship" and "a distortion of the simple truth of democratic processes."

Hall identified eight persons (seven of those would testify that week) as having been active in his "Midtown group." He could not specify who else in Actors' Equity might be a Communist. With regard to politics within the union, Hall testified that there was no such thing as a Communist slate there. Candidates for council were democratically nominated. Further, he received no party instructions about who or how to vote in union matters.

Chairman Walter commended Hall for his courage in coming forward. He emphasized,

> It is not easy. I should not like to be called a stool pigeon, and I am sure that that appellation will be applied to you. But let me tell you something: Every patriot in the history of America has been proud of the enemies that he has made. . . . Your contribution here cannot be appraised. It may well be that it is equal to that of a division of infantry.

Setting aside Hall's apparent willingness to sacrifice former associates with whom he once shared the same ideals and ambitions for the country, one must ask: How reliable is the testimony of a government stool pigeon who desperately seeks to save his or her own skin?

Blacklisted folk singer Pete Seeger appeared on the morning of the last day and made it known that "with no discredit to the others" he would not rely on the Fifth Amendment.

> I am not going to answer any questions as to my associations, my philosophical or religious belies or my political beliefs, or how I voted in any election or any of these private matters . . . however, if

you want to question me about my songs, I would be glad to tell you, sir.

Under repeated questioning on where, when, and with whom he had sung, Seeger answered,

> I have sung for Americans of every political persuasion. . . . I have sung in hobo jungles, and I have sung for the Rockefellers, and I am proud that I have never refused to sing for anybody. That is the only answer I can give along that line.

And so it went, to the obvious frustration of Chairman Walter. Prior to Seeger's appearance, two witnesses had been cited for contempt for not having sufficient legal reason supporting their refusal to answer. But it was Pete Seeger who would be brought to trial and sentenced to a year in prison as a result. Six years later, an appeals court reversed his conviction; the other two were also reversed.

The New York Times editorial of August 18, read:

> But no matter how much we may condemn persons who refuse to talk about their past . . . the present hearings do raise some genuinely troublesome problems. One of these is the extent to which an individual is protected from such inquiry by the guarantees of the First Amendment. . . . The other concerns [the inquiry's] wisdom and necessity. Why single out a profession so remotely removed from the realm of national security?

Patrick Malin, ACLU director, wrote to HUAC:

> Investigation of conspiratorial acts about which the Congress can legislate is wholly proper. But an inquiry into political associations as such, about which the Congress may not legislate, is improper.

Early in the hearings, Walter had pointed to a standing rule that any person named in previous testimony would be given an opportunity to appear for the purpose of denying or explaining that testimony. Sam Jaffe was one of those waiting to be heard. He had survived years of unemployment, years of being tailed and taunted by FBI agents—like so many others. While he had brief runs in Anton Chekhov's *Seagull* and George Bernard Shaw's *Saint Joan* the year before, by August 1955, he was out of money and deep in debt. He moved from his "lovely apartment" into a "hole in the wall" on the far-upper East Side. He had one suit left to his name.

It was Jaffe's lawyer, however, claiming more pressing business elsewhere, who requested to be temporarily excused. HUAC's time restrictions in the City did not allow for Jaffe's return. He spoke to the press:

"I'm not a Communist and have never been a Communist, nor have I ever given to Red causes. I have always been a good American citizen." Jaffe said he would appear when called and answer all questions put to him. He never was. The committee's interest in him died while he waited. Nearly five years were squandered in the waiting.

Bettye Ackerman Jaffe told me, "Sam and I met later that year in a production of Jean-Baptiste Molière's *Tartuffe* at the Ninety-second Street YMCA. Despite our fifteen-year age difference, we knew the instant we laid eyes on one another. Some say that I was the decoy in getting this illustrious actor to join our company. As we were introduced, Sam said, '*This* is a marriage.' Six months later, in June 1956, when he landed his first, good-paying job, Jean Anouilh's *Lark* on Broadway, we were wed."

French film director Henri-Georges Clouzot would give Jaffe his boost back into motion pictures the following year in *The Spies*. And, as the air cleared in Hollywood, Jaffe would return there as well. From 1961 to 1965, he was seen as the wise old Doctor Zorba on the *Ben Casey* television series.

•

On September 1, 1955, "Fred Lang"—better known as actor-director Philip Loeb—was found dead in a New York hotel room; the apparent cause of death: an overdose of sleeping pills. He was sixty-one.

"I was with Phil only two weeks before," said Ezra Stone, "at a luncheon he'd summoned me to. He was staying at the home of a childhood friend while recovering from a second cataract operation. It wasn't the old Phil, my teacher and cherished friend of twenty-two years, who greeted me. There were no wisecracks, no fiery tirades. All attempts to cheer him were put aside. He was grim, taut. He spoke in an almost monotone.

" 'Did I still have the handwritten last will and testament bestowing on me all his assets to hold until his son, Daniel, was well again? Did I remember my promise to act as executor of his estate and legal guardian of his son?' he asked. I assured him I did, but I was in no hurry to do so.

"He ignored the joke and handed me a scrap of paper. It read that, if Daniel did not recover [he died a still-mysterious death, years later, in a veterans' hospital], Phil wanted his estate divided between his sister, two longtime friends, and Sam Jaffe." (Jaffe would refuse the money and pass it to the Loeb Memorial Student Assistance Fund at the American Academy of Dramatic Arts in New York, a fund established by Ezra Stone's parents and still in existence today.)

"That night I stayed at my folk's apartment," Stone went on, "where Phil had been a frequent visitor. He loved my mother's good, home-cooked meals and the hot political debates with my father. I told them how concerned I was over Phil's state of mind. My father suggested that depression following surgery was not unusual, and with all Phil's other problems, it should, in fact, be expected.

"The next week, I heard Phil moved to Zero and Katie Mostel's. I took that as good news. Next to Sam, Zero was Phil's closest friend and his craziness was just what Phil needed. Then, the last night of August, I learned that he hadn't shown up for dinner. Zero, Sam, and I phoned everywhere—to all his friends—late into the night. We couldn't track him down. We decided to wait till morning.

"Why did he do it? I'm not really sure," said Stone. "He was starting to get work. He'd been in an off-Broadway production recently of Chekhov's *Three Sisters* [salary, $87.50 per week]; I myself directed him, the previous sumer, in a package of *The Play's the Thing*, by Ferenc Molnár, starring Ezio Pinza. The only explanation I can offer is that all his resources were spent. All efforts to reclaim his good name had been tried and failed. And in his pained and tortured mind, the one accomplishment left him was to become a martyr to a cause." Loeb chose Labor Day to die; he chose the Taft Hotel, named for the former president and chief justice of the Supreme Court; and he registered under a pseudonym that when roughly translated into German means "a long peace."

As it turned out, the estate of the man who brought joy to millions on television and in over thirty Broadway shows—who was a key figure in building his beloved Actors' Equity into a strong, modern labor organization, who was instrumental in integrating the National Theater in Washington, D.C.—amounted to, as Ezra Stone phrased it, "less than a used Chevy in today's market."

Loeb never owned a home; he lived much of his life in the old Lincoln Hotel in the heart of New York's theater district. His entire wardrobe fit into a single closet. His treasured personal property—books and files stuffed full with Equity minutes and other such documents—filled two humpbacked steamer trunks. That was all.

•

The popularity of motion pictures had fallen a poor second to the hugely entertaining live television. While Hollywood's independent film producers fared well (they had been selling to television for years), by 1955, a crisis existed in the major film studios. In one brilliant stroke, Warner Brothers put aside the well-known industry disdain for the electronic medium and, with a made-for-television series, *Warner Brothers Presents*, became the first to cross over into televisionland.

Cheyenne, an adult western introduced on the series and turned by Warners into a series of its own, rescued the company. The apparent appetite for the wild and wooly West, the stockpiles of Old West footage, and the modest fees paid to unknown actor-cowboys brought the others along as well. Within three years, Hollywood would be turning out thirty-five episodes of television westerns per week, plus scores of new comedy and adventure series. Once only a secondary market, LA would become the East's main competitor.

In crowded New York, meanwhile, available studio space for live anthology drama was dwindling; advertisers' "cost per thousand [homes with TV sets]" was spiraling upwards. Producers complained that stars made by television now refused to work for the going television salaries. Prominent shows headed West, claiming the "no surprises, no failures" aspect of film production; film's larger, more modern facilities; and its superior profitability—only to die there shortly after. Some shows that stayed were canceled for budget-shifting reasons.

To many observers, however, the demise of the live dramatic show would be less known and less remembered. With the now-inviolate rule that a sponsor's advertising vehicle must not offend, much of what was thought provoking or controversial—the very "bite" of a well-written drama—had been excised. Scripts were weak, bland; viewing audiences, limited at best, grew smaller still.

By 1958, of the twenty-four shows seen weekly in the 1955–56 season, only eight would remain. The Golden Age of television drama—the ten-year showcase of New York's best writing, performing, and producing talents—would be over. A cheaper form of entertainment, the "super" quiz show, with its seductive prizes and corruptive ratings, would take its place.

•

November 1955, in the flush of the vote to condemn AWARE, a thirty-three-candidate middle-of-the-road slate, made up primarily of political newcomers, mounted a fresh new challenge to the New York board. Charging it with creating a "wall of fear" and demonstrating "an alarming indifference" to membership's needs in a fast-changing broadcast technology, the middlers pledged to protect and perpetuate "the democratic principles of the nation and the union," to fight the "denial of employment by discriminatory and intimidating practices—especially by outside organizations—and to reawaken the "dynamic spirit of AFTRA," bringing "sanity, decency . . . and fair play" back to the local.

The candidates were CBS news commentator Charles Collingwood (one of "the Murrow boys"); folklorist and television panelist John Henry Faulk; comedian Orson Bean; television host Garry Moore; and announcers Jay Jackson, Richard Stark, Stan Burns, and Cy Harrice. Also running were actors Luis Van Rooten, Faye Emerson, and Louise Allbritton (Collingwood's wife); specialty acts Cliff Norton and Ronny Graham; singers Del Horstmann, Earl Rogers, and Martha Wright; dancers Janice Rule and Helena Seroy, to name a few. They had been chosen not only for their anti-AWARE, anticommunism positions but for their so-called untainted political pasts, untouched by previous smear or innuendo.

The New York press viewed this "hottest campaign in years" as a potential victory for all moderates that could "reverberate on the national level" of AFTRA as well. The Artists' Committee group viewed it as a potential crippling defeat. The dominant force for more than a dozen years, they were not likely to give over leadership in orderly succession. Seven of their number had been exposed and publicly wounded. The others would do whatever was deemed necessary to hold on to their political power base.

Armed with freshly manufactured evidence against the insurgents, AWARE's Vincent Hartnett fired off a letter to HUAC urging them to take heed of this new situation and to issue an official statement to help "crush the slate" (Faulk 1983).

On December 11, 1955, in the largest vote yet cast in the local's history, 1,677 ballots, the middlers won an overwhelming victory—twenty-seven board seats out of a possible thirty-five; the popular Garry Moore garnered the highest vote. Five incumbents—Bud Collyer, Alan Bunce, Conrad Nagel, Rex Marshall, and Walter Kiernan plus three new performers on the right, Broadway singers Ethel Waters and Bill Tabbert and dancer Beatrice Kraft, won seats as well.

In a follow-up ballot for officers, Collingwood was elected president, and Bean and Faulk were elected first and second vice presidents, respectively. Van Rooten, Jackson, and Norton were elected vice presidents. Singer Elise Bretton was elected recording secretary, dancer Barbara Ferguson, treasurer.

Just as the twenty-seven, heady with their monumental win, gathered for the first New York board meeting of 1956, the HUAC Annual Report of 1955 was released to the public. In it, the committee blasted the middle-of-the-road slate:

> Investigation uncovered a militant Communist faction within the New York local [whose] principal activity . . . was a campaign against so-called "blacklisting." Through their campaigning, these Communists had falsely convinced many fellow artists that they are denied employment if they at one time innocently supported a cause supported by the Communist Party.

President Collingwood responded to the committee:

> [If] . . . HUAC really thinks that the only people . . . who are dis-

turbed by the excesses of the blacklisting system are Communists or their dupes, then it is laboring under a misapprehension. . . . The New York Local has just elected . . . a slate of officers and board members who ran unequivocally opposed to the indiscriminate blacklisting . . . surely, the electorate which swept them into office . . . cannot be exclusively composed of Communists or deluded pawns, either.

[HUAC] deplores indications that the blacklisting machinery . . . is losing some of its force. It is my belief and fervent hope that this is indeed the case. The climate of opinion . . . is changing. Perspective is returning. The blacklist is dying and the present officers and majority of the New York Local Board of AFTRA intend to do everything they can to assist in the process.

It is clear that the degree of Communist infiltration in radio and television was exaggerated from the beginning . . . [and] the safeguards which exist in our union . . . are more than sufficient to deal with the situation.

"The point I tried to convey," wrote Collingwood in his column, "From the President," in the January 1956 *Stand By!*,

was that if it should turn out that there *is* a militant Communist faction concealed somewhere, [we] can be depended upon to see that it is contained and rendered harmless. Aside from this little brush, we approach our tasks with no spirit of rancor or vindictiveness and have been met with nothing but cooperation and good will. . . . Politics has not lifted its ugly head nor shaken its gory locks.

Within the month, the local was on its way toward "reawakening" the spirit. A dozen new committees were established, including one to honor "the heritage and radiance George Heller cast over the whole labor movement." Chaired by Bud Collyer, it would establish the national George Heller Memorial Foundation to help fund the higher education of qualified AFTRA members or their children. Its first and largest contributor was CBS officer Lawrence Lowman. The George Heller Gold Lifetime Membership Card Award was created to pay tribute to persons, in- or outside of AFTRA, for their unique contribution to the union. Henry Jaffe and Zack Becker, formerly of CBS, were among its first recipients. And old committees—black employment and antiblacklisting included— were reactivated. (The national board agreed to lift its proscription on action by locals regarding that matter.)

Even so, John Henry Faulk wrote in *Fear on Trial*:

It was rough sledding from the start. [Except for Norton and Stark] the slate was inexperienced. A bigger problem, though, was the constant, vehement objection to any new ideas. We had soundly defeated the AWARE faction . . . but we hadn't silenced them. And in a naive gesture of magnanimity, we appointed some to head up important committees.

"There was also Henry Jaffe," Faulk said. "Although only an employee . . . [he] never hesitated to speak out—usually in opposition."

•

In a highly controversial move, far overshadowed by the turbulent 1955 election, Jaffe and executive McKee bypassed the traditional W & W Committee process and effected a "clarification agreement" to the existing (1954–56) network television code. Essentially, clarification accomplished two things. It specified that all electronic methods, technology, and apparatus used to record television programs and commercials, now and hereafter, fell under AFTRA's jurisdiction (motion picture cameras excluded). And it revoked, beginning March 1, 1956, Heller's "full original fee" for program repeats. Original fee was slashed to 75 percent of minimum for the first and second replays, 50 percent of minimum for the third and all others.

The clarification agreement was approved by all three sections of the national board. In the New York local, however, it sent up a howl. Programs recorded earlier on the new videotape were now being rebroadcast at the performers' full original fee. Replacing live performances with recordings was hard enough to swallow, but having to take a huge cut for it—imposed on them by their own negotiators—was infuriating.

On the West Coast too, SAG registered a "strong protest" against the right of television networks to enter into such a "secret" agreement—secret from SAG, secret even from the AFTRA membership. The guild's replay schedule then was no payment for the first rerun, 35 percent of minimum for the second, 30 percent for the third, 25 percent for the fourth and fifth combined, and a 25 percent buyout for the sixth and all others. The new AFTRA fees, while still richer, were now more competitive with the guild's.

Questions of conflict of interest were raised in New York. Henry Jaffe's ambitions to be a full-time television producer had been known since the previous February, when producer Leland Hayward, one of Jaffe's "management" clients, had panicked, taking off for vacation on the very eve of his NBC production of the closing Broadway hit *Peter Pan*, starring Mary Martin. Hayward wired back: "Take over for me."

"I knew I could handle it," Jaffe told me. "I had only to sell the deal to David Sarnoff. We met and, after a lot of screaming, the general said, 'Why *don't* you take over?' " Incredibly, Henry Jaffe made his official

television debut, March 7, 1955, before a record sixty-five million view-
ers and at the topmost rung of the television ladder. Executive Secretary
George Heller, learning of his plans for further television productions,
was not impressed, however. Jaffe chuckled, uncomfortably, as he remembered, "George fired me."

But there was more to the conflict of interest charges. The middlers had
recently learned of Jaffe's well-hidden involvement in an earlier ABC TV
series *The Ruggles*, starring Charlie Ruggles and based on his 1930s film
hit, *Ruggles of Red Gap*. True, that had occurred under a more amenable
board. But these were different times. Was *counselor* Jaffe clarifying replays to benefit *producer* Jaffe?

Middler Cy Harrice told me, "He sobbed like a baby when we confronted him—he turned the color of clay. Said he never intended to do
wrong. He pleaded with us not to fire him. It was very traumatic for everyone there. We finally 'allowed' him to resign."

The New York board voted "no" to the clarification agreement and
petitioned the national for a ratification vote. The national ruled that the
1954–56 code of Fair Practice for Network Television Broadcasting had
already been ratified; the motion was, therefore, unnecessary. Further,
"the action of the negotiators, including the agreement, is in full accord
with the board's wishes."

Jaffe was on the hot seat; his good reputation was in jeopardy. He explained at a New York membership meeting that, by negotiating without
the usual membership consultation, he avoided yet another protracted labor dispute with the guild. Only months before, he said, SAG had won
Jackie Gleason's *Honeymooners* away from AFTRA through secret negotiations of their own—involving Dumont's new electronic movie camera, the Electronicam. But with virtually the entire industry having signed
the agreement before the guild could send out letters of protest, "there is
no basis on which they can legitimately contest our jurisdiction." That
was Jaffe's rationale then.

His rationale to me, thirty-five years later, was that "The AFTRA code
was very strict; it had become economically impossible. The guild paid no
attention to the wonderful things George and I got earlier. And we were
losing a lot of weight in the jurisdiction."

"What," I asked, "were the benefits to membership?"

"They weren't outstanding," Jaffe admitted. "There were some results
but not the rush of business I expected because, by that time, the industry
had gotten used to working under the guild."

•

On February 10, 1956, within weeks of the stinging HUAC Annual Report, a second and even more damaging blow was dealt the middlers:

Aware's *Publication No. 16*, a five-page bulletin distributed now to more than two thousand persons in news, broadcasting, government agencies, and, surprisingly, the New York City police. It contained Vincent Hartnett's "new evidence" against the middlers and particularly against the local's top three officers.

Former University of Texas teacher and First Vice President John Henry Faulk, who had never been cited by either vigilantes or government committees, was singled out for special abuse. Hartnett listed seven public events at which entertainer Faulk was to have participated, describing them as "officially designated Communist fronts," and cited the *Daily Worker* as his source.

So too grocer Laurence Johnson, aided by Vincent Hartnett, turned his exquisite pressure tactics on Libby Foods, Rheingold Beer, Diamond Crystal Salt, and other advertisers on Faulk's long-running CBS radio talk show. Since the loss of "researcher" Harvey Matusow to federal prison, Johnson had teamed with Hartnett, and the two were frequently seen "up and down Madison Avenue" doing business.

President Collingwood wrote in *Stand By!*:

> I [am] amazed at how well-mannered national politics are compared to the variety practiced in our union. . . . Anxious as he is to wrest the . . . nomination from Adlai Stevenson, no one dreams that Estes Kefauver wishes to deprive him of his law practice. . . . But in AFTRA, political differences bring on personal attacks of a ferocity unknown on the national scene—attacks not only to defeat . . . but to drive the individual out of his profession.
>
> It seems crystal clear that the motive . . . is not the purification of the union [but] a transparent attempt to destroy anyone who has the temerity to run against the group which feels it is its holy mission to direct the affairs of AFTRA.

Within weeks, *Publication No. 16* was followed by an official inquiry to the AFTRA National Board from Frank Tavenner, HUAC counsel. What steps have been taken, Tavenner wanted to know, regarding the fourteen New York members who defied HUAC at their recent hearings, refusing to affirm or deny party membership?

AFTRA President Frank Nelson, never hesitant to press HUAC's business, met directly with Collingwood, "It is incumbent on the Local to determine what action shall be taken . . . in view of the Anti-Communist provision of the Constitution and National Rule re disciplinary action."

And Henry Jaffe, who had been close to Aware, who had written their constitution for them (Foley 1979), who had strategized with them on attacks against other AFTRA members, now approached John Henry Faulk. Local officers could "parry" Aware's charges, he advised, by bringing charges against the fourteen—and being the principal target, Faulk should take the action personally. Jaffe offered to locate AFTRA informers, those who had given evidence in the past and would be willing to testify again (Faulk 1983).

Faulk caucused with several trusted middlers—Cy Harrice, actor Dennis Patrick, and announcers Jay Jackson and Stan Burns among them—to report the abhorrent exchange. AWARE is not out to expose Communists, Faulk told the group, they are out to divert the leadership. "But the attack on us could stir the union into an all-out fight against them. . . . The time has come for a showdown!"

The caucus authored the "showdown" motion and presented it at the March 22 board meeting. If a member has been denied employment because of misleading statements by AWARE, Inc., "the Board will take all action within its power against that employer." The motion generated a long, loud debate about its wisdom or effectiveness: the Artists' Committee group against the middlers, as was expected; one middler against another, which was not. It carried, nonetheless, and was subsequently mailed to all signatories. (Bud Collyer, the same evening, proposed "that meetings open and close with a moment of silent prayer." That motion also carried.)

But Faulk and the caucus were now perceived as "wild-eyed radicals" (his words). He had overestimated the slate's homogeneousness and its fortitude under fire. He wrote, "Several Middlers were already voting on the Collyer/Jaffe side." Within days, the rift would widen further.

Announcer Nelson Case, once an ardent slate supporter, requested a letter from Faulk stating that he, Case, was not and had never been a member of the group. And Orson Bean, a regular on Ed Sullivan's show, was told that he was off until he "did something" about AWARE's allegations (Faulk 1983).

•

The April 6 *New York Times* headline read: "JAFFE QUITS POST IN A.F.T.R.A. LOCAL." TV-radio columnist Val Adams wrote:

Acceptance is expected at the board meeting today. . . . Serious differences between the [national and local] boards has created new problems in his role as counsel for both. It is known that he has strong opposition from certain members of the NY board.

The motion to accept was unanimous, with the added refinement of "with reluctance and regret." Jaffe agreed that he or an associate would stay on until a replacement was found. But that was not to be the end of it. The "resignation" would be used as the final step in the New York–Washington strategy to smash an already-weakened middle-of-the-road slate, and it would take place at the next local membership meeting, three months into the middlers' first term of office.

"I simply made a few calls to my friends," Jaffe said. "I told them I needed their support." He and Collyer then paid a visit to the genial middler Garry Moore, host of CBS's *I've Got a Secret*. They prevailed upon him to offer a motion calling for a "unanimous vote of confidence" for Jaffe's nineteen years of dedicated service. Unfamiliar with the two until recently but sensitive to the urgency expressed, Moore agreed. Ed Sullivan also helped, writing in his *Daily News* column that "sinister forces" were seeking to take over the local, and members should attend prepared to counterattack (Faulk 1983).

It was an unusually large turnout; 683 AFTRAns crowded into the casino at the New York City Center. President Collingwood apprised members of Jaffe's resignation and read from his official letter. Both local and national boards, Jaffe wrote, had been advised, months earlier, of his imminent departure to more fully pursue his new interests. Due to the death of George Heller, he had agreed to stay on. Now Donald F. Conaway, AFTRA's new national executive secretary (formerly of the Brotherhood of Railroad Trainmen), asked that he continue through the coming (1956) television negotiations; Jaffe decided he would do so. His resignation from the local, however, was "final and irrevocable."

Moore introduced the vote of confidence. One after another of Jaffe's partisans rose to pay tribute and express deepest gratitude for his loyalty, integrity, and devotion. The tributes soon gave way to denunciations of the middle-of-the-road group. Middler supporters then tore into the clarification agreement, attacking Jaffe, the national officers and board for "their flagrant disregard of membership's rights."

Middler Richard Stark charged that certain local directors were conducting "factional policy making" in clandestine meetings. Punitive action was called for against the offending members. Stark had prepared a resolution to condemn, but the issue touched off such furious confrontation that no action was taken. The meeting ended in chaos.

The strategy to smash the middlers had worked. The group was broken into political bits and pieces, their supporters left bewildered, angry, heartsick. How could it have gone so wrong so soon? Collyer, "the great peacemaker," aided by Alan Bunce, scurried to reassemble the shattered bits—somewhat more in their own image—and do so in time for the June elections for national board and convention delegates.

Henry Jaffe too spent a busy few months—as a commuter to and from Los Angeles, launching his second major career there. By the time he "finally shed AFTRA," as he described his controversial leave-taking, Jaffe's Showcase Productions, Inc., was operating in high gear. He launched the NBC specials *Shirley Temple Storybook* (replayed later by ABC); the

NBC concert series *Bell Telephone Hour*; and, finally, the NBC ninety-minute talk and variety show *Dinah!*, starring Dinah Shore, seen live and "live on videotape"—all Emmy Award winners in years to come.

•

On June 22, 1956, Richard Shepard of *The Times* wrote that a "coalition" slate had walked off with ten of twelve openings for the AFTRA National Board of Directors; middle-of-the-road candidates actors Faye Emerson and William Prince took the remaining two. Richard Stark, Luis Van Rooten, and Cliff Norton were elected as "coalition" candidates. Others included Nelson Case (with the highest vote), Bud Collyer, Alan Bunce, Conrad Nagel, and song-and-dance man Ray Heatherton. The coalition also won eighty-two of the one hundred New York delegate seats for the coming national convention in Chicago.

"I pray that [the former middlers] do not delude themselves into believing that such a coalition is AFTRA's political panacea," defeated convention candidate Leslie Barrett cautioned. "It is imperative they keep firm control of the reins or will once again find themselves at the mercy of irresponsible leadership."

•

John Henry Faulk, now stripped of nearly all sponsors and soon to be dismissed from his CBS radio show, filed a libel suit on June 26, 1956, in New York State Supreme Court: *Faulk v. AWARE, Laurence A. Johnson, and Vincent Hartnett.* While it would be the first such case to survive a full trial, it would take a half dozen years of calculated delays—by AWARE's Godfrey P. Schmidt, first defense attorney; next by Roy M. Cohn (counsel in the Army-McCarthy hearings); and finally, by Cohn's partner, Thomas A. Bolan, who tried the case—before proceedings would get under way.

Two years earlier in Los Angeles, actor John Ireland had brought suit against the Y & R ad agency and Norvin Productions for dropping him from the lead in the new *Ellery Queen* film series. He too had been falsely accused of pro-Communist activities and labeled "politically unacceptable" (*Variety*, March 10, 1954). The suit ended months later with a disclaimer of the allegations and a generous out-of-court settlement. Ireland did not appear in the role.

Faulk's case was taken on by Attorney Louis Nizer, one of the great legal minds of his generation. "Unemployable" through most of the ensuing years, Faulk's colleague Edward R. Murrow helped out with Nizer's retainer fee: "Let's get this straight, Johnny," Murrow said, "I'm not making a personal loan. . . . I'm investing this money in America. These people must be brought into court. This blacklisting racket must be exposed" (Faulk 1983).

With their concern over the "prestige" of AFTRA—were Faulk to win or not—and their diametrically opposed positions on AWARE, the New York board offered little support. An expression of "total confidence in the loyalty and integrity of *all* its officers" was the best it could muster.

•

The 1956–58 AFTRA Code of Fair Practice for Network Television Broadcasting—the last contract Henry Jaffe put his hand to and the first for Executive Secretary Donald Conaway—boasted increases of an average of 20 percent overall compared to the first television code of 1950. For example, on-camera actors, solo singers, dancers, and announcers, who speak five lines or more, would earn a minimum of eighty-seven dollars for a fifteen-minute show, $155 for a thirty-minute show, and $210 for a sixty-minute show. Increases for soap opera actors, however, were up as much as 40 percent for the fourth and fifth days of a calendar week, acknowledging the progressive difficulty for those carrying the heaviest roles.

The Code of Fair Practice for Phonograph Recordings of 1957–59 would also show an improvement for group singers of more than 20 percent from their first (1951) contract. The minimum for a solo singer, actor, and narrator (not having a separate royalty agreement) was sixty-five dollars per side.

Lesser increases in the radio code were indicative of radio's waning popularity and loss of programming to television. Rates for actors and announcers ranged from $22.40 for a five-minute show (plus rebroadcast of $10.67) up to fifty-six dollars for a sixty-minute show (plus twenty-eight dollars for a rebroadcast) and $9.60 per hour for rehearsal. Solo singers earned almost double the actors' fees throughout the schedule.

Fees at SAG had risen handsomely in the 1950–56 period as well. Film actors working on features and film made for television now earned a minimum of seventy-five dollars a day, $285 a week. And in the Actors' Equity contract, soon to be drawn up with the League of New York Theatre Owners, the minimum for all Broadway players would be one hundred dollars a week, $130 on the road.

•

"RIGHT WING WINS IN TV-RADIO UNION, Coalition Candidates Defeat Middle-of-the-Road Group," wrote Val Adams in *The Times* on December 5, 1956. "The outcome was the reverse of a year ago, 29 from the coalition and five from the Middlers. . . . [They] were charged with entering into many projects that were never fulfilled." Faulk, Orson Bean, Janice Rule, and two newcomers, singers Bob Carroll and Craig Timberlake, were elected on the middler ticket. Continued professional harassment of Bean—CBS dropped plans for his pilot—forced him soon to resign from the board.

Among the coalition, in addition to right-wing Collyer, Bunce, Marshall, and Vicki Vola, was the independent faction: actors Leon Janney (with the highest vote), Virginia Payne, Bernard Lenrow, dancer Socrates Birsky, and announcer Jackson Beck, to name a few. This nucleus would one day put the local back on its once-compassionate, progressive course and serve it, in positions of leadership, for years to come.

Former middler Luis Van Rooten was elected president; Janney, Nagel, Stark, Norton, and Bunce, vice presidents; dancer Rae MacGregor, recording secretary; singer Travis Johnson, treasurer. Outgoing Charles Collingwood, having acknowledged to Faulk that the middler group was no longer an effective instrument against blacklisting, ran and was elected independently. In his farewell *Stand By!* editorial, he wrote:

> It has been a year of ferment, and ferment implies change and is, by its nature, disorderly. . . . The success of the insurgents has made dissent respectable again, and that is a long step forward. . . . If like Stephen Leacock's horsemen, [they] set off in all directions at once, not all of its courses were mistaken. . . . The demonstration that members outside the traditional governing group . . . could stand successfully for office has helped produce a splendid list of candidates. . . . The task of the incoming Board will be to select, refine and consolidate the innovations begun in '56.

Within weeks, the coalition rescinded most of what the "wild-eyed radicals" had put in place. Jaffe's replacement, Judge Ferdinand Pecora, former justice of the New York State Supreme Court and founder of the federal Securities Exchange, was let go for being "too liberal." He had advised that the matter of the fourteen AFTRAns who had "defied" HUAC be set aside for a time—that there was a contempt of Congress case pending before the Supreme Court, *Watkins v. the United States*, whose outcome could profoundly affect the legality of any action taken.

Judge Pecora was succeeded by Mortimer Becker, a former associate in the firm of Jaffe and Jaffe and himself a man of excellent credentials. Becker's working history with the union dated back to 1943 and the days of AFRA. It was he who, in 1945, legally established that performers (if they read from scripts or took direction) were employees not independent contractors; as such, they were entitled to unemployment insurance and all other benefits provided by social legislation (Lipton 1963).

And so, as we began the year 1957, the matter of blacklisting—which had so inflamed the union for six long years—was again left for others to bring to an end. Clearly, it would require more than a few scattered bands of well-meaning, highly principled citizens to put out the fire.

•

19

Finally, the Law

In a six to one decision on June 17, 1957, the U.S. Supreme Court reversed the recent contempt of Congress conviction of John T. Watkins, a midwestern labor leader, for refusing to reveal to HUAC the names of persons he knew to be Communists. Chief Justice Earl Warren, while agreeing that the power of congressional committees to investigate for purposes of creating legislation is inherent in the process, maintained:

> Investigations conducted solely for the personal aggrandizement of investigators, to expose for the sake of exposure, and to "punish" those investigated are indefensible. . . . First Amendment freedoms of speech, religion, or political belief and association cannot be abridged in legislative inquiries.

The court's decision was expected to affect some thirty other persons besides Watkins, among them several academics, newspaper reporters, editors, and playwright Arthur Miller, all convicted or under indictment for similar refusals.

In a second decision, the Court reversed the five-year-old conviction under the Smith Act of fourteen Communist leaders from California, freeing five and granting new trials to the other nine. The trial judge's charge to the jury was found to be defective because it did not specify that, for advocacy of the violent overthrow of government to be illegal, it must be advocacy of action, now or in the future, not simply theoretical urging (*The New York Times*, June 18, 1957).

•

One year later, June 18–19, 1958, HUAC appeared again in New York in one of its final investigations of communism in entertainment. It was an uneventful, barely publicized interrogation of nineteen persons, twelve of them from television and theater. All invoked the Fifth Amendment.

A final witness was Joseph Papirofsky, known professionally as Joe Papp, then employed as a stage manager at CBS TV and producer of the popular Shakespeare in the Park. A portion of the questioning, by Representative Morgan Moulder, follows:

> Q: Do you have the opportunity to inject into your plays or into the acting or the entertainment supervision which you have, any propaganda in any way which would influence others to be sympathetic with the Communist philosophy or the beliefs of Communism?
>
> A: Sir, the plays we do are Shakespeare's plays . . . "To thine own self be true," and various other lines of Shakespeare can hardly be said to be subversive or influencing minds.
>
> Q: My point is, do you intentionally control the operation of the entertainment which you produce or supervise for the purpose of influencing sympathy toward communism? That is my point.
>
> A: The answer to that is obviously "No." The plays speak for themselves. (Vaughn 1972)

CBS fired Papp several weeks later for invoking the Fifth Amendment. He was defended in arbitration by his union, the Radio and Television Directors Guild, who won Papp's reinstatement and partial back pay (Foley 1979).

Twenty years of un-American interrogations, and still there was no significant piece of legislation to protect the national security. None of the three hundred or so artists identified before HUAC as being Communists had been shown to have disseminated Communist propaganda, to be a danger to their country, or to be subversive in either intent or action (Vaughn 1972).

A *Times* editorial, "The TV Hearings," read:

> The obvious point . . . was to expose . . . a few more actors, musicians, directors and assorted persons in the industry. To what purpose? To make the United States . . . look ridiculous? To undermine this country's well-earned reputation for liberalism in thought and freedom of speech? To emulate Communist and other kinds of totalitarian societies by persecuting people for holding radical beliefs?
>
> The question would be different if a serious inquiry were pointed toward . . . sensitive posts in defense industries . . . or key communications spots. . . . But the . . . Committee apparently believes there is no fruitful ground left in such areas for the kind of publicity-seeking investigation in which it specializes. (June 25, 1958)

●

"I was one of those called before HUAC that June," said actor Cliff Carpenter, former chairman of the Anti-Blacklisting Committee at the old TvA. "I was appearing on Broadway in Dore Schary's *Sunrise at Campobello*, starring Ralph Bellamy. And I dressed with Alan Bunce, my nemesis from AFTRA, who played a featured role in the production. Over the months, we'd developed a friendly, cordial relationship; he even proposed me for membership in The Players.

"The night before the hearing, I decided to speak to him about it: 'Alan, there's something I must do tomorrow that may cast a pall on the play. I'm appearing before the House Un-American Committee.'

" 'Wha-a-t?' He spun around in his chair. He looked me full in the face for a moment, then he sputtered, 'I, uh, I'm going with you. I, I want to go with you. I, uh, I want to tell them some things about you.' "

"What he was saying was, he wanted to defend me. I was reduced to tears.

•

The year 1958 would provide other breakthroughs for AFTRA. Members saw the first retirement benefits paid out under the AFTRA-Industry Pension Fund. Health and welfare benefits—life insurance, a major medical-surgical plan, and hospitalization—had been in effect since January 1956 to those earning one thousand dollars a year or more under contracts covered by the fund. There would now be payment—up to 45 percent of scale—for television programs when replayed in foreign markets. There were changes in governance: in New York, a system of staggered three-year terms was established, and thousands of Associate Members were moved to Active Membership, where they might vote and hold office. And AFTRA concluded, "against great odds," it was said, its first contract covering commercials recorded on videotape.

Continued technological advancements and the perfection of tape for use in electronic and film cameras had erased all the old AFTRA-SAG divisions. Still, the jurisdiction wars raged on in the areas of recorded programs, syndication, and, most heatedly, the wildly proliferating field of taped commercials.

In March, preceding AFTRA by several months, SAG completed its first commercials contract with the ad agencies, covering both filmed and videotaped announcements. But their residual fees "wound up far too low," New York President Virginia Payne protested in July 1958 issue of *Stand By!* "Videotaped commercials should be paid for, as in the past, at 'live' rates"—the rates embodied in the AFTRA television code —"because the sales impact of tape is exactly that of live."

"The Guild is totally, abysmally ignorant in the 'live' field and, by extension . . . in videotape. Yet it has . . . limited its members (many who are also AFTRA members) to the inferior scales of the old-fashioned motion picture camera." If the fees were allowed to stand, Payne warned, the "whole pattern of live television salaries would be shattered."

AFTRA challenged the agreement and petitioned the NLRB for an election, so that the memberships could choose the bargaining agent they preferred to represent them. Preliminary hearings had been held, briefs written. While the two waited for a Labor Board decision to come down, AFTRA proceeded with its own first recorded commercials negotiation. As had been expected with a great deal of foreboding, the ad agencies used the lower SAG fees to bargain AFTRA down (unsuccessfully, for the most part). This had become sheer professional madness.

It was absolutely the right moment, once again, for a major push towards merger. Los Angeles actor Tyler McVey, a future president of AFTRA (1965–67), remembered an earlier effort, three years before, when the electronic movie camera was first developed. "We worked night and day for two days. We proposed that the merged headquarters be situated here in LA, that we conegotiate all contracts, including radio. The board felt, to a man, that merger—or a partnership of some kind—was the *only* solution to this undercutting and jurisdictional mess we'd gotten ourselves into. But SAG President Walter Pidgeon, using all the old familiar reasons, plus a new one—the political schisms in AFTRA—turned us down, flat and final."

Now, however, eyeing the substantially better commercials rates AFTRA had just won, ranking guild members agreed that, perhaps, the time had come to reconsider. In a first joint venture, the two commissioned noted labor mediator David L. Cole to prepare a feasibility study. And in January 1960, Cole presented his findings in a ninety-four-page report, "Is Merger Practicable?" He wrote, "It is inconceivable that there could be any doubt about the desirability of merging SAG and AFTRA." To illustrate, Cole summarized in *Stand By!*:

> It would enhance the bargaining strength of the members . . . and would permit them to have uniform residual programs. . . . It would end the sapping of energies and fortunes of the two . . . and would unify their voices at state and federal levels in legislative efforts. . . . It would permit the development of uniform pension and welfare plans . . . and would add strength and standing to the negotiators. In a word . . . [it would be] collective bargaining in its true sense.

The AFTRA board voted "to again offer to join with the Guild in organic merger," as outlined in the report. Executive Conaway wrote to executive Dales urging reactivation of SAG's merger committee and suggesting that it meet with the similar AFTRA committee. Dales answered that serious study would begin as soon as current "difficulties" (regarding SAG's motion picture negotiations) allowed. The rank and file held its collective breath.

Michael Collyer, Bud's son, told me, "Dad was totally committed to merger. He ran for AFTRA president in 1959 just to accomplish it. He met with the joint merger committees several times and thought he had it all pretty much put together until the day Ronald Reagan walked in. He had come to tell a story about an old farmer and a pasture. When he finished, Walter Pidgeon said, 'Good point, Ronald, good point.' My father said, 'What the hell's he talking about? What farmer? What pasture?' Dad took Reagan to lunch. They patched some things up and Dad assured him that he wouldn't run for president again—that Ronnie could be president of the merged union."

From the June 1960 issue of *Stand By!* came the news: "The SAG merger committee has rejected the Cole proposals as well as all AFTRA suggested modifications based on the Cole Report." The guild did, however, offer several counterproposals: joint negotiation in the entire field of commercials, live, tape, and film; joint negotiation in taped television programs; study of the interchangeability of union cards in those fields; study of cross-crediting of earnings under both unions' pension and welfare plans. (As a result of the 1960 motion picture strike, SAG won a pension and welfare plan of its own. It also won what older movie actors would refer to as "the great giveaway"—payment for television showings of theatrical films, but only for those films made *after* 1960.)

Basic positions on merger had hardly changed in the dozen years since George Heller's TvA was established. It was clear, however, that it was in AFTRA's best self-interest to give serious consideration to the guild's conditions and to move forward with them. "With deep regret . . . for the rejection," and in the continued hope that "joint action . . . may prove to be a prelude to organic merger," the Twenty-third AFTRA National Convention, meeting in Washington, D.C., voted to accept.

In what AFTRA President Payne described as a "historic five-month effort," and with profound gratitude to both teams, the jointly negotiated 1960–63 television commercials contract was, indeed, accomplished.

Scales were modeled after the federation's first code (1958) but sweetened slightly—a small step up for AFTRAns, a far greater one for guild members. Essentially, the AFTRA Code of Fair Practice for Recorded Commercials retained nearly live performance fees for the all-important first several showings on network programs. For example, there would be a session fee of ninety-five dollars, per commercial, for on-camera performers, which included the first use, then seventy and sixty dollars for the next two uses; a session fee of seventy dollars, per commercial, for voice-over performers, which included the first use, then fifty-five and forty-eight dollars for the next two uses; followed by, for both on-

and off-camera performers, a sliding scale down to ten dollars for the twenty-first use and thereafter.

There were fees for "wild spots" (local station-break announcements with unlimited use within a thirteen-week cycle). Sponsors could advertise in as few as one to five cities for a minimum of ninety-five dollars for on-camera performers and seventy dollars for off-camera performers, per performer, per commercial, per cycle, or as many as all cities in the country (Mexico City; Tijuana; Pembroke, Bermuda; and Havana, Cuba, thrown in for good measure) for $323.75 on camera and $212.75 off camera, per performer, per commercial, per cycle. Not only did this first joint agreement win improvements for all performers in the commercials field, it made giant steps toward a new fraternal trust and respect between the two organizations, so long and so devoutly wished.

The first jointly negotiated contract for prime-time programming (Exhibit A of the AFTRA television code) would not come about until 1973, under the leadership of then President Ken Harvey and Executive Secretary Sanford "Bud" Wolff. By that time, joint enterprise would be flourishing. More than a dozen AFTRA offices would share space and the considerable talents of the AFTRA executives with the newly established branches of an expanding SAG. And while organic merger of the two great unions has still not been achieved, it continues to be studied.

●

The practice of blacklisting in television was beginning to break apart by the fall of 1960. Certain producers, notably David Susskind, had taken back full artistic authority and were hiring again entirely on their own initiative.

Actress Jean Muir, whose nineteen-year marriage and long bout with alcohol both ended in the same week one year earlier, had just signed for a guest shot on Susskind's new CBS crime series *The Witness*. It would be Muir's first television appearance since her public firing ten years earlier. The next morning, however, she was asked to return to Susskind's Talent Associates office.

"What the hell is *this?*" Muir thought, as she put down the phone. "I signed the contract. Everything was OK. Well, maybe he needs a rider or something." When Muir walked in, Susskind said, "Sit down, Jean. I had a call yesterday from a Miss so-and-so at CBS telling me that I couldn't use you on my show."

"Oh, my God, here we go again."

"Wait a minute! I'm calling Paley now, and I wanted you to be here when I did. . . . Hello, Bill? What's this I hear from your Miss so-and-so that I can't have Jean Muir?"

"Oh, no!" said Paley. "You know what it is, David—the whole

damned office has been geared up to it for so long. I'll call you back." A few minutes passed. Then, "Hello, David? That Miss so-and-so you mentioned? I wanted you to know. She's, ah, no longer with the company."

To take up the interminable spells between jobs, Muir found herself teaching and directing young people in and around her home of White Plains, New York. In doing so, she discovered the field in which she belonged and, at long last, excelled.

"I made a much better teacher than I ever was an actress," Muir said. This was the first self-compliment from a woman who, throughout our interview, often deprecated her achievements and was unforgiving of her mistakes. From amateur productions and summer theater, she moved into teaching drama at Stephens College in Columbia, Missouri (she earned her Bachelor of Arts there). When they "retired" her in 1976, Muir was in charge of the freshman class and was named one of the school's best teachers.

"When I left the acting profession," Muir said, "I made two vows. One, that I'd continue working within the theater, where I started in the early 1930s. The other, and more important, that I'd try to win back the love and respect of my three children."

After a decade of poor health and great personal sorrow, Jean Muir has accomplished both.

•

On June 28, 1962, following nearly three months of closely watched hearings presided over by New York State Supreme Court Justice Abraham Geller, the jury in the John Henry Faulk libel trial returned their verdict. It was in Faulk's favor, and it was precedent setting.

Defendants AWARE, Laurence A. Johnson, and Vincent Hartnett were found to have deliberately and maliciously destroyed Faulk's career in order to silence his opposition to their blacklisting business. Faulk was awarded compensatory and punitive damages amounting to $3.5 million, the largest libel verdict in history and far more than attorney Louis Nizer had asked.

The trial marked the first confrontation between Faulk and two of his defamers, Hartnett and Paul R. Milton, cowriters of AWARE's *Publication No. 16*. The third, grocer Laurence A. Johnson of Syracuse, New York, made no appearance in court. At 9:00 A.M., on the very morning Nizer would begin his summation to the jury, a pajama-clad body was found in a Bronx motel room. It was identified as Johnson. Apparently, as officials explained, he had choked to death on his own vomit (Nizer 1966).

An appellate court later reduced Faulk's award to $550,000. Because of the insolvency of Hartnett and AWARE, Inc., he would receive only $175,000 (before expenses)—a settlement with the Johnson estate. But the court upheld all law and facts in the case. The decision read, in part: "We have, as found by the jury and amply supported by the evidence, a vicious libel . . . planned and executed with devastating effect . . . all without a semblance of justification."

The case was finally adjudicated in late 1964, following additional appeals by defense attorney Thomas Bolan. The last two went to the U.S. Supreme Court and were based on a plea that libel laws violate the First Amendment. All appeals were denied; the judgment of the appellate division was affirmed (Nizer 1966).

The results stunned the radical right. Hartnett and AWARE went out of business; *Counterattack* too ceased publication the same year. The old Artists' Committee incumbents appeared cowed, repentant, or in denial. Several more of them resigned. Former leaders, while still securely ensconced on both the local and national boards of AFTRA, claimed they had never had anything to do with either of the organizations.

And so, after years of immeasurable pain, it was the law and one courageous man, John Henry Faulk, a devout advocate of the Constitution and the Bill of Rights, who finally broke the vigilantes' stranglehold not only on his own career but on AFTRA and the giant, multibillion-dollar broadcasting industry as well.

•

Frank Reel of the old AFRA told me, "The blacklisting machine, in one area of the business, kept right on going—well into the middle of the 1960s." It was during those years that Reel was legal counsel for the ZIV Company, syndicators of *Sea Hunt*, *Highway Patrol*, and other television series.

"Syndicators," Reel said, "had no central body to carry out blacklisting for them, but the BBD & O agency volunteered to run it for the group. We'd send the names over to this guy and he'd either approve or not approve every actor on the list. He was a pretty decent sort, though, and not particularly tough about it. Then, as controversial people started reappearing in movies and on television, the question was: why are we still banning them in syndication?

"Finally, the machine wore itself out."

In July 1974, on a motion made by actor-comedian Marvin Kaplan, future (1989–95) president of the Los Angeles local, the nearly five hundred delegates represented at the Thirty-seventh AFTRA National Convention, meeting in Denver, voted overwhelmingly to delete the anti-Communist sections of the AFTRA constitution.

•

George Heller died at the height of an era rarely spoken of today and shrouded, still, in shame and collective guilt. I hope that this narrative casts new light on those years—those wonderful, terrible years—and on the roles Heller, his colleagues, and their beloved unions played in them.

Wherever history places them, one truth remains. George Heller was an extraordinarily gifted man. And he shared those gifts, generously, throughout his short and brilliant life. For this, his beneficiaries—the seventy-five thousand members in the thirty-six locals of the American Federation of Television and Radio Artists—offer a renewed and full-throated tribute.

Tribute goes as well to the hundreds of AFTRAns and their families, most unnamed in this writing, who suffered at the hands of the black-listers. May it be of some comfort that the victimizers are all but gone from the scene, while many of their victims remain alive and well and continue to please on stage, film, radio, and television.

•

Bibliography
Index

Bibliography

Bierly, Ken, John Keenan, and Ted Kirkpatrick. 1950. *Red Channels: Report of Communist Influence in Radio and Television*. New York: American Business Consultants.

Brown, Ralph S., Jr. 1958. *Loyalty and Security*. New Haven: Yale University Press.

Ceplair, Larry, and Steven Englund. 1980. *The Inquisition in Hollywood*. Garden City: Doubleday.

Cogley, John. 1956. *Report on Blacklisting II, Radio-Television*. New York: Fund for the Republic.

Cohen, Sanford. 1979. *Labor in the United States*. 5th ed. New York: Simon and Schuster.

Cole, David L. 1960. "Is Merger Practicable?" Unpublished SAG-AFTRA study.

Faulk, John Henry. 1983. *Fear on Trial*. Austin: University of Texas Press.

Foley, Karen Sue. 1979. *The Political Blacklist in the Broadcasting Industry: The Decade of the 1950's*. New York: Ayer.

Kanfer, Stefan. 1973. *Journal of the Plague Years*. New York: Atheneum.

Klehr, Harvey. 1984. *The Heyday of American Communism: The Depression Decade*. New York: Basic Books.

Lipton, William. 1963. "AFRA-AFTRA, Twenty-five Years of Labor Unionism." Unpublished compilation.

McWilliams, Carey. 1978. *The Education of Carey McWilliams*. New York: Simon and Schuster.

Miller, Merle. 1952. *The Judges and the Judged*. New York: Doubleday.

Mostel, Kate, and Madeline Gilford. 1978. *170 Years of Show Business*. New York: Random House.

Nizer, Louis. 1966. *The Jury Returns*. New York: Doubleday.

O'Connor, John, and Lorraine Brown, eds. 1978. *Free, Adult, Uncensored: The Living History of the Federal Theater Project*. Washington, D.C.: The New Republic.

Paley, William S. 1979. *As It Happened*. New York: Doubleday.

Taft, Philip. 1959. *The A.F. of L. from the Death of Gompers to the Merger*. New York: Harper and Brothers.

U.S. House. *Committee on Un-American Activities. Investigation of Communist Activities, New York Area.* 1955. 84th Congress. Parts VI and VII.

Vaughn, Robert. 1972. *Only Victims.* New York: Putnam.

•

Index

Rita Morley Harvey served on the governing boards of the Screen Actors Guild, New York branch, 1962–71; the New York local of AFTRA, 1975–81; and the AFTRA national, 1980–89. She was a delegate to more than twenty-five AFTRA National Conventions.

Harvey attended the Julius Hartt School of Music, University of Hartford, where she trained in voice and piano. She appeared in leading roles on scores of television dramatic shows and was featured in running parts on many daytime soap operas. She was the television spokesperson for dozens of national advertisers. In her first such stint, three years for the Coty company in the early 1950s, she often appeared up to twelve times a day and was then dubbed "America's Most Televised Girl." Harvey played in a number of musical comedies on tour and in stock and was featured on Broadway in *The Seven Year Itch* and *The Impossible Years*.

A former vice-chairperson of the Connecticut Civil Liberties Union, she is active on its Fairfield County Chapter Board. Currently an officer of the AFTRA–George Heller Memorial Foundation, she received the 1988 Ken Harvey Award for Outstanding Service to the membership of the New York local.